YET WITH A STEADY BEAT

Society of Biblical Literature

Semeia Studies

Number 42

YET WITH A STEADY BEAT
Contemporary U.S. Afrocentric
Biblical Interpretation

YET WITH A STEADY BEAT

Contemporary U.S. Afrocentric

Biblical Interpretation

Edited by
Randall C. Bailey

Society of Biblical Literature
Atlanta

YET WITH A STEADY BEAT

Contemporary U.S. Afrocentric
Biblical Interpretation

Copyright © 2003 by the Society of Biblical Literature

Library of Congress Cataloging-in-Publication Data

Yet with a steady beat : contemporary U.S. Afrocentric biblical interpretation / edited by Randall C. Bailey.
    p. cm. — (Society of Biblical Literature Semeia studies ; no. 42)
    Includes bibliographical references.
    ISBN 1-58983-072-5 (pbk. : alk. paper)
    1. Bible—Black interpretations. 2. Afrocentrism—Religious aspects—Christianity.
I. Bailey, Randall C., 1947– II. Series: Semeia studies.
    BS521.2.Y48 2003b
220.6'089'96073—dc21   2003001672

11 10 09 08 07 06 05 04 03   5 4 3 2 1

Printed in the United States of America
on acid-free paper

CONTENTS

RESPONSES

ABBREVIATIONS

ABD	*Anchor Bible Dictionary.* Edited by David Noel Freedman. 6 vols. New York: Doubleday, 1992.
ANET	*Ancient Near Eastern Texts Relating to the Old Testament.* Edited by James B. Pritchard. 3d ed. Princeton, N.J.: Princeton University Press, 1969.
BJS	Brown Judaic Studies
DC	The Deuteronomic Code
ER	*Encyclopedia of Religion.* Edited by M. Eliade. 16 vols. New York: Macmillan, 1987.
ET	English translation
FCB	Feminist Companion to the Bible
HR	*History of Religions*
HTR	*Harvard Theological Review*
JAAR	*Journal of the American Acacemy of Religion*
JRT	*Journal of Religious Thought*
JSJ	*Journal for the Study of Judaism in the Persian, Hellenistic, and Roman Periods*
LEC	Library of Early Christianity
NCB	New Century Bible
NIB	*The New Interpreter's Bible*
NICOT	New International Commentary on the Old Testament
NTS	*New Testament Studies*
SBL	Society of Biblical Literature
SBLDS	Society of Biblical Literature Dissertation Series

INTRODUCTION

Randall C. Bailey
Interdenominational Theological Center

In 1989 *Semeia* 47, "Interpretation for Liberation," co-edited by Katie Cannon and Elisabeth Schüssler Fiorenza, appeared. This collection of essays written, all but one, by Black scholars, many of whom were in biblical studies and all but one of whom were women, opened the door for examination of new questions growing out of the African American community. This volume also laid a foundation for soon to follow new works that bespoke some challenges to the discipline and some new insights into the budding field of cultural criticism.

In 1991 the volume *Stony the Road We Trod: African American Biblical Interpretation* (Fortress), edited by Cain Hope Felder, appeared. It opened the door to examination of this form of cultural exegesis and interpretation of the text. The volume, which has become a classic, represented the beginning stages of work by Black biblical scholars, many of whose voices had not previously been heard. At the time of publication there were only nine African Americans who held the terminal degree in Hebrew Bible and only eleven who held it in New Testament. This volume concentrated on issues of hermeneutics, the role of ancient Africa in the life of ancient Israel, and identification of biblical passages that had special relevance to this community. As noted in many reviews of this work, two additional areas that needed to be addressed were the adherence to historical-critical methods within this volume and further attention to the history of interpretation within Black religious and cultural traditions.

In 1994 the *Journal of the Interdenominational Theological Center* published a collection of essays by Black biblical scholars that had been produced in the early years of the African American Theology and Biblical Hermeneutics Group of the SBL. Those essays were primarily exegetical in method and related to passages in which Africans appeared in the text, although there were some beginning works relating to cultural criticism.

Since the release of these important works a new generation of Black biblical scholars has arisen, which brings to the fore new questions, application of new methods of interpretation, and new directions for contouring older problems. The advent of cultural criticism, explorations of ideological interpretation, and postmodern methods have helped this group to find its voice in new and exciting ways. Questions that could not be raised a decade ago are now being brought to the fore in dynamic new forms. It is now time for a hearing of these new voices. While the numbers of Black biblical scholars are still low, the growth is a source of encouragement to those of us who spent years as lone voices in communities.

In 2000 Vincent Wimbush produced a work entitled *African Americans and the Bible*. This monumental work looks across disciplines at the variety of ways Black people in the U.S. have utilized the Bible as a tool for a variety of quests in their lives. While this work spans the disciplines in a most impressive manner, its nature required the limiting of the voices of academically trained biblical scholars. Thus, this volume of Semeia Studies complements that work by bringing to the center this latter group of contributors to the discourse.

The main title for this volume, *Yet with a Steady Beat*, derives from James Weldon Johnson's lyrics to "Lift Ev'ry Voice and Sing" (J. W. Johnson 1963), commonly referred to as the Black National Anthem. Like "Stony the Road We Trod," this phrase also comes from the second verse and bespeaks the persistent march of our people on the "Freedom Trail." In fact, the words of that couplet are:

> Yet with a steady beat have not our weary feet
> Come to the place for which our [parents] sighed?

While the design of this volume was to have more voices of womanist scholars, this did not mature in the collection of the final essays for this volume.

Some of the essays to be presented in this volume were first presented in the context of the Society of Biblical Literature. Many were part of the programs of the African American Theology and Biblical Hermeneutics Group of the Society. Others were presented in such varied groups and sections as Ideological Criticism, Deuteronomistic History, Pauline Studies, Psalms, and Narrative Criticism. These essays have been expanded and further developed.

The term *Afrocentric* is used in a variety of ways in these essays. As a common denominator, the term refers to scholarship whose questions grow out of the experiences of people of African descent. Since most of the writers of these essays are citizens of the United States, these questions often speak to the existential reality of being Black in the United States. Thus, the question of ethnography in the ancient world is looked at as a way of getting a handle on how these constructs could speak to difference in our own culture (Braxton). Similarly, the use of laws that impact the poor in Deuteronomy shed light on the ways these texts can and might be appropriated by those living in such conditions in this country (Bennett). Some of these essays look to Black folk tradition as a starting point for interpretation and intersection with the biblical text (Bailey, Kirk-Duggan, Page, and Smith). Others tackle exegeting passages that have been central to the Black Theology Movement (Liburd and Williams). Most of these works are interdisciplinary in nature.

In order to further the dialogue, the respondents to the volume engage the works from their own social locations, representing various racial, ethnic groupings. They have been invited to participate in this project by reviewing and commenting on the work of these scholars and relating this to those of their own contexts. In this way the circle of discourse becomes larger.

While this volume is reduced from its original proposal, the scope of essays shows maturity and breadth in the African American and Afro-Caribbean biblical communities. Thanks have to be given to those who contributed their work for inclusion. Thanks also have to be given to the Interdenominational Theological Center, which provided a Faculty Research grant to assist in the production of the volume. Thanks also go to Candi Dugas Crawford, Debra Grant, BaSean Jackson, and Alisha Burt, research assistants who helped at various phases of this project.

It is my hope that this collection will move us in the guild of biblical scholars and other communities to look at these works and see new questions coming to the fore. In this way the dialogue can only get better.

ESSAYS

TRIENNIAL TITHES AND THE UNDERDOG: A REVISIONIST READING OF DEUTERONOMY 14:22–29 AND 26:12–15[*]

Harold V. Bennett
Morehouse College

Deuteronomy 14:22–29 and 26:12–15 treat the allocation of grain, fruit, wine, and meat in the biblical communities. These legal injunctions list the *almanah, ger,* and *yatom* together, and they provide guidelines on the offering of public relief to these types of persons. Since these codes list these types of people together, it is plausible that they shared a distinctive social characteristic. Further, these legal injunctions proffer food to these people; consequently, it is likely that these persons were a category of socially weak, vulnerable human beings and that these laws affected the predicament of this social subgrouping in ancient Israel. Deuteronomy 14:22–29 states:

> [22] You must indeed tithe all your crops that the field brings forth each year. [23] You will eat them in the place that Yahweh will choose, the place where the divine name is present. You will give a tithe of your grain, new wine, fresh oil, and the firstborn of your small and large cattle, so that you will learn to fear Yahweh your God forever. [24] If the place is too far away, and you are unable to carry the tithe, [25] exchange the tithe for silver; bind it in your hand and go to the place that Yahweh your God will choose. [26] You may give the silver for whatever you desire, for large or small cattle, wine, or strong drink; you and your household will eat and rejoice there before Yahweh your God. [27] Do not abandon the Levite, since he has neither portion nor inheritance among you. [28] At the end of three years, bring all the tithe of your increase and leave it in your gates. [29] The Levite, since he has neither portion nor inheritance among you, the stranger, orphan, and widow will come; they will eat and be satisfied, so that Yahweh your God will bless you in everything you do.

---

[*] An expanded form of this essay appears in my *Injustice Made Legal: Deuteronomic Law and the Plight of Widows, Strangers, and Orphans in Ancient Israel* (Grand Rapids: Eerdmans, 2002).

Deuteronomy 26:12–15 says:

> [12] When you finish taking the tenth of all your increase, in the third year, which is the year of the tithe, give the tithes to the Levite, stranger, orphan, and widow, so that they will eat it in your towns and be satisfied. [13] Then you will say before Yahweh your God: "I removed the holy thing from my house and gave it to the Levite, stranger, orphan, and widow according to all your commandments. I have neither transgressed nor forgotten your commandments. [14] In my affliction, I did not eat from the tithe; when unclean, I did not consume it, and I did not give any of it to the dead. I obeyed the voice of Yahweh, my God. I did according to every thing you commanded me. [15] Look down from the sky, your holy dwelling place, and bless your people Israel and the ground that you gave to us as you swore to our ancestors, a land that flows with milk and honey."

An interesting research question about these legal prescriptions suggests itself: What role might these codes have played in the circumstances of the *almanah, ger,* and *yatom* in ancient Israelite society?

In what follows, I argue that these regulations relegated this category of socially weak, vulnerable human beings to positions of socioeconomic inferiority. In discussing the question about the relationship of these legal injunctions to the predicament of these persons, I shall: (1) identify ideas in the historical-critical study of the Hebrew Bible that inform my point of view about these laws; (2) sketch the social-scientific framework, that is, the theory of law that informs my opinion about these codes; and (3) demonstrate how my proposed social-scientific framework allows me to read these legal injunctions with a concern for socioeconomic injustice.

The Historical-Critical Framework

Craigie (233–34, 244–47, 310–11, 318–24), Mayes (245–46, 259–61, 326–27, 335–37), Malchow (8–30), Epsztein (113–18), and Crüsemann (215–34) examine the Deuteronomic Code (DC). These scholars represent important points of view on the relationship of Deut 14:22–29 and 26:12–15 to the plight of the *almanah, ger,* and *yatom.* These commentators advocate the position that these laws spawned a public relief system that rectified economic disproportion and ameliorated the quality of life for this category of defenseless persons. What is more, Craigie, Mayes, and Epsztein posit that an element in ancient Israelite society—a social subgroup with an interest in caring about those who were without traditional means of economic support—drafted these laws. This camp intervened in the lives of an element among the peasantry out of a humanitarian concern. The critics cited in this essay, therefore, contend that beliefs about the distribution of tithes of agriculture, produce, and livestock were part of a revolutionary social program. Regarding the role that these commodities played in their agenda, Craigie declares:

> Those without regular means of subsistence, such as aliens, widows, and orphans, were thrown onto God, the Lord of the community, for provision. In receiving it from the tithe, which properly belonged to God, their needs were met. (234)

Malchow provides insight into the drafting of Deut 14:22–29 and 26:12–15 and into the relationship of these types of legal injunctions to the circumstance of the *almanah, ger,* and *yatom.* He elucidates the literary background of texts in the Hebrew Bible that treat social justice. He adduces evidence from the Egyptian wisdom literature—The Protests of the Eloquent Peasant, Merikare, Amenemhet, and Ipuwer (see, respectively, *ANET,* 407–10, 414–18, 418–19, and 441–44)—to show that a significant concern for improving the predicaments of vulnerable social subgroups was present in ancient Egypt. Malchow clears the way for arguing that points of view in ancient Africa about the welfare of marginal social subgroups contributed to the drafting of codes in ancient Israel regarding morality toward individuals who existed on the periphery of the social structure. He, therefore, implies that the Deuteronomic legislations cited in this essay reflect the common ancient Near Eastern practice of providing for the material endowment of individuals who were without traditional means for economic support.[1]

Crüsemann places Deut 14:22–29 and 26:12–15 into a sociopolitical framework. He offers ideas about the dynamics that led a faction to place these laws in the Deuteronomic Code. He argues particularly that the *am ha'arets* (the people of the land) incorporated these legal injunctions into Deut 12–26. Moreover, he maintains that these legal injunctions are adaptations of extant laws that governed the distribution of agriculture, produce, and meat in the biblical communities. Crüsemann contends that a social subgroup reformulated existing regulations about the distribution of these commodity goods and inserted innovations to establish a social program that ameliorated the plight of the *almanah, ger,* and *yatom.* The most distinctive point about the position he takes regarding these

---

1 Although Malchow (1–7) argues that Deut 14:22–29 and 26:12–15 echo notions about the treatment of vulnerable individuals that appear in literature from ancient Egypt, he contends that notions about the deliverance from slavery in Egypt and about the redistribution of wealth in ancient Israel contributed to the formation of these laws.

laws is the significance he assigns to these regulations. He claims that these laws are windows on the theological underpinnings of Deuteronomic law, for they promulgate the typical Deuteronomic notion that the deity had a claim to the complete allegiance of the people.

Four key points about the drafting of Deut 14:22–29 and 26:12–15, and about the role that these laws played in the circumstances of the *almanah, ger,* and *yatom,* emerge from the scholarship of the scholars cited in this essay. One proposition is that these laws are reworkings of separate regulations on the presentation and consumption of tithes of agriculture, produce, and livestock. These scholars propose that older laws on these issues were present in ancient Israel. While they point out that no regulations governing the presentation and distribution of tithes appear in the Covenant Code, the oldest legal corpus in the Pentateuch, these critics indicate that codes governing the presentation and distribution of tithes appear in Deut 12:15–19. Thus, these critics posit that this law is the literary basis of Deut 14:22–29 and 26:12–15.

A second claim is that the dilemma of the *almanah, ger,* and *yatom* was a social problem in ancient Israel prior to the drafting of Deut 14:22–29 and 26:12–15. The commentators mentioned in this study point out that codes that deal with the plight of these types of persons are present in the book of the covenant (Exod 20–23), a corpus of material that antedates the eleventh century B.C.E. These data compel these scholars to argue that the plight of this category of defenseless people attracted the attention of a social subgroup in the biblical communities prior to the appearance of the monarchy. These critics, however, argue that the dilemma of the *almanah, ger,* and *yatom* became a significant social problem after the appearance of the state. At the center of this claim is the notion that the concomitants of the monarchy (e.g., urbanization, social stratification, bureaucracy, and the ascendancy of a mercantile economy) spawned widespread social injustice and a proliferation of economic exploitation on the local scene. This circumstance contributed to the dilemma of the *almanah, ger,* and *yatom.*

A third point is that of the effect of Deut 14:22–29 and 26:12–15 on the lives of the *almanah, ger,* and *yatom.* The scholars cited in this essay posit that these types of moral injunctions established a public relief system that ameliorated the circumstances of these defenseless human beings. As was mentioned earlier, Craigie avers that this system for the relief of these types of persons—the welfare program that stemmed from these laws—improved their circumstances. Thus, conventional scholarship works from the position that these laws enabled the *almanah, ger,* and *yatom* to live with a degree of independence. In fact, Crüsemann maintains that these legal injunctions were part of a well-thought-out social safety net (231).

A fourth proposal is that the drafting of Deut 14:22–29 and 26:12–15 was a conscious activity. This tenet bolsters the chance that the ideas represented in these laws were part of a larger program. This claim clears the way for contending that a subgroup modified existing laws that governed public relief efforts. Working from the position that the creation of these Deuteronomic legal proscriptions was a deliberate phenomenon, it becomes possible to argue that the enactment of moral ideas into authoritative guidelines for human behavior provided significant opportunity to make innovations in extant legal injunctions that served personal interests.[2]

Conventional scholarship contends that Deut 14:22–29 and 26:12–15 worked to the advantage of and rectified the conditions of the *almanah, ger,* and *yatom.* Noteworthy, however, is that the critics cited in this essay never identify the sociolegal framework that informs this claim. Perhaps these scholars presuppose that how one should interpret these laws is self-evident. This is problematic because dominant and subordinate social subgroups often hold competing loyalties and different bases for judging law and other social phenomena. Underclass persons might view law and public policy decisions differently from those socioeconomic elites who draft legal injunctions and formulate social policy regarding public programs in a human community. Thus, silence about a theoretical framework for understanding the role that these legal injunctions played in ancient Israelite society is a feature of mainstream scholarship on these texts.

My position builds upon the research of these scholars and Critical Legal Theorizing about law. This approach places my argument on social-scientific terrain. Social-scientific methodology is an amalgamation of approaches where angles of vision from the social sciences intertwine to produce detailed representations of social history in ancient Israel. Social-scientific angles of vision on the Hebrew Bible, therefore, help to develop possibilities on the internal dynamics of biblical Israel, an otherwise inaccessible community. Thus, the next section identifies the legal paradigm that guides the discussion in this paper about the role that these legal proscriptions played in the circumstances of the *almanah, ger,* and *yatom.*

THE SOCIAL-SCIENTIFIC FRAMEWORK

Deuteronomy 14:22–29 and 26:12–15 are facts, raw data only. It is important to add immediately that DC nowhere tells the reader how to interpret the data it contains. Haas, however, argues that one should

---

2 For a detailed treatment on how the drafters of Deut 12–26 incorporated extant legal injunctions into their sociopolitical program, see Levinson 1997.

analyze biblical law much in the same manner one would examine law in other human societies (68). The present study on Deut 14:22–29 and 26:12–15, therefore, draws from contemporary theories of law and society. It is important to mention that the academic framework for my examination of these regulations proceeds from Critical Theory.[3] This approach evaluates institutions and social phenomena with a special sensitivity to class, socioeconomic inequality, ideology, interests, and the consequences of legal proscriptions for the everyday, practical affairs of social subgroups in human communities.

Since 1970, Critical Theory has spawned three major legal trajectories: Critical Legal Studies (CLS), Feminist Legal Theory, and Critical Race Theory (CRT). Critical Theorizing about law embraces a movement of sociologists, legal scholars, political scientists, and philosophers, whose research and professional work analyzes the role that legal prescriptions play in maintaining relations of domination and subordination in societies that are economically heterogeneous and asymmetric.

While Critical Legal scholars draw from different sources of knowledge and explore distinct research questions, three ideas about law that appear in their literature inform the present paper:

(1) Critical Theorizing about law contends that legal sanctions are often the result of special interests in human communities. The belief that laws reflect the ethos of powerful subgroups informs this claim. Critical Theorizing about legal proscriptions contends that affluent socioeconomic subgroups have the resources to create regulations that establish their positions of privilege and justify their ideas about proper moral action.

(2) Critical Theorizing about law argues that legal sanctions often focus on categories of individuals in human societies. These angles of vision contend that social criteria over which people have little or no control, such as race, gender, sexual orientation, and class, become the basis for social subgrouping and the patterning of social relations. Thus, critical perspectives about law propose that a link is present between one's social features and one's socioeconomic location.

(3) Critical Theorizing about law rests upon the premise that frameworks for discussing the effects of legal injunctions in a society should include the perspective of those vulnerable social subgroups that are immediately affected by the regulations in question. Critical Theory about legal injunctions does not defend an essentialist position, for it posits that competing ideas and difference of opinion regarding social

---

3 For examples of and treatments on Critical Theorizing about law, see Vago; Crenshaw et al.; and Delgado.

phenomena are present among people who comprise vulnerable social subgroups. Critical Theorizing about legal injunctions, however, advocates the position that subordinate socioeconomic individuals often view social phenomena differently from dominant, powerful individuals; thus different angles of vision on social institutions might be present between socioeconomic subgroups in the same society.

The yields of current social-scientific study of ancient Israelite society justifies using Critical Theorizing about law to shape a framework for discussing the relationship of Deut 14:22–29 and 26:12–15 to the plight of the *almanah, ger,* and *yatom.* As was said above, conventional scholarship proposes that these laws came into being after the appearance of the state. Chaney postulates that the formation of the state in ancient Israel spawned a network of phenomena. He suggests that urbanization and politico-economic centralization were concomitants of the Israelite monarchy. He argues also that these phenomena contributed to the development of a tiered community where one group controlled large percentages of the means of production. With the appearance of the Israelite monarchy, the construction of the first temple, and the foreign and domestic policy of Solomon, the social composition of the Israelite communities became more diverse and stratified. Prophetic circles, levels in cultic leadership, owners of large amounts of land, monarchic officials, sages, and other social groups became more apparent. Concomitant with political and economic centralization and with urbanization in ancient Israel, the socioeconomic infrastructure was conducive to the emergence of an elite ruling class whose bases of social standing and economic affluence were not completely dependent upon land ownership. Critical Theory about law presupposes the presence of competing socioeconomic subgroups in human communities, and it argues that it is unsafe to explore law without regard for the antagonisms that proceed from the presence of these social elements in a human society.

Knight and Barton (5–6) maintain that ideas about morality in the Hebrew Bible might not be conterminous with ideas about morality among the masses in ancient Israel. Working from the position that Knight and Barton are correct, their research into the ethics of ancient Israel leads to the conclusion that subgroups in the biblical communities separated acceptable moral ideas from unacceptable ones. As was said above, Critical Theory about law rejects the idea that legal proscriptions are above politico-economic considerations; consequently, it posits that legal codes often reflect the values of elitist subgroups in human societies. When we allow this premise to shape our understanding of law in ancient Israel, we can argue that the moral points of view in DC identify those ethical positions that were crucial to a substratum of individuals. Moreover, we can contend that the ethical positions in Deut 14:22–29 and

26:12–15 were responses to issues that the drafters of these codes sought to prevent or restrain.

Deuteronomy 14:22–29 and 26:12–15 are human creations—individuals or subgroups in the biblical communities produced these legal injunctions. This fact justifies attentiveness to the overwhelmingly important role that self-interest can play in moral conduct. In fact it is a grave error to neglect the fact that human beings often behave in ways that proceed from their own self-regard. Since these legal injunctions are human creations, this justifies raising questions about self-interests, while exploring the effects of these regulations in ancient Israelite society. Furthermore, these laws regulate the dispensing of grain, fruit, oil, and meat in the biblical communities. This fact too justifies suspicion concerning economic proclivity in these codes.

My framework, therefore, focuses on the human element in the formulation of a layer of law in DC. It probes these legal injunctions with a special interest in their contribution to the advantage of the overprivileged and to the disadvantage of the underprivileged in ancient Israel. This approach honors the vantage of a category of vulnerable persons. It treats these types of persons as the central subjects in the investigative process and permits unheard voices in Deut 14:22–29 and 26:12–15 to speak.

DEUTERONOMIC LEGISLATIONS AND THE PLIGHT OF THE WIDOW, STRANGER, AND ORPHAN

This essay argues that Deut 14:22–29 and 26:12–15 relegated the *almanah, ger,* and *yatom* to positions of socioeconomic inferiority in ancient Israelite society. Now I will show four ways that these regulations contributed to the predicaments of these types of persons in the biblical communities. Viewing these laws with a special sensitivity to the ways that these individual legislations worked to the disadvantage of this subgroup, then, gives rise to a very different reading of these so-called humanitarian codes.

Centralization and the Victimization of Widows, Strangers, and Orphans in the Biblical Communities

Deuteronomy 14:23a and 24b contain the phrase *bammaqom asher yibhar* ("in the place that [Yahweh] chooses"). This innovation suggests that the deity designated a site for the distribution of material goods to the *almanah, ger,* and *yatom.* Noteworthy, however, is that this innovation worked to the disadvantage of this social subgroup, for it increased the chance that this category of socially weak persons suffered hardship, mistreatment, and personal injury. It is possible to argue that these persons were without the protection of adult males (Bennett: 35–117).

Working from the positions that these people were without the protection of adult males and that the site for the distribution of produce and meat was a great distance from the local villages or cities where these individuals lived, two unfortunate sets of circumstances come into play. On the one hand, traveling to and returning from this site with grain, wine, and meat placed these persons at the mercy of murderers, rapists, robbers, kidnappers, and other nefarious individuals. On the other hand, if the *almanah, ger,* and *yatom* made trips to these sites for the distribution of material goods, they might have remained and formed permanent communities of beggars, prostitutes, or sources for slave labor. Forcing these defenseless persons to appear at the official cultic site in order to collect food ignores a main feature of their social dilemma. Therefore, issues associated with the pilgrimage to the official shrine might have influenced these persons negatively, in that the fear of becoming the victims of crime kept them from making the journey to feed at the public trough. Deuteronomy 14:22–29, therefore, reflects the decontextualization of these types of persons, in that this regulation prescribed a solution that appears to be indifferent to their circumstances. This disregard for the practical, everyday implications of calling for defenseless individuals to travel throughout Syria-Palestine endangered, and broke ground for the dehumanization of, this social subgroup in ancient Israelite society.

Centralization and the Indoctrination of the Widow, Stranger, and Orphan
Deuteronomy 14:22–29 uses theology to justify limiting the sites for the distribution of grain, meat, oil, and wine to the *almanah, ger,* and *yatom.* This innovation entices this social subgroup into thinking that this change was the will of the deity. This feature of the law lures these defenseless human beings into overlooking the probability that the choice of the site for distributing public aid proceeded from a private agendum. This assertion conceals the fact that centralizing the presentation and distribution of produce positioned priests and prophets to advance their religio-politico-economic ideas and to diversify the sources from which they could draw material sustenance. By advocating the position that sites for distributing goods to the *almanah, ger,* and *yatom* was the choice of Yahweh, Deut 14:22–29 could promulgate an otherwise biased, sectarian viewpoint about this program: this ideology hides the interests of a subgroup in the Yahweh-alone cult, by implying that the deity commanded a change of venue for the presentation and distribution of tithes of agriculture, produce, meat, and wine.

Periodic Assistance and the Oppression of the Widow, Stranger, and Orphan
Deuteronomy 14:22–29 and 26:12–15 link the distribution of corn, wine, oil, and livestock to the *almanah, ger,* and *yatom* to periodic events

in the biblical communities. These laws demand that persons allocate commodities to the *almanah, ger,* and *yatom* every three years. Two major interrelated phenomena, therefore, might proceed from assigning these dates for sharing produce and meat with these human beings. Each phenomenon could contribute to the dehumanization of this vulnerable, socially weak category of persons.

Periodic Assistance and the Protracted Indigence of the Widow, Stranger, and Orphan. According to Deut 14:22–29 and 26:12–15, the *almanah, ger,* and *yatom* received tithes of produce and meat every three years. The question quite naturally arises: Where did these individuals obtain food and other provisions between periods for the distribution of the triennial tithes? The infrequent distribution of meat, vegetables, and fruits contributed to a critical level of deprivation and hardship for these types of persons and forced them into exploitative relationships. Since Deut 14:22–29 and 26:12–15 earmarked two out of every six years for allocating food to a category of persons who were without traditional means for economic support, it is possible to argue that these laws forced these persons to involve themselves in dehumanizing occupations in order to eke out their existence. Perhaps it was from debt slavery, prostitution, or from other exploitative economic arrangements that the *almanah, ger,* and *yatom* obtained sustenance in the meanwhile.

Periodic Assistance and the False Sense of Hope in the Widow, Stranger, and Orphan. Deuteronomy 14:22–29 and 26:12–15 suggest that farmers and herders were going to share commodities with the *almanah, ger,* and *yatom.* It is possible that some concern for these vulnerable individuals was present among farmers and herders. It is improbable, however, that the commitment to providing aid for the *almanah, ger,* and *yatom* was widespread among the masses. Two reasons justify this claim.

First, most farmers and herders were poor and eked out their existence; consequently, it is probable that points of contact were present between the circumstances of farmers and herders and the plight of the *almanah, ger,* and *yatom.*

Second, 1 Sam 8:11–22 implies that after the formation of the state, most local farmers and herders supported urban elites and supplied the monarchy with food, supplies, and labor. What is more, scholarly research into economic conditions in agrarian societies brings into play the probability that the payment of debts to landlords and to persons elsewhere in the local villages or cities, bartering with artisans and merchants, and the reciprocation of acts of charity left local peasant farmers with little or no sustenance.[4] Thus, it is probable that crops and livestock that were present after bartering and after the payment of debts supported the households of local farmers and herders. Working with the assumption that peasants simply did not have much food left after taking care of their daily obligations, Deut 14:22–29 and 26:12–15 simply become romantic legal injunctions. These laws invite the *almanah, ger,* and *yatom* to ignore the fact that local farmers and herders had food only enough to share with their families and with those whose services they needed in order to maintain a basic level of existence. Regulations that imply that the peasantry would share their small amounts of meat and produce with the *almanah, ger,* and *yatom* provoked these socially disadvantaged persons to exercise their imaginative abilities and create fiction.

Conclusion

Deuteronomy 14:22–29 and 26:12–15 prescribed morality toward the *almanah, ger,* and *yatom*. These laws centralize the presentation and distribution of tithes of grain, fruit, meat, and oil. What is more, these legal injunctions state that this development was the will of the deity. These laws imply that local farmers and herders had a moral obligation to distribute produce and meat every three years to the *almanah, ger,* and *yatom*. In my reading of these texts, I operated from a different center. I examined these legal injunctions from a perspective analogous to the vantage point of underclass, vulnerable subgroups in a society. This approach positioned me to argue that the innovations in these laws cleared the way for the victimization and protracted indigence of the *almanah, ger,* and *yatom*. This angle of vision also provides a framework for arguing that the distinct ideology in these regulations invited this category of vulnerable, socially weak individuals to form illusions about the probability and efficaciousness of a public relief program. It is probable, therefore, that these regulations contributed to the oppression of these persons in ancient Israelite society.

The question immediately arises: Are these texts of any use to the local church in its community service programs? I answer—yes. The public theologians who direct these programs, however, must invoke constantly a hermeneutic of suspicion. An examination of Deut 14:22–29 and 26:12–15 from the perspective of the underdog brings to the forefront the claim that social-service oriented institutions should be critical of the services they proffer to the underdog. That is to say, in providing services

---

4 For treatment on subsistence strategies in the biblical communities, see McNutt.

to homeless, indigent, or disenfranchised persons, social-service organizations should be guided by a systematic process that seeks to ameliorate the circumstances of this category of people. The Black church, in particular, should ensure that it affirms these persons, while addressing the causes of their predicament. The Black church, therefore, should guarantee that their programs contribute to the humanization of marginalized groups. In doing this, it can institute corrective measures and continue to develop self-determining human beings in distressed communities.

THE ROLE OF ETHNICITY IN THE SOCIAL LOCATION OF 1 CORINTHIANS 7:17–24

Brad Ronnell Braxton
Wake Forest University

A TRANSLATION[1] OF 1 CORINTHIANS 7:17–24

[17] Only, let each of you lead your life, as the Lord assigned, as God has called. Thus, in all the churches I command this. [18] If anyone was circumcised when he was called, let him not remove the marks of circumcision. If anyone was called in the state of uncircumcision, let him not be circumcised. [19] Circumcision is nothing, and uncircumcision is nothing, but keeping (the) commandments of God. [20] Let each of you remain in the calling in which you were called. [21] Were you a slave when called? Let it not be a care to you. But even if you are able to become free, rather use the opportunity. [22] For the slave called in the Lord is a freed person of the Lord; likewise, the free person called is a slave of Christ. [23] You have been bought with a price; do not become slaves of people. [24] Each in the calling in which you were called, brothers and sisters, in this let each of you remain before God.

REVISITING ETHNICITY

An overlooked feature of the social location of many New Testament writings is the concept of ethnicity. Ferdinand Christian Baur, the founder of the Tübingen School and the pioneer of "historical theology," argued in the nineteenth century that the prime mover in the development of early Christianity was the controversy between Jews and Gentiles or, more specifically, the controversy between Jewish Christianity and Gentile Christianity. Commenting on the growing

---

1 I have tried to strike a balance between an accurate rendering of the Greek and the use of gender-inclusive language where appropriate.

schism between Jewish and Gentile Christianity in the first century, Baur wrote:

> They [Jewish Christians] could not look on with indifference when they saw a Gentile Christian church arising over against the church of Jerusalem in utter disregard of the ordinances and privilege of Jerusalem, and yet putting forth a claim to equal place and dignity with themselves. (51–52)

As history would show, Baur's insights, though seminal and in many regards correct, were too sharply configured, and thus too myopic. In his work, Baur was more interested in the *theological* differences between Jewish Christianity and Gentile Christianity than he was in the question of ethnicity per se. As Robert Morgan has argued, Baur did not account for other factors that influenced both the shape and the direction of early Christianity (72).

Other scholars, in their attempts to modify or correct Baur's over-emphasis, recognized the ethnic distinction between Jewish and Gentile Christianity, but the ethnic distinction was always a means to an end and never an end unto itself. The ethnic distinction between Jewish and Gentile Christianity was in service of a discussion of history. Wilhelm Bousset, in his classic work *Kyrios Christos,* traced the changes that the religion of Jesus and of Palestinian Christianity underwent as it moved into new geographic and ethnic boundaries. Yet, this investigation was not so interested in issues of ethnicity per se as it was in tracing historical developments. To the degree that the *religionsgeschictliche Schule* (history of religions school) was interested in exploring and tracing the development of Christianity as a living religion, it, perhaps, failed to account fully for the concept and role of ethnicity.

In the current milieu of New Testament scholarship, interdisciplinary approaches to exegesis are gaining credibility and wider application (Robbins: 15–16). Thus, recent insights from cultural anthropologists and sociologists have awakened New Testament scholars to the importance of ethnicity (Bilde et al.). Previous New Testament scholars may have avoided the concept of ethnicity because it is notoriously difficult to define. In my opinion, the difficulty of defining ethnicity and of categorizing ethnic groups and boundaries in the New Testament social matrix contributes to the thick social and cultural texture of the Corinthian correspondence in general and of 1 Cor 7:17–24 in particular.

Before engaging the topic of ethnicity any further, a brief discussion distinguishing between older conceptions of ethnicity and new, emerging conceptions will be helpful. Typically, in more dated discussions of the role and import of ethnicity, the approach could be labeled as "essentialist." In an essentialist approach, there are thought to be rela-tively fixed, sometimes observable qualities or characteristics that define one ethnic group over against another. In other words, such an approach is designed to locate the "essence" of what it means to belong to a particular ethnic group.

In the wake of the growing realization gained from the social sciences that group and individual identities are social constructions, the criteria for establishing ethnic boundaries have changed. Social anthropologists are insisting that group and individual identities should be explored on a variety of levels, including the *subjective* evaluations of group members themselves (J. Smith). Social anthropology encourages complex, subjec-tive analysis in addition to simple, objective analysis (Elliott).

A chief architect of this shift in the study of ethnic identity is the Nor-wegian social anthropologist Fredrik Barth. Barth argues:

> The symbolic and social construction of people's realities entail the neces-sity of comprehending interpersonal events by interpreting them, on many simultaneous levels of meaning and significance, by means of the codes and keys employed in their own culture as well as analyzing them by canons which we can accept as objectively, materially adequate. (8)

In addition to calling for a greater appreciation of complexity in ascertain-ing ethnic identity, Barth also contends that scholars have not paid enough attention to the construction and maintenance of ethnic boundaries (198). Boundary maintenance among ethnic groups is complicated and problem-atic. In the social mechanisms of an ethnic group, there are particular roles, functions, and cultural features that lead to the creation of bound-aries around the group. Yet, the boundaries created by these roles, functions, and cultural features are neither impervious nor absolute. The cultural features, which identify an ethnic group, may change according to various circumstances.[2]

In light of the volatile nature of those ethnic boundaries based on cul-tural features, social anthropologists have looked to another important and overlooked feature of ethnic boundaries, namely, self-identification, or what group members are saying about themselves. Individual and group self-identification gives insight into the attitudes of group mem-bers. Privileging self-identification as a primary criterion of ethnic identity, social anthropologists have discovered that persons in ethnic

---

2 Barth remarks, "It is thus inadequate to regard overt institutional forms as constitut-ing the cultural features which at any time distinguish an ethnic group—these overt forms are determined by ecology as well as by transmitted culture" (202).

group A may actually adopt cultural features that generally typify ethnic group B. Yet, these persons continue to identify themselves as members of group A (Barth: 213).

Ethnicity is as much a function of attitudes expressed in discourse as it is an analysis of observable cultural features. Thus, there must be a shift from an infatuation with "objective" reports from readers distant in time and space from those being investigated to an attentive investigation to what these (ancient) groups are *saying* about themselves. Boundary mechanisms and markers for ethnic groups are contained frequently, but certainly not exclusively, in language. If identity is about discourse and language (i.e., people are in an ethnic group because they *say* they are in an ethnic group), the criteria for distinguishing ethnic boundaries must shift from the quest for external, "essential" characteristics to the analysis of attitudes.

Contending that ethnicity is more about attitudes than internal characteristics, Koen Goudriaan summarizes the implications of this new approach to ethnicity in six points. These six points will be borne in mind, and they will enhance my ensuing discussion of the import of ethnicity in first-century Corinth. Goudriaan's words are set off by quotations marks. My amplifications of his points are in italics. Goudriaan's six points are:

1. "Ethnicity is looked at from the inside" (Goudriaan: 75). *The categories used by insiders to describe themselves and to describe others become normative for ethnic boundaries.*

2. "Ethnicity, as a way of organizing cultural differences, implies that specific features of culture (in the broad sense) are singled out as ethnically significant, while others are neutral" (76).

3. "Ethnicity is an independent dimension of social life" (76). *The ethnicity of a group can never be reduced to any particular cultural feature of the society. Moreover, it could be said that ethnicity is greater than the sum of various cultural parts.*

4. "Survival of an ethnic identity group, in this view, is not the result of its biological reproduction, but the outcome of a continued interest on the part of its members in maintaining the boundaries" (76). *In light of this point, Goudriaan introduces the concept of ethnical strategy, which is the* "policy adopted by an individual or a group for applying ethnical categories to themselves and others in a range of different circumstances" (76).

5. "Ethnicity is a normal feature of social life. It does not automatically entail tension between the ethnic groups. So long as these are in

agreement on the roles they have to play in society, they may live peacefully together" (76).

6. "This marking off of [ethnical] boundaries is a universal trait of human experience. The way in which it manifests itself may, of course, vary greatly through the ages" (77). *For Goudriaan, point six is the heuristic* raison d'être, *which allows him and other scholars to employ the social category of ethnicity in diachronic analysis. Regardless of the culture and time period (be it twenty-first-century North American culture or first-century Mediterranean culture), groups distinguish themselves from one another ethnically. How groups distinguish themselves may differ, but such social differentiation is a constant. Thus, whereas the category of ethnicity as discussed above is, in some sense, a modern scholarly construct, the social phenomenon entailed in or meant by this construct will (or did) occur in actual social life (even ancient social life).*

Before leaving this abstract discussion of ethnicity, let me note the important distinction between culture and ethnicity. This approach to ethnicity presupposes the presence of cultural features and even allows for the presence of a shared culture between ethnic groups. Since, however, ethnicity emphasizes some features of culture as more or less important than others, it is possible for groups to share the *same culture* yet understand themselves to belong to totally different *ethnic* groups.

Ethnicity is an important but underutilized social category in New Testament exegesis. Employing this category, especially in the interpretation of passages where ethnic language is explicit, might greatly enhance our understanding of the complexities and ambiguities of early Christian communities and the writings these communities produced. One such passage where ethnic language is explicit is 1 Cor 7:17–24. Let us briefly explore how applying the concept of ethnicity might shape our exegesis.

ETHNICITY AND THE EXEGESIS[3] OF 1 CORINTHIANS 7:17–24

In my reading of the social location of 1 Cor 7:17–24, I contend that Paul is not retreating into the world of ideas, employing illustrations with

---

3 In this discussion, I have made a basic methodological decision. My discussion purposefully avoids the "Paul and the law debate," which has (pre)occupied much of Pauline scholarship in the last two decades. This debate is more an attempt to correct modern prejudice in Pauline exegesis (a correction that has its merits) than it is a debate about ancient ethnicity, the topic presently at hand. To superimpose this debate upon every Pauline passage where circumcision or law appears is to predetermine one's exegetical results, for questions posed control answers given. For a recent synopsis of this debate, see Kruse: 24–53.

no thought at all of their actual social content, value, and implications. Paul is not only dealing with the practical realities of marriage and sexuality. He is also an apostle whose symbolic world[4] is in upheaval. In such a crisis, hypothetical appeals would seem out of place.

These verses are part of a larger rhetorical attempt by Paul to secure those things that are coming loose in his symbolic world. For instance, it appears that certain persons in the Corinthian community are calling into question various aspects of Paul's interpretation of the gospel, and those same persons may also be casting doubt on Paul's apostolic authority. Moreover, Paul is not presenting a philosophy of maintaining the status quo per se. Instead, he is reflecting on the radical nature of the call of God, which creates the *ekklēsia,* and he is attempting to avoid the restructuring of the community boundaries he has inscribed by means of his kerygma.

In light of our earlier discussion about ethnicity, why does Paul appeal to the ethnic reality of circumcision in the first place? If, as I have intimated, the rhetorical situation of 1 Corinthians consists of Paul's perceived threats to the boundaries of his symbolic world, the issue at hand is, What role, if any, do change and difference (of opinion from Paul's) have in Paul's understanding of community boundaries? Does an acceptance of the kerygma necessitate change, not just internal, moral transformation, but concrete sociocultural, ethnic alteration? Or, in light of the gospel, is social change *adiaphora,* a matter of indifference left up to the conscience of the believer?

Since a salient issue for Paul is the role of societal changes with respect to the boundaries of the *ekklēsia,* Paul deals with concrete social practices and institutions that involve and are symbolic of societal changes: marriage and sexual practice,[5] ethnicity (construed here as circumcision or uncircumcision), and social status (configured here in terms of slavery).

The mention of circumcision and slavery is not arbitrary. Instead, it is Paul's attempt to wrestle with how the Corinthian community should treat rituals of change or transition. It is not unreasonable to believe that some in the Corinthian church were concerned about the role of ethnicity with respect to the kerygma. Does the gospel require an ethnic transformation, or is it indifferent to such transformation? Let us analyze the various social possibilities envisioned by Paul in 7:18.

---

4 A symbolic world, according to Luke Johnson, "is not an alternative ideal world removed from everyday life. To the contrary, it is the system of meanings that anchors the activities of individuals and communities in the real world" (L. T. Johnson: 11). For a classic discussion of symbolic universes, see Berger and Luckmann: 85–118.

5 In 1 Cor 7, he deals with those who are already married, those who are not married, and those who are contemplating divorce.

In 7:18ab, Paul writes, "If anyone was circumcised when he was called, let him not remove the marks of circumcision." The first concrete social scenario offered by Paul is that of a circumcised man wanting to submit to epispasm. An overlooked textual feature in verse 18 buttresses the claim that Paul has actual social practice and ethnic states in mind. Paul uses the technical medical term for reversing circumcision, epispasm. Paul implores the circumcised man, "*mē epispasthō*" (let him not be uncircumcised).

Since epispasm was a live option in Diaspora communities, what kind of person would fit the social profile of 7:18ab, that is, a circumcised person seeking epispasm? The most natural response would be a Jew.[6] What kind of Jew would have wanted to remove the marks of circumcision and why? Several options present themselves. The first option would be a man[7] who still wanted very much to be a Jew ethnically but by the same token wanted full and unfettered access to civic benefits, including Roman citizenship and upward social mobility in Corinthian institutions, such as the gymnasium. This kind of a Jew might view himself with a double identity, Jewish and Roman. Such dual identity would not necessarily have been problematic for the Romans. In the eyes of the Romans a person could be a Jew, observe Sabbath, send money to Jerusalem, and still hold Roman citizenship or still move up the ladder of power and honor in an important imperial city such as Corinth. Such a person, perhaps, would not want the embarrassment of his circumcision when exercising nude in the gymnasium or enjoying a moment of relaxation in the baths.[8]

If one were circumcised, it might be a great social hindrance, especially if a person had designs on some municipal office in Corinth. Yet, submitting to epispasm was not necessarily an indicator that a person had abandoned his Jewish ethnicity. This kind of person would be highly

---

6 Other groups in the Mediterranean world practiced circumcision. For example, in *The Histories*, Herodotus writes, "They [the Egyptians] practice circumcision, while men of other nations—except those who have learnt from Egypt—leave their private parts as nature made them" (143). The Jews, however, turned this cultural practice into a quintessential ethnic boundary marker. See Schäfer: 96–99.

7 Undoubtedly, male circumcision as the sign of the covenant in Israel raises a host of gender questions about the covenant status of women. For a discussion of the inherent gender difficulties and inequalities in privileging circumcision as a sign of the covenant, see Cohen: 12.

8 A fragmentary text in *Corpus Papyrorum Judaicarum* indicates the degree to which a circumcised man in a Diaspora setting might be the target of public scorn. The fragment reads, "and this man carrying a Jewish load [ostensibly this means a circumcised phallus]. Why do you laugh and why are some of you disgusted at what has been said or at the man whom you see?" (Tcherikover et al.: 117). For further discussion, see Kerkeslager.

acculturated but not necessarily assimilated, still maintaining an appreciation of himself as Jewish.

A second, equally live option would be that of a man who no longer wanted to be Jewish but instead wanted, in every way, to be identified with Greek or Roman customs and *ethnicity*. The Jewish man who submitted to epispasm as a way of denouncing his Jewish ethnicity would have been not only acculturated to Greek or Roman culture but also *assimilated* into Greek or Roman *ethnicity*. Without removing the marks of circumcision, a Jewish man in Corinth may not have had full access to Corinthian social life and power, and he would also have been the object of potentially severe social ridicule.

Yet, as we assess the social data we must remember that 1 Cor 7 is "insiders' rhetoric," written by a Christian apostle to a Christian community. Although the Jewish man in the Corinthian congregation who submitted to epispasm may have been denouncing his Jewish ethnicity, such a man would still have been a member of the *ekklēsia*. When Paul advocates that a circumcised man not seek uncircumcision, Paul's interest lies not in privileging Jewish ethnicity over against Greek or Roman ethnicities.

Instead Paul is trying to preserve the primacy of the new community (i.e., the *ekklēsia*) and the new identity of the Christian (as, of course, Paul has defined them). The new community, the *ekklēsia*, as Paul understands it, provides an identity that surpasses the honor and power-mechanisms of Greco-Roman cities. Richard Horsley rightly captures the *social* dimension of Paul's conception of the *ekklēsia*, which is often overlooked in theological discussions. Horsley writes:

> At several points in 1 Corinthians Paul articulates ways in which the assembly of saints is to constitute a community of a new society alternative to the dominant imperial society.... The assembly stands diametrically opposed to "the world" as a community of saints. As often observed, in Paul holiness refers to social-ethical behaviors and relations. (244, 246)

In 1 Cor 7, Paul is not merely responding to concerns in the Corinthian congregation, but also he is providing, according to the dictates of deliberative rhetoric, examples of the erosion of the boundaries of the symbolic world. For Paul, compelling examples of this erosion consist in *porneia* (sexual immorality), in all of its manifestations, and also in the adoption of standards from the social world, which cut against the grain of Paul's desire to make the Corinthian *ekklēsia* "an exclusive alternative community to the dominant society and its social networks" (Horsley: 249–50). For Paul, the means by which one is included in the *ekklēsia* is not ethnic identity but purity (here understood as an adherence to Paul's way of organizing the symbolic universe).

If "purity," and not ethnic status, is what characterizes existence in the *ekklēsia*, then the circumcised person should not remove his circumcision and the one called in a state of uncircumcision should not seek circumcision. Thus Paul remarks in 7:18cd, "If anyone was called in the state of uncircumcision, let him not be circumcised." Having investigated the first social scenario (i.e., the circumcised person attempting to remove his circumcision), let us now analyze the second scenario (i.e., the uncircumcised person contemplating circumcision). What kind of person in the Greco-Roman world who was uncircumcised would be seeking circumcision?

The obvious answer is a proselyte. In the history of Jewish–Greco-Roman encounters, there is sizable evidence that Jews were attracted by Greco-Roman practices and institutions and that Greeks and Romans were drawn by Jewish practices and institutions. For instance, there is ample evidence of Greek and Roman benefaction with respect to the building and maintenance of Jewish synagogues (Feldman: 51–55).[9] Moreover, there is evidence that there existed a group of non-Jews who participated in synagogue worship and were sympathetic to Jewish customs, the so-called God-fearers.[10]

Arguing against A. T. Kraabel (1981), scholars such as John Gager (1998) and Tessa Rajak have provided evidence that the term *theosebēs* (God-fearer) could very well have referred to proselytes who were "less fully Jewish than the others" but on their way to being fully Jewish (Rajak: 257). It is possible, even quite probable, that there existed semi-proselytes (258).

According to this line of reasoning, the uncircumcised man spoken of in 1 Cor 7:18c could be a non-Jew who has been (semi)proselytized to Judaism, stopping short of circumcision. It is possible that such semi-proselytes were considered Jewish not only by others but, more importantly, by themselves. This approach to ethnicity actually clarifies an important point in the debate concerning circumcision and its necessity with respect to Gentiles who wanted to enter the *ekklēsia*.

Early in the development of Christianity, Jewish leaders in Jerusalem[11] accepted that Gentiles could remain uncircumcised and still enter

---

9 The New Testament itself contains an example of Roman benefaction for a Jewish synagogue in the land of Israel. See Luke 7:1–10.

10 For example, there is a second- or third-century C.E. inscription from Aphrodisias in Asia Minor. The inscription, which dedicates a memorial, applies the term "God-fearers" to a group of non-Jewish sympathizers who appear to be very involved in the life of this particular Jewish community.

11 Gal 2:7–10. Notwithstanding Paul's rhetorical and theological agenda in Gal 2, New Testament scholars generally accept the historicity of Paul's account of the so-called Jerusalem conference.

the *ekklēsia*. The provisions of the Jerusalem conference left no room (at least theoretically) for ambiguity; uncircumcised Gentiles would be entering the *ekklēsia as Gentiles*. It is another matter altogether when uncircumcised proselytes (who are in the *ekklēsia*) remain uncircumcised and claim to be *Jews*. As long as uncircumcised Gentiles claimed to be *non-Jews*, there was no difficulty. When uncircumcised men claimed to be Jewish, this was another issue.

In Diaspora communities it was taken for granted by some, but not all, that circumcision was the *sine qua non* of Jewish ethnicity. An uncircumcised man seeking circumcision as described in 7:18cd would, in Paul's estimation, not be understanding his identity with respect to Christianity or the *ekklēsia* because there was already a standard practice in Pauline churches that the uncircumcised could enter the church without circumcision. The uncircumcised man seeking circumcision, although a member of the *ekklēsia*, would be defining his identity with respect to the synagogue.[12] Such a man would feel the need to submit to circumcision, not to be more fully a Christian, but to be more fully a Jew. For Paul, the problematic issue would not be becoming a Jew per se. Instead, the issue would be to allow becoming a Jew to supersede the most important identity bestowed upon the believer by virtue of the call, namely, membership in the *ekklēsia*. Thus, John Collins notes, "Paul's rejection of circumcision[13] symbolized a rejection of the ultimate efficacy of the contemporary synagogue" (185–86).

In other words, Paul de-emphasizes Greek and Jewish ethnicity with respect to the identity that really matters, namely, being a Christian or being in the *ekklēsia*. In this passage, it would appear that membership in the *ekklēsia* creates a new identity. The *ekklēsia* is comprised of Jews and Gentiles, but the sum of the *ekklēsia* is greater than its parts. In the history of Pauline scholarship, some have argued that Paul understood Christianity to be a "third race" or ethnicity. Whether or not Paul actually considered membership in the *ekklēsia* to constitute a "third race" is debatable. What I believe is beyond doubt is that from Paul's perspective

---

12 John J. Collins remarks, "Conversion to Judaism involved joining a new community and being accepted as a member of a synagogue. We may assume that synagogues would normally have insisted on circumcision, but in a place like Alexandria there may have been exceptions" (176). My suggestion is that in Corinth there may have been persons who proselytized to Judaism, stopping short of circumcision. Some of these "semiproselytes" may have felt the need to be more fully involved or accepted in the life of the synagogue by means of circumcision.

13 Paul also rejects uncircumcision in 1 Cor 7:18. This is the unusual and often overlooked point. In light of his assertions in Galatians, we would expect a rejection of circumcision. It is the concomitant rejection of uncircumcision that adds complexity to 1 Cor 7:18.

membership in the *ekklēsia* was to be *the* identity by which believers organized their existence.

Membership in the *ekklēsia* obligates one to keep the commands of God or the law of Christ. When one properly understands the importance of the *ekklēsia* in determining social existence, one sees the inherent futility of attempts to gain fuller access to the gymnasium or the synagogue.

To submit to epispasm so as to scale more swiftly the ladder of Greco-Roman life or to seek circumcision so as to be more fully incorporated into the synagogue are equivalent actions for Paul. They are two manifestations of the same problem, a denial of the most important identity bestowed upon the believer by the call of God, membership in the *ekklēsia*. Since submitting to epispasm and circumcision are equivalent, Paul arrives at a bold and unilateral affirmation in 7:19: "Circumcision is nothing, and uncircumcision is nothing, but keeping the commandments of God." Then, as if to remind his hearers of the importance of the call that makes one a Christian, in 7:20 he reiterates that believers are to remain in their call; that is, they are to remain in the *ekklēsia*.

In light of Paul's de-emphasis of ethnicity in 7:17–19, I am led to ask the following questions: Did Paul underestimate the role of ethnicity in community formation? Did the fledgling Christian community have enough tradition and stability to compete with the attractions of the gymnasium and the synagogue? Why should one who had entered the *ekklēsia* feel that "membership" in the *ekklēsia* was sufficient to meet all social needs?

Each of these questions itself could generate voluminous answers, but, in short, I believe that Paul underestimated the role of ethnicity in configuring social existence. Interestingly, in several places in his other writings (e.g., Rom 3:1–4; 9:1–11:36; Gal 2:15; 1 Thess 1:9), Paul is unable to extricate himself from his own ethnic assumptions and biases. Yet, it was his belief and hope that these ethnic assumptions and biases in others could be held in abeyance, if not eradicated, so that a new social unit could be configured, the *ekklēsia*. Paul's goal may have been laudable, but his method of achieving the goal may have been at best naive and at worst ambiguous concerning the role (and power) of ethnic identity.

Conclusion

In sum, 1 Cor 7:17–24 may not be an unimportant digression. In these verses, Paul may arrive at the heart of the matter: What is the relationship between alterations in one's social conditions and one's membership in the *ekklēsia*? In 1 Cor 5–7, Paul has attempted to combat one threat to his symbolic word, namely, *porneia* in all its manifestations. In 7:17–24, changes of social condition, which include circumcision/uncircumcision and slavery and manumission, may also be challenging the boundaries of

Paul's symbolic world. Such changes could potentially involve not just individual believers' preferences but also larger institutions such as the gymnasium and the synagogue.

Greater complexity emerges if one considers that some of the Corinthians may not have viewed issues of ethnicity through the same ideological lens as Paul. Ironically, Paul may have unwittingly provided the Corinthians with a different set of lenses than he had intended. In 1 Cor 7 Paul could be understood as intimating that certain social changes are *adiaphora* with respect to one's position in the *ekklēsia*. Other changes, according to Paul, are more problematic.

What if, on the one hand, some of the Corinthians agreed with Paul that certain social changes are *adiaphora,* but, on the other hand, they disagreed with Paul concerning which changes fell under that category? When Paul says that both circumcision and uncircumcision are nothing, it would appear that he does not simply understand ethnic alteration as harmlessly "irrelevant." Emphasizing ethnic status *in addition to* one's status in the *ekklēsia* may have been more than irrelevant for Paul; it may have been problematic, especially in light of the allure of the gymnasium and the synagogue.

However, for one to affirm ethnic status in addition to one's status in the *ekklēsia* may not have posed the same problem for the Corinthians as it may have for Paul. In other words, instead of viewing ethnic alterations as a threat to one's membership in and allegiance to the *ekklēsia*, some of the Corinthians may have viewed such alterations as unrelated and certainly not harmful to their standing in the *ekklēsia*. The Corinthians may have taken elements of Paul's teaching and arrived at different conclusions.

Undoubtedly, the *ekklēsia* was important to certain persons in Corinth, but, perhaps, it was not an exhaustive identity marker. The very fact that ethnicity was "irrelevant" with respect to the *ekklēsia* may have been their justification for affirming their ethnic status. Some Corinthian Christians may not have viewed ethnicity and religious affiliation as inimical. Each social reality may have affirmed a different aspect of their identity. Thus, their ideological understanding of the factors of social identity may have been more fluid and complex than Paul's.

Possibly, some of the Corinthians may have understood the importance of the *ekklēsia* and still sought epispasm so as to enjoy the benefits of unfettered access to the Corinthian gymnasium. Or one could still be a Christian and be circumcised in order to have greater access to the Corinthian synagogue. There were certain *ethnic* benefits that may have come with either circumcision or uncircumcision that may have been very attractive to some in the Corinthian community. If such persons had an understanding of the nature of the *ekklēsia* that was different from Paul's, they may have felt as if they could belong simultaneously to "competing" institutions. Thus, in fascinating ways, Paul's admission that circumcision and uncircumcision are "nothing" may not have prevented some from making these changes but, ironically, may have encouraged some to seek these changes.

Paul's *de*-emphasis of Jewish and Greek ethnicity in favor of the "third ethnicity" of being in the *ekklēsia* may have, ironically, caused people to focus all the more on ethnic realities. Paul continued to struggle with the relationship between ethnic heritage and Christian identity, but some in the Corinthian *ekklēsia* may not have had that struggle. For them, the rites of passage into a new ethnic heritage would not have necessarily impugned their standing in the *ekklēsia*. In order to clarify the ideological stance that I imagine some of the Corinthians holding, let me use the contemporary example of Kwanzaa, the African American ethnic holiday.

In 1966, noted scholar and African American activist Maulana "Ron" Karenga created the holiday of Kwanzaa (McClester). Even in the midst of the gains of the Civil Rights movement and the consciousness raising of the Black Power movement, African Americans in the late 1960s were still victimized by the pernicious ideological legacy of white supremacy and racial, educational, and economic discrimination.

Kwanzaa was implemented as an antidote to the virus of white racism. It would be an annual celebration, centering around seven principles of communal uplift and individual responsibility. For the children of the *African Diaspora* resident on American soil, Kwanzaa would be a time to celebrate the unique ethnic heritage called *African American*. In this celebration, the emphasis would be as much on the American as it would be on the African, and vice versa.

Interestingly, the celebration of Kwanzaa would begin December 26 and continue for seven days. Needless to say, in its inception, the chronological proximity of this *ethnic* festival to the religious holiday of Christmas caused considerable unrest in the religious community. Many persons, including religious leaders, labeled this holiday as a "pagan" festival—one designed subtly or not so subtly "to take the Christ out of Christmas." Those African Americans who felt as if this ethnic celebration desecrated one's religious devotion during a sacred time of the year could be said to be the contemporary manifestation of the Pauline ideology of 1 Corinthians. That is, ethnic heritage and Christian identity were seen in a more inimical or antithetical fashion.

On the other hand, as the celebration of Kwanzaa has grown in popularity, many African Americans, and especially African American Christians, have realized that Kwanzaa and Christmas are not competing realities at all. The former is an ethnic celebration, the latter a religious one. For some, precisely because the two holidays are unrelated and affirm different realities, they can be appropriated at the same time.

For others, precisely because ethnic heritage and religious devotion are inextricably linked, these holidays must be appropriated at the same time. That is, in some Christian congregations, Kwanzaa and Christmas are now celebrated simultaneously as a way of saying that there is something unique and powerful about *African American Christian* heritage. Such people affirm that they are not just Christians, but they are *African American* Christians. Such people also affirm that they are not just African American, but they are African American *Christians.*

Those African Americans who feel that ethnic and religious realities can and/or must be appropriated at the same time can be said to be the modern manifestation of the ideology that I imagine some in the Corinthian church may have held. Precisely because the gymnasium and the *ekklēsia* or the synagogue and the *ekklēsia* affirm different realities, membership in both institutions can be held concomitantly. Perhaps it was the more fluid understanding of social identity among some of the Corinthians—an understanding that could accommodate a multiplicity of identity markers—that prompted Paul to write, "Circumcision is nothing and uncircumcision is nothing, but keeping the commandments of God."

For Paul, seeking either circumcision/uncircumcision and yet maintaining a Christian identity were contrasting notions. For certain Corinthians, circumcision/uncircumcision and Christian identity may have been unrelated and therefore appropriately incorporated into their social identity. Therefore, it may have been quite possible for them to robustly affirm their ethnic identity while concomitantly affirming their religious identity. Such persons would be Greeks or Jews *and* Christians, participants in the gymnasium or synagogue *and* members of the *ekklēsia.*

Or equally, for some persons circumcision/uncircumcision and Christian identity may have been related and therefore necessarily integrated into their social identity. Such persons would have been *Jewish* Christians or *Greek* Christians. In short, Paul's statement, "Circumcision is nothing and uncircumcision is nothing, but keeping the commandments of God," may have precipitated different ideological responses from the Corinthians, or this statement may have been Paul's response to those different ideological stances among the Corinthians.

As a proud member of the *African American Christian* tradition—a tradition that has unashamedly mingled the ethnic and the religious to the point that it is nearly impossible to distinguish the ethnic from the religious—my response might be to Paul, "For me and my house, ethnic heritage is not a deterrent to 'keeping the commandments of God' but rather the very context through which those commandments are kept." I am an African American. I am a Christian. I am an *African American Christian.* To single out and prioritize the parts that make up my whole may substantially and negatively alter that whole.

THE BIBLE AND MODELS OF LIBERATION IN THE AFRICAN AMERICAN EXPERIENCE

Demetrius K. Williams
Tulane University

The Bible has been traditionally the most important source for the articulation of liberation in the experience of people of African descent in North America. Cain Felder suggests that the black church and others within black religious traditions give allegiance to biblical faith and witness, primarily because their own experiences seem to be depicted in the Bible (Felder 1989a: 155–57; 1989b: 5–7). For obvious reasons, then, African Americans were able to find within the Bible's theological language and the encoded experiences of its people analogous life situations and, more importantly, biblical models that echoed in many respects the intrinsic equality and humanity of all people before the God of the Bible. Scripture enabled African Americans to affirm a view of God that differed significantly from that of their oppressors. The intention of the slave master was to present to the slaves a conception of God that would make the slaves compliant, obedient, and docile. These desired qualities were supposed to make them better slaves and faithful servants of their masters. Many slaves rejected this view of God because it contradicted their African heritage and also because it contradicted the witness of the scriptures (Cone 1975: 31).

Thus it was through the scriptures that enslaved African American people found models and paradigms to construct visions of hope. Various biblical models have served as paradigms for African Americans in particular historical moods and moments. That is, African Americans' religious and political uses of the Bible correspond to distinct formations in their social history and coincide also with biblical formations of social history (T. Smith: 17). Several biblical models have informed African American experience, resulting in conceptual paradigms such as exodus, wilderness and promised land, Ethiopia and Egypt, and captivity and exile/Diaspora (ibid.).

BRIEF REVIEW OF CLASSICAL BIBLICAL MODELS
IN THE AFRICAN AMERICAN RELIGIOUS TRADITION

The most important biblical model or paradigm of liberation in African American social and religious history is the exodus. The biblical account of the miraculous delivery of the children of Israel from slavery in Egypt under the leadership of Moses evoked similar hopes and dreams in the minds of the enslaved African American community. Outnumbered and closely controlled by the restricting North American hegemonic slavocracy, the hopes of African Americans' liberation lay in a miraculous act of the divine for which the exodus motif served well. This motif configures the transfer of African American people from oppression to freedom under the leadership or inspiration of Moses figures (ibid.). With the actualization of the Emancipation Proclamation, African Americans realized that a decisive event had become a reality in their own historical experience. This presidential order, following the outbreak of the Civil War, confirmed to enslaved Africans in North America that the God who delivered the ancient Hebrew slaves from Egyptian bondage had responded to their oppression also. For this reason, they were convinced that the likelihood of continuing reenactments from biblical narrative could be expected. To this reality Theophus Smith noted:

> Henceforth many African American believers and converts would be convinced of the possibility that through prayer and expectation, the rough acts of obedience and righteousness, black folk could inherit divine promises of prosperity and freedom. Furthermore, an apparent precondition for such bestowals would appear to be their linkage to biblical models. That singular instance, the link between Lincoln's role in the emancipation and Moses' role in the Exodus, would distinguish itself as a kind of paradigm. In this manner a new development in the ancient tradition of biblical typology emerged in the collective psyche of a displaced people. (55)

However, less than ten years after the dream of freedom from slavery became a reality, it was soon dashed against the rocks of a failed Reconstruction effort and a new form of American aggression and oppression: "Jim Crow." The biblical model most analogous to this historical mood and moment was the Hebrew experience of "wandering in the wilderness." While African Americans (like the ancient Hebrews) were set free from slavery, they encountered debilitating setbacks and unrealized expectations. One ex-slave remarked during this trying period that black preachers encouraged their people by comparing their situation to that of the children of Israel wandering in the wilderness: "De preachers would exhort us dat us was de chillen o'

Israel in de wilderness an' de Lord done sent us to take dis land o' milk and honey. (Raboteau: 304).

W. E. B. Du Bois in *The Souls of Black Folk* also invoked the "forty-years-of-wilderness" theme. In the African American experience the theme of "wilderness" can signify either the post-Reconstruction period of the late nineteenth century or the early colonial period (T. Smith: 101). Du Bois, like the ex-slave, applied the wilderness motif to the collapse of the reconstruction experiment and the failure to realize a democratic "promised land" in the South after the emancipation of the slaves in 1865. He says,

> Years have passed away since then,—ten, twenty, forty; forty years of national life, forty years of renewal and development, and yet the swarthy spectre sits in its accustomed seat at the Nation's feast. In vain do we cry to this our vastest social problem.... The Nation has not yet found peace from its sins; the freedman has not yet found in freedom his promised land. Whatever good may have come in these years of change, the shadow of deep disappointment rests upon the Negro people. (1969: 47–48)

Instead of reaching a biblical "promised land," the fate of African Americans was conceived in the pattern of ancient Israel's wilderness experience. Moreover, according to Smith, "true to the Bible's Wilderness figure their experience included the advent of new legal and juridical traditions. The new laws were distinguished for their uniformly oppressive and toxic effects. This situation fell far short of the dream of freedom long desired by black folk in America since the colonial period" (T. Smith: 101). Arguably, this period of "wandering" remained applicable until the mid-twentieth century, ending with the rise of the Civil Rights movement.

With the emergence of the Civil Rights movement of the 1950s and 1960s and a renewed militancy, the exodus motif emerged again. In this period the wilderness figure gave way to the latter configuration in the exodus saga—"possessing the promised land." African Americans felt that they were in a position to move into the promised land filled with the "milk and honey" of equal opportunity and social advancement. America as a "promised land" has been a central idea for many ethnic and social groups throughout United States history. It has especially been such for African Americans seeking remedies from race and class oppression (T. Smith: 17). For many the first exodus experience liberated African Americans from a particular form of racial/class oppression, namely, their racially based status as slaves. The new appropriation was to liberate the nation and African Americans from racial and economic oppression ("Jim Crow," that is, "separate but equal," or in reality "separate but unequal"—entailing second-class citizenship). They wanted the nation to "judge not by the color of one's skin, but by the content of one's character." This would make America an open and democratic society for all of its citizens. If America could come to terms with its racism, then America as the promised land of economic and social freedom, regardless of race or class, could be realized.

Finally, for our purposes (although more African American appropriations of biblical paradigms could be advanced), in contemporary African American religious thought the model of exile and Diaspora has been evoked to express the historical mood most analogous to the experience of biblical Israel. The use of the term "African Diaspora" has become popular since the 1960s black-consciousness movement.[1] It was in the early 1970s, however, that C. Shelby Rooks proposed that blacks should abandon the theme of "promised land," along with that of "the American dream," because the former had become tarnished by its crass reformulation into the latter. Rooks suggests that

> The Biblical image which has been at the heart of the black [American's] faith in the eventual appropriation of the American myth must be replaced.... My own very untested suggestion about a possible new image is that of an African Diaspora based on the Biblical story of the Babylonian Exile and the Final Jewish Diaspora. It is to the end of the Biblical history of Israel that black America must look rather than to the beginning. (Rooks: 8; quoted in T. Smith: 249)

Rooks's tentative suggestion at the beginning of the 1970s to reconceive African American experience as analogous to the Babylonian captivity and the Jewish Diaspora has become increasingly applicable for many as the twentieth century has come to a close (T. Smith: 249). Thus the paradigms of exile and Diaspora have been seen as more appropriate paradigms for interpreting the contemporary aspects of the African American experience.

---

1 On this issue Theophus Smith (250) states: "the figural correspondence between the worldwide dispersal of Jews and that of African peoples has been recognized at least since the early nineteenth century. The word 'Diaspora' itself derives from the Greek word for dispersion and was typically applied to the 'scattering' (as in Nehemiah 1.8) of the Jews among Gentile nations beginning with the fall of the Northern Kingdom to Assyria in 721 B.C.E. The dispersal of Jews in the Hellenistic world of the Roman Empire sets the scene for the appearance of the word in the Christian Scriptures (for example, John 7.35). According to this view, Diaspora configures a people's eschatological (end of the age) dispersal from every earthly homeland."

CRITIQUE OF CLASSICAL BIBLICAL MODELS IN THE
AFRICAN AMERICAN RELIGIOUS TRADITION

What is the meaning of this all too brief sketch? To be sure, it shows that the use of biblical models and paradigms reveals the importance of the Bible in the experiences and aspirations of African Americans in the past, present, and undoubtedly for the future. But in many ways these classical biblical models and configurations have not presented fully liberative paradigms. This has been recognized more clearly in the last few decades. Recently there have been several critiques of some of the classical paradigms, especially the exodus motif. Delores Williams, for example, strongly suggests that we must question the assumption that African American theologians can without qualification continue to make paradigmatic use of the Hebrews' exodus and election experience as recorded in the Bible (147). Indeed, she has uncovered some major fallacies in its usage that are difficult to ignore.

Williams advances several reasons for the inadequacies of the exodus paradigm for contemporary usage. First and foremost, the exodus paradigm can no longer serve as paradigmatic because it is not liberating for *all* the oppressed (144, 148). Black people historically, and some black liberation theologians of late, have identified so thoroughly with Israel's election and liberation that they have ignored "the figures in the Bible whose experience is analogous to that of black women" (149). Total identification with the Hebrews, but not with the other people who were later victimized by the former slaves (like the Canaanites), privileges the children of Israel and overlooks the violence and subjugation that they later perpetuated on other peoples. In addition, it underscores they way in which black women (who are analogous to those victimized non-Hebrew slaves in the Bible) have been overlooked and made invisible. This means, moreover, that if the God of the Bible sanctioned the victimization, servitude, and annihilation of non-Hebrew peoples, then the God of the Bible is "partial and discriminatory" (144–45). If this obtains, then God is not against all oppression for all people: Israel alone is favored.

> The point is that when non-Jewish people (like many African-American women who now claim themselves to be economically enslaved) read the entire Hebrew testament from the point of view of the non-Hebrew slave, there is no clear indication that God is against their perpetual enslavement. (146)

It turns out that on a close reading of the Bible with this new perspective, God may not be on the side of all the oppressed, only the oppressed of the descendants of Israel. Williams further avers that if

African Americans, then, identify with the non-Hebrew slave and not the Israelite, there is a nonliberating thread that runs through the Bible (144).

Randall C. Bailey concurs to a certain degree with this assessment, suggesting further that the exodus/liberation narratives (particularly the P or Priestly source) are not concerned necessarily with liberation but rather with the competition between the religion of Israel and that of Egypt. This means that the exodus saga was not read as a narrative strictly about liberation from Egyptian slavery but about the conflict of competing religions (1994: 16–17). "The leaving out of the liberation formula is not by chance. It is by design. The liberation is secondary" (17). Nevertheless, the liberation theme reasserts itself. As Bailey states:

> Unfortunately for P, this desire to supplant liberation thought with a call to piety did not win out in the tradition. The "signs and wonders" narrative was not allowed to stand alone.... In the final redaction of the Pentateuch, the "God of liberation" made more sense than the "God of Contest." As often happens, liberation wins out. (ibid.)

While the liberation theme eventually carries the day, it reveals that there were alternative readings of the exodus saga within the biblical tradition that were not concerned with social liberation. Moreover, the liberation narratives were originally concerned with class struggles and national struggles (R. Bailey 1995: 36).

Thus, a close and critical reading of the exodus narratives by both Williams and Bailey exposes some hidden flaws in the paradigmatic use of this biblical model. It certainly has been useful in the struggle for freedom, but it can only be used cautiously now. This is not unusual with the appropriation of biblical paradigms: they are useful for certain social and historical moments, but new information and situations entail a reevaluation of their use and function. The primary function of the exodus paradigm in African American religious history was that it could be invoked as a direct challenge to slavery, as Clarice Martin clarifies:

> [W]hereas the legitimacy of the slave regulation in the *Haustafeln* [household codes] could be challenged rather handily based on explicit paradigms about liberation from slavery in such narratives as Exodus 14, biblical narrative does not contain an equally *explicit and consistent* paradigm about the liberation of women from patriarchy, androcentrism and misogyny. (1991: 227; emphasis in original)

Although Martin does not deal explicitly with the analysis of the exodus narrative but with the household codes of the New Testament and their injunctions to slaves, she clarifies cogently the dilemma of the classical biblical narratives. Her assessment gets to the heart of the issue for our purposes. She perceives correctly that the appropriation of classical biblical paradigms in the African American experience (like the exodus in particular) addresses only the liberation from class and/or race oppression. African Americans' religious and political discourse was and is dominated by these concerns. While these matters remain legitimate and necessary, they stop short of including a paradigm that would take seriously the concerns and sexist oppression of African American women. For example, considering the situation of voting rights for freedmen and women in the nineteenth century and the African American "male led" Civil Rights movement in the twentieth century, the total equality and concerns of African American women were pushed aside as secondary. According to Cheryl Townsend Gilkes, the problem has been that for blacks in general the race issue has been most important. She states that

> black feminist theory has explicitly affirmed that "our situation as black people necessitates that we have solidarity around the fact of race." Black feminist church-women have not approached black religious institutions with the same level of indictment that white women have carried to theirs, in spite of the struggle over women in the pulpit. (1987: 77)

While Gilkes is correct in general, in the last two decades of the nineteenth century black Baptist women increasingly challenged such examples of gender inequality, working within the orthodoxy of the church to argue for their rights. In this way they held men accountable to the same text that authenticated their arguments for racial equality (Higginbotham: 120). To be sure, an early voice for equality within the African American women's community, Anna Julia Cooper, did not give primacy to gender discrimination over and against race discrimination, since black women were oppressed both because of their race and sex. In addition, they also had to contend with economic and educational discrimination—a third form of oppression (Baker-Fletcher: 61). Moreover, while Womanist theologians of late have launched even more challenging critiques of sexism, black women have still been expected not to challenge African American churches and religious organizations to consider their own sexist practices because the evil of racism has had precedence over sexism.

The result is that in many African American churches and religious organizations sexist practices are perpetuated. Black women are still expected to remain subordinate to black men and are discouraged from pursuing the preaching or pastoral ministries, both of which are prohibited to them in the Bible. Such prohibitions against female leadership and submission to male authority can be found in 1 Cor 14:33–36, 1 Tim 2:11–15, and the household codes of Col 3:18–4:1, Eph 5:21–6:9, and 1 Pet

2:13–3:7. The uncritical perpetuation of such biblical passages in African American churches has not been curtailed, despite the use of the Bible in the historical struggles for the realization of full humanity, freedom, and equal opportunity regardless of race or class. African Americans engaged this struggle, appealing to the authority of the Bible, despite the fact that proslavery white Americans used the Bible at the same time to support their racially based oppression. This meant that African Americans had to struggle with and against the Bible because of passages that apparently supported slavery. Notwithstanding, African Americans used the Bible to argue vehemently against race and class oppression. In their use of the Bible African Americans rejected biblical passages that sanctioned slavery, oppression, and race prejudice. This makes it puzzling, then, that the African American interpretive traditions, which found within the Bible models and paradigms of liberation from race and class oppression, were unwilling to explore the Bible to find equally liberating models to challenge the traditional roles and status of women, especially black women who suffered under the same harsh system of race and class oppression. The unfortunate result is that the early African American interpretive traditions, while claiming to represent the universal concerns of black people, have been willing to accept uncritically paradigms of gender oppression based upon the same Bible that was used to argue for race and class liberation. It seems that "while the 'nonracist' principle called attention to a common tradition shared by black churches, it masked the sexism that black churches shared with the dominant white society" (Higginbotham: 121).

GALATIANS 3:28 AS A POTENTIAL MODEL OF LIBERATION

What biblical model, then, could: (1) be inclusive of the multiple struggles of the African American experience; (2) fully embrace the concerns of African American women; and (3) counter (especially biblically derived) sexist ideologies? I propose that the biblical model that could adequately serve these purposes as we embark upon the twenty-first century is found in Gal 3:28—"There is no longer Jew or Greek [race], there is no longer slave or free [class], there is no longer male and female [sex/gender]; but you are all one in Christ Jesus." A liberative biblical model based upon this passage is particularly in tune with the situation of African American women who have suffered triple oppression on account of their race, class, and gender—in the church and in society. To be exact, in the view of Anna Julia Cooper, black women represent the most oppressed group of women in America (Baker-Fletcher: 61) and are the only group in America that has historically experienced the full impact of this triple oppression (Hoover). But black women, however, did not use this as an excuse simply to claim a victim's status. They not only reenvisioned womanhood—indeed black womanhood—to mean something different from the dominant ideal in American culture; they also advocated an ontological freedom and equality for all women. In addition, they reconceived the notion of human *being:* "humankind, male and female have been created ontologically free" (Baker-Fletcher: 70–71). Christ was a prime example of the notion of human *being,* who exhibited the principles of freedom and equality in his life and work: for all are created in the image of God (62, 67). For this reason, the means of achieving social equality between the races and genders should be sought in Christian principles. Such ideals of universalism rooted in the Christian tradition were important early on for showing the common humanity shared by blacks and whites. While such notions remain appropriate, in recent thought among black women such notions are more nuanced.

Black feminists and Womanist theologians have critiqued the rhetoric of "universalism" in both white and black theologians. According to Jacquelyn Grant, blacks identify such universalism "as white experience; and women identify it as male experience. The question then is, if universalism is the criterion for valid theology how is such a universalism achieved? This criterion must include not only Black women's activities in the larger society but also in the churches as well" (1989b: 210). I suggest that Gal 3:28 is one means of meeting this challenge. Moreover, while Grant does not refer to Gal 3:28 in her article, "Womanist Jesus and Mutual Struggle for Liberation" (1995), it does provide a conceptual framework for her understanding of the mutual struggle of Jesus and African American women. For African American women Jesus was a central figure whom they experienced (1) as a Co-sufferer; (2) as an Equalizer; (3) as Freedom; (4) as Sustainer; and (5) as Liberator (1995: 138). Grant adds, moreover, an interesting twist to the Gal 3:28 paradigm by showing how the three categories of race, class, and sex/ gender have been used to oppress not only other human beings but even Jesus Christ. She argues that Jesus Christ has been imprisoned by patriarchy (= the sin of sexism), white supremacy ideology (= the sin of racism), and the privileged class (= the sin of classism). This indicates that the Jesus of African American women has also suffered a *triple oppression.* "As such, Jesus has been used to keep women in their 'proper place': to keep Blacks meek, mild, and docile in the face of brutal forms of dehumanization; and to ensure the servility of servants" (1995: 138). Thus for many African American women any theory of liberation and equality has to deal with the total situation of oppression experienced by all black people. Hence Womanists define liberation as the survival of the whole people—male and female, young and old, gay and straight (D. Williams : xiv).

Although early African American interpretive traditions have excluded a sustained critique of gender/sex oppression, the issue of sexism must still be examined in light of these interpretive traditions, which early on developed a hermeneutic of liberation. This hermeneutic of liberation, coined most poignantly in the idea of "the equality of all people before God" and the idea that "all were created in the image of God," encouraged the independent black church movement and provided the impetus for social protest (Wilmore 1983: 99–124). Since African Americans' political-religious protest rhetoric, interpretive traditions, and churches were organized and founded upon the biblical principles of equality (which are expressed in Gal 3:28), in order to be true to the traditional struggles for nonclassism and nonracism (i.e., the protest posture against class and race discrimination), they must also combat sexism in the religious institutions and in the interpretive traditions. To achieve these goals new biblical models and paradigms should be considered that do not have the limitations of the previous classical biblical models and are sensitive to the issues of sex/gender oppression and the concerns of African American women. To this challenge, Gal 3:28 has great potential. Furthermore, a model based upon Gal 3:28 can also serve as a theo-ethical paradigm; that is, any discourse or practice that is not guided by this model is to be deemed incompatible with African American aspirations for freedom and equality in the present and for the future. But these claims must be substantiated.

Therefore, while I have proposed that Gal 3:28 has the potential to meet the challenges of the historical quests for liberation for African Americans, it cannot be accepted uncritically. Thus, in what follows I will briefly (1) explore the interpretation of the saying in modern New Testament scholarship; (2) examine its use in the African American Christian religious tradition and contemporary African American scholarship; and (3) evaluate its strengths and weaknesses as an effective model of liberation, especially for challenging sexism.

GALTIANS 3:28 IN CONTEMPORARY NEW TESTAMENT INTERPRETATION

The Function of Galatians 3:28 in Paul's Argument on Justification

Galatians 3:28 has come to occupy center stage in the debate over the role of women within early Christianity (MacDonald: 14). It is not surprising that it would come to occupy such a place in this debate because it appears to suggest that those who are "in Christ" have overcome the triple barriers of race, class, and gender that have been used historically to deny human freedom and equality. And although Paul's letter to the Galatians says a lot about slavery and freedom (2:4; 4:1–7, 21–31; 5:1, 13), it does not deal directly with a program for realizing freedom from these triple categories as a whole or spell out such an agenda in any significant way. In the context of Paul's argument in Gal 3, the egalitarian statement (3:26–28) appears at the end of an elaborate argument on justification by faith that is introduced at 2:15–21 and explicated in chapter 3.

In Gal 3:1–29, Paul grounds his teaching on justification by faith with the introduction of the theme of the crucified Christ (3:1), through whom the Galatians (and all those "in Christ") have received the promise of the Spirit (3:4–5). Paul introduces the ancient father of faith, Abraham, to anchor his teaching on justification in the scriptures (3:6–18) and because in the Abraham saga he could find support to argue that the fulfillment of the promise and blessing of many nations has been realized in his own missionary activity and in the life of the Galatian Christians. In addition, it provided him with a means of including the Gentiles into the covenant people without recourse to circumcision and Torah observance. Moreover, the notion of the promise to many nations (esp. 3:8–9) is not contingent upon the observance of the law or circumcision but upon faith in what has been wrought by the cross of Christ—"for it is written, 'Cursed is everyone who hangs on a tree'—in order that in Christ Jesus the blessing of Abraham might be to the Gentiles, so that we might receive the promise of the Spirit through faith" (3:13–14). The gift of the Spirit to the Gentiles evinces the fulfillment of the promise made to Abraham and inaugurates the new era of God's grace upon all people indiscriminately (as in Joel 2:28–32; cf. Acts 2:17–21). Finally, after a discussion of the purposes and limitations of the law in 3:19–22, Paul's argument on justification by faith culminates with the baptismal confession:

> For in Christ Jesus you are all children of God through faith. As many of you as were baptized into Christ have clothed yourselves with Christ. There is no longer Jew or Greek, there is no longer slave or free, there is no longer male and female; for all of you are one in Christ Jesus (Gal 3:26–28 NRSV).

This baptismal confession has a particular function in Paul's argument: as a result of the crucifixion of Christ, which has wrought a new dispensation of faith ("now that faith has come…"; 3:25), the promise of the blessing upon many nations is realized within the Christian community because those that have been baptized "into Christ" are the "true" heirs to the promise (3:29). In this new era, all who have faith in Christ, whether Jew or Greek, slave or free, male or female, have equal access without distinction to the Spirit of God and the covenant promises. They are indeed a new covenant people (6:16). But is this as far as it goes? Is there a social dimension to the saying besides free access to grace and the formation of a new eschatological community?

Contemporary Interpretations of Galatians 3:28

With respect to Paul's use and understanding of Gal 3:28, there are several ways in which this passage has been understood in contemporary interpretations. First, it is argued that Gal 3:26–28 supplies a paradigm for a revolutionary social program that represents Paul's ideal for Christian relations. Some even perceive that it has a revolutionary dimension leading to the field of political and social ideals (Betz: 189–90; Horsley 1998). On the whole, it is argued that Gal 3:28 represents Paul's own understanding of the liberating power of the gospel. The liberating implications of the gospel, combined with "the Hellenistic desire for the One, which among other things produced an ideal of a universal human essence, beyond difference and hierarchy" (Boyarin: 181), were the motivating factors behind Paul's vision. But this radical ideal was unsustainable in practice. In other words, complete transformation and liberation from social norms is unattainable prior to the Parousia (MacDonald: 2). Therefore, since Paul had to curtail some of its overtly enthusiastic social appropriations—"for slaves because of the social unrest and suppression of Christianity that would result, for wives because of *porneia*—[he] settled for something else, something less than his vision called for" (Boyarin: 193).

Second, it is argued that Gal 3:28 does not entail an egalitarian social agenda at all. Paul does not advocate an abrogation of hierarchical structures but merely acknowledges that Jew and Greek, slave and free, women and men are equal in the sight of God and have equal access to grace because God is impartial (Matera: 147). Hence, the saying merely acknowledges the equal access to God's grace but entails no revolutionary social agenda. This argument is based upon 1 Cor 7, where Christians are commended to "remain in the condition in which you were called" (7:20; reiterated also in 7:17—where Paul adds interestingly: "This is a rule in all the churches"—and 7:24). In 1 Cor 7, where the social implications of the three categories of the baptismal saying are addressed directly (7:17–19 = Jew/Greek; 7:21–23 = slave/free; and 7:27–39 [and earlier in 7:1–16] = male and female [marriage]; Scroggs: 293), Paul does not imply an overtly radical appropriation of the baptismal saying. On the contrary, as the argument goes, his advice is cautionary and conservative: do not disrupt the status quo but "remain as you are."

Third, interpreters have argued that Gal 3:28 is not Paul's own novel creation but a quotation from early Christian baptismal liturgy: a pre-Pauline baptismal confession (Betz: 195; Scroggs: 292; Schüssler Fiorenza 1983: 208), expressing "the theological self-understanding of the Christian missionary movement" (Schüssler Fiorenza 1983: 209). The radical equality of humankind through baptism into Christ is not a completely new invention of Paul. This notion existed already in earliest pre-Pauline Christianity. To be precise, the Hellenistic Christian mission acknowledged the societal-leveling quality of baptism apart from Paul (Scroggs: 292). Before baptism into Christ, the world was divided socially into Jew/Greek, slave/free, and male/female, but through baptism these distinctions are removed. This ideal would have significant implications for women in Pauline circles. As Scroggs states, "Paul is, so far from being a chauvinist, the only certain and consistent spokesman for the liberation and equality of women in the New Testament, although, he probably inherited this affirmation of equality from the earliest church" (283). This view of Paul as a champion of feminism can be achieved only when the Paul of the seven uncontested letters (1 Thessalonians, 1 and 2 Corinthians, Galatians, Philippians, Philemon, and Romans) is divorced from the "Paul" of the Pastorals (1 and 2 Timothy and Titus) and the Deutero-Pauline letters (Colossians and Ephesians [2 Thessalonians is not important in this matter]). Yet even within the uncontested Pauline correspondence, 1 Cor 14:33–36 has to be pruned from the rest of the text and 1 Cor 11:2–16 has to be positively evaluated in order to create "Paul the feminist." With these matters settled, the image of the Paul of female liberation can be created primarily from Rom 16 and Phil 4:2–3 (where several women are mentioned as missionaries and co-workers).

Fourth, Gal 3:28 has been viewed as both a traditional and an original formulation. MacDonald argues that Paul altered the wording of this confession, which profoundly affected its ethical consequences. In its present form, the denial of social divisions in Gal 3:28 is Paul's "own original declaration and not an echo of a more socially egalitarian tradition still audible in spite of Paul's attempts to muffle it" (15). S. Scott Bartchy concurs, arguing that the three pairs of opposites represent actual social challenges to Paul's mission. Thus the three pairs of opposites in Gal 3:28 are the ones we should expect him to use (1973, 174). The view that Paul is the creative redactor of the traditional baptismal saying is proffered against the previous position that Gal 3:26–28 represents as a whole a pre-Pauline tradition. But, while Paul is no feminist, " 'There is no male and female' is Paul's vision of sexual equality in his communities as they *should* be, not a witness to conditions in these communities as they were in fact" (MacDonald: 16; emphasis in original). It is this reality of the "already and not yet" that Paul had to hold in creative tension because the new creation in Christ

(2 Cor 5:17) had already begun, but some patterns of the old creation must remain until the Parousia.

Galatians 3:28 and the Old and New Creation

As noted above, in 1 Cor 7 Paul had to address issues related to the baptismal confession. He may not have done this by choice; the Corinthians themselves may have thrust this responsibility upon him. In certain places in 1 Corinthians it is clear that Paul is responding to various questions that the Corinthians posed to him (7:1, 25; 8:1; 12:1). It is possible that Gal 3:28 lay behind some of the Corinthians' questions and Paul's response in 1 Cor 7. It appears that the Corinthians "had discussions as to how their new self-understanding expressed in the pre-Pauline baptismal formula in Gal 3:28 could and should be realized in the midst of a society rooted in patriarchal status divisions" (Schüssler Fiorenza 1987: 397). For some in the Corinthian community the distinctions of race, class, and sex have been dissolved in the new creation that has occurred through baptism into Christ (Matera: 146). Even the idea of patriarchal marriage is no longer constitutive of the new creation, which is represented by the saying, "no longer male and female" (Schüssler Fiorenza 1987: 397). Wayne Meeks argues that such notions in Corinth were strengthened by the myth of the original androgyne.

The myth of the original or Adam androgyne was not uncommon in the ancient world. This myth refers to the idea that in the beginning humankind were created neither male nor female (or in some cases a unity of male and female), as Gen 1:27 says: "So God created humankind in his image; in the image of God he created them; male and female he created them" (NRSV). For Philo (and others) the first Adam of Gen 1 is a spiritual androgyne, neither male nor female (Boyarin 1994: 189). Moreover, Philo believes that the division of humanity into male and female in Gen 2 was the beginning of the fall (*Opif.* 134; MacDonald: 25). Likewise, in Plato's *Symposium* the idea of the two sexes returning to their primordial unity is similar to the idea of "when the two become one," which equals "neither male and female" (16). The notion of the eschatological reunification of the distorted image (of God) was also a part of the androgyne myth. For some in Corinth this truth had become a reality through baptism. Thus the combination of this myth with the baptismal confession joined together a powerful and revolutionary set of images:

> The reunification of male and female became a symbol for "metaphysical rebellion," an act of "cosmic audacity" attacking the conventional picture of what was real and what was properly human.... In baptism

the Christian has put on again the image of the Creator, in whom "there is no male and female," then for him the old world has passed away and, behold! the new has come. (Meeks: 207)

The "new that has come" was a new order of creation, indeed, a "new creation" (2 Cor 5:17; Gal 6:15). Galatians 3:28 represents the order of the new creation that has overcome the old order of creation in Genesis (Stendahl: 32). The old order divided humanity, but the new order unites it. To be sure, Paul and the Corinthians realized that the new creation implied radical social and political changes (Betz: 190). But what was the nature of these radical changes? Did the new creation imply or entail the dissolution, eradication, or abolition of the distinctions of race, class, and gender/sex (Matera: 146) or that the distinctions have been relativized (Dunn: 207), which means that they remain but have lost their significance? The former position was most likely that of some of the Corinthians, while the latter was that of Paul. This situation is arguably reflected in Paul's discussion in 1 Cor 11:2–16, where the issue of women and the wearing of veils is addressed (MacDonald: 12–13; Schüssler Fiorenza 1983: 235–36).

Although Paul used the baptismal formula in Gal 3:28 and 1 Cor 12:13, his use in 1 Cor 7 reflects an uneasiness with it because of the social implications being drawn by slaves and women in the Corinthian community. Moreover, 1 Cor 11:2–16 reflects his uneasiness with it because of the ethical and ecclesial implications being drawn by women whose praxis was supported by the androgyne myth (Meeks: 207). But if Paul advocated the order of the new creation in his preaching and mission (as reflected in Gal 3:28 and 1 Cor 12:13), how could he then use the order of the old creation (i.e., man as the head/source of woman, as in Gen 2) in 1 Cor 11:2–16 to curtail the practice of women removing veils during worship?

The long and the short to this question is that Paul wanted to curtail some of the radical appropriations of the baptismal formula that resulted in some unexpected applications—wives and husbands were refusing one another conjugal rights (others were opting for celibacy and refusing to marry), and slaves were anxious for social emancipation (1 Cor 7). Even more, some women were removing their veils during worship as an ultimate display of returning to the divine image: they were behaving as if they were no longer female but "neither male nor female," implying a restoration of the divine image at creation (MacDonald: 130). So Paul wanted to modify these (mis)applications of the baptismal confession by arguing that the distinctions of male and female have not been dissolved but relativized. The comments of Meeks and Scroggs may help to clarify this point.

Paul insists on the preservation of the *symbols* of the present, differenti-
ated order. Women remain women and men remain men and dress
accordingly, even though "the end of the ages has come upon them."
Yet these symbols have lost their ultimate significance, for "the form of
this world is passing away." Therefore Paul accepts and even insists
upon the equality of role of man and woman.... The new order, the
order of man in the image of God, was already taking form in the patterns of leadership of the new community. (Meeks: 208)

Scroggs agrees with this assessment but notes that Paul and the Gnostics
share some of the same insights, although there is one crucial difference:

Both agree in eliminating value judgments of man over against
woman. The gnostics seem to have wanted to go further, however, to
obliterate all distinctions between the sexes. Paul is ... passionate
about keeping the reality of the *distinctions;* he just will not suffer any
value judgment to be drawn on the basis of the distinction. (283 n. 1;
emphasis original)

For Meeks, Paul reacted to the gnostic appropriation because of their
rejection of the created order. Paul, on the other hand, wanted to hold the
symbols of the old and the new creation in eschatological tension. Paul
insists, then, with much tension, that the current hierarchy is still in effect
(Rom 13:1–7; 1 Cor 7; 11:1–16; Stowers: 304), but, as Scroggs suggests, a
new evaluation of those differences is in order.

Galatians 3:28 and the "Neither Male and Female" Category

To be sure, Paul did not write Gal 3:26–28 as a declaration for
sexual equality. The reference to "male and female" was a part of the
traditional saying. Furthermore, this pair was omitted in 1 Cor 12:13
because women were exercising their "freedom in Christ" (Schüssler
Fiorenza 1983; Wire 1990). But in Galatians Paul could use the saying in
his argument unedited because there were no issues within the community related specifically to women. Thus in 1 Cor 12:13 Paul does not
talk about "all are one" (Gal 3:28), which can imply a notion of equality,
but the social unification implied by Christian rituals (that is, baptism;
so here he uses the image of "one body" and the language of "one
Spirit"). Furthermore, in Galatians Paul uses "neither ... nor" to formulate the pairs of opposites, while in 1 Cor 12:13 he uses the positive
"either ... or." Paul's intention here is to emphasize not the abolition of
social differences but the unity of these different groups into one body
(MacDonald: 116). This indicates that Paul had an ambiguous stance
with respect to the last pair of opposites. Later conservative Christian

appropriation is also ambiguous on the application of this saying to social realities, although it expands upon the racial/ethnic category. For example, Col 3:11 says: "There is no longer Greek and Jew, circumcised and uncircumcised, barbarian, Scythian, slave and free; but Christ is all in all." It is interesting that while the saying is expanded to enlarge the category of race/ethnicity, the aspect related to sex/gender—"no longer male and female"—is missing, as in 1 Cor 12:13. The reason for its omission in Colossians has to do with the development of the household codes (3:18–4:1), which sought to reinstitute the patriarchal order of man over woman, curtailing women's freedom. The very fact that the "neither male and female" pair was eliminated from the baptismal confession's liberative litany in 1 Cor 12:13, and later in Colossians, is a subtle indication of its potential for revolutionary social implications for women and slaves.

This indicates further that the category related to sex/gender was the least important not only for Paul but also for the early church as it moved toward institutionalization. As a matter of fact the last two categories in Gal 3:28 "came along for the ride because they are not a part of the rhetorical context—only the Jew/Greek pair" (Scroggs: 291). It turns out that even though Paul does address all three categories in 1 Cor 7, the Jew/Greek category is the most important (Dunn: 206) and the only category that Paul worked out theologically to support a program for the *social realization* of this vision prior to the Parousia. His teaching on justification by faith in Romans, Galatians, and Philippians was formulated to articulate and support his vision that Jew and Greek are equal and have equal access to the covenant promises (for Gentiles without recourse to the Jewish identity symbol of circumcision and the observance of certain parts of the law). This ideal was sustained in Paul's theology and praxis even to the point of open conflict (as in his debate with Peter in Gal 2). Thus Paul fully worked out a sustained solution only to the Jew/Greek question, not to the woman and slave questions. But those who accepted the message of the gospel and heard at baptism the confession of Gal 3:28 did not wait for a sustained argument in order to actualize this vision into social reality.

It is clear that some churches in the early Christian missionary movement believed that on the basis of the baptismal saying of Gal 3:28 they had overcome the three categories of human oppression. The action of women in the early church challenging their social roles (Schüssler Fiorenza 1983; 1987; Wire 1990) and the attempts of slaves to gain freedom at all costs, even through the church (Horsley 1998), shows the great impact the message of freedom had for both women and slaves. While Paul's use of Gal 3:28 and that of the emerging early church were ambiguous, it is not necessary to limit the liberating implications of this saying to Paul's or a segment of the early church's position. It is the liberating applications of this saying in some early churches and beyond that we must consider (Schüssler Fiorenza). This saying, although sparingly throughout Christian history (Stowers: 309), radically challenged notions of race, class, and gender: the triple category of division among human beings. For this reason, even in the eighteenth and nineteenth centuries C.E. Gal 3:28 also appealed to enslaved African Americans. It provided them with a model that envisioned the unity and "equality of all people" regardless of social distinctions or physical characteristics. But even African American churches and interpretive traditions, like Paul whose legacy was cautiously accepted, have not fully realized the egalitarian potential of Gal 3:28, despite their historical rhetoric of freedom and equality for all.

THE AFRICAN AMERICAN RELIGIOUS TRADITION AND GALATIANS 3:28

Pre-Scholarly Assessments of Paul and Galatians 3:28 in the African American Religious Tradition

An assessment of Paul and his legacy was not an option for enslaved African Americans: it was a necessity. Proslavery advocates constructed an image of Paul that made him the pillar of slave-holding Christianity and the post of antebellum Southern values. The Pastoral Epistles, the Deutero-Pauline Epistles, and, of course, Philemon supplied the backbone for the construction of the image of the "proslavery Paul." This "Paul," created in the image of the slave-holding class to support their economic exploitation of black flesh, mandated slaves to "obey your masters in everything" (Col 3:22; cf. Eph 6:5) while having little to say to masters. The "Paul" of proslavery hermeneutics never sought to question the social condition of the slave nor threaten the privileged status of the master (Martin 1998: 213). Despite these harsh realities, while Paul may have been viewed as an ambiguous and ambivalent witness to the gospel, it is remarkable that few African Americans ever rejected Paul as hopelessly anti-emancipatory (Callahan: 235). They developed a more nuanced understanding of Paul. Rather than outright rejection, they sought instead to "put Paul back together again" (A. Smith 1998). Although Paul was used to support slavery and oppression, black abolitionists believed that a different image of "Paul" could be reconstructed to support slavery's abolition and win Paul over for the cause of freedom. Black abolitionists, then, sought to reconstruct "Paul" by using several strategies: (1) utilize positive statements of Paul against those that were negative to critique slavery's mythological structures; (2) assume a typological correspondence between Paul and the said abolitionist; and (3) seek the general "spirit" of Paul (summary of A. Smith 1998: 255–56). These strategies were used to sustain a hermeneutic of liberation using a reconstructed "Paul" as a cornerstone. The African Americans' "Paul" of liberation could be seen most clearly through the egalitarian vision of Gal 3:28.

In their quest for freedom from slavery and in their hermeneutic of liberation, the egalitarian vision of Gal 3:28 was not lost upon minds of enslaved African Americans. As a matter of fact, Vincent Wimbush states that especially in the eighteenth and early nineteenth centuries during the period of the rise of independent black churches,

> African Americans seemed anxious to institutionalize as an ethical and moral principle one of the rare New Testament passages they found attractive and even identified as a *locus classicus* for Christian social teaching—"There is neither Jew nor Greek, there is neither slave nor free, there is neither male nor female; for you are all one in Christ Jesus" (Gal 3:28). Ironically, this biblical verse stressing the principle of Christian unity was embraced and referred to over and over again as the separate church movements got under way. This and other passages were used to level prophetic judgment against a society that thought of itself as biblical in its foundation and ethic. (1991: 90)

An example of the institutionalization of this saying can be seen in its use by an ex-slave, G. W. Offley, who claimed that "he learned from his mother and father the *potentially revolutionary* doctrine 'that God is no respecter of persons, but gave his son to die for all, bond or free, black or white, rich or poor,' and that God protects those whom he chooses to sanctify for some task" (quoted in Raboteau: 305; my emphasis). The unique aspect of this saying is that it combines two important passages together that were building blocks of equality for African Americans—Gal 3:28 and Acts 10:34 ("God is no respecter of persons"). In addition, it includes the idea of the death of Jesus Christ as an essential element of this *revolutionary* doctrine on freedom and equality (which, as we saw above, was important in Paul's argument in Gal 3), and it expands on categories that were essential to the African American situation: "black or white, rich or poor." Interestingly enough, however, the statement on "neither male and female" is missing! It appears that just as in the early Christian tradition, this baptismal saying was so versatile that it could be modified to fit multiple visions of freedom and equality. But the category related to sex/gender remained the unstable element in the saying.

However, in Julia A. J. Foote's use of the baptismal confession in her nineteenth-century biography, the category related to women was the essential element of the saying. In arguing for her calling and right to preach the gospel in Holiness circles she says:

> We are sometimes told that if a woman pretends to a Divine call, and thereon grounds the right to plead the cause of a crucified Redeemer in public, she will be believed when she shows credentials from heaven; that is, when she works a miracle. If it be necessary to prove one's right to preach the Gospel, I ask of my brethren to show me their credentials, or I can not believe in the propriety of their ministry. But the Bible puts an end to this strife when it says: "There is neither male nor female in Christ Jesus" [Gal 3:28]. (quoted in Andrews: 208–9)

For Foote, quoting this one element of the saying could settle the problem related to women in ministry because she recognized the radical implications that could be drawn from it to empower women for ministry. "No longer male nor female" meant for her a new pattern of relationships that rested on equality between men and women in terms of the roles for preaching and ministry within the church. This is one example of the importance of this saying in black women's interpretive traditions of the Bible. Another example can be found in Mary McLeod Bethune.

Bethune, in recounting her early childhood realization of self-worth when her teacher read to her of God's love from John 3:16, tropes Acts 9 and Paul's Damascus Road experience (Callahan: 244). In this same passage, she also tropes Gal 3:28 when, in her moment of self-discovery, she realizes that "[her] sense of inferiority, [her] fear of handicaps, dropped away" (quoted in G. Lerner: 136). It was the word "whosoever" through which she saw herself joined to a common humanity through God's love that ignited her determination and passion:

> "Whosoever," it said. No Jew nor Gentile, no Catholic nor Protestant, no black nor white; just "whosoever." It meant that I, a humble Negro girl, had just as much chance as anybody in the sight and love of God. These words stored up a battery of faith and confidence and determination in my heart. (ibid.)

Like Foote before her, Bethune sought to validate her aspirations for self-realization and equal opportunity through (in her case, a trope of) Gal 3:28. Although she does not include the "male and female" reference, it can be inferred through her reference to herself, "a humble Negro girl," who had not even reached womanhood "had just as much chance as anybody" in God's sight.

Finally, in Howard Thurman's reflections we find a further development of this saying. "It is my belief," he says in his work *The Creative Encounter*, "that in the Presence of God there is neither male nor female, white nor black, Gentile or Jew, Protestant nor Catholic, Hindu, Buddhist, nor Moslem, but a human spirit stripped to the literal substance of itself before God" (1954: 152). To his credit he did not delete the aspect related to gender! As a matter of fact, it appears first in his liberative litany. He also adds elements important for his historical circumstance and religious-philosophical position—"neither white nor black, Gentile or Jew, Protestant nor Catholic, Hindu, Buddhist, nor Moslem." It is possible, again, to see the versatility of this saying in the African American religious tradition.

It is apparent, then, that African Americans' encounter with the Christian religion exposed and confirmed within them an idea of "the equality of all people before God." Peter Paris calls this tradition, which has been essential in African American religious history, the black Christian tradition. In Paris's words,

> the normative tradition for blacks is that tradition governed by the principle of non-racism, which we call the black Christian tradition. The fundamental principle of the black Christian tradition is depicted most adequately in the biblical doctrine of the parenthood of God and the kinship of all peoples which is a version of the traditional sexist expression "the fatherhood of God and the brotherhood of men." (1985: 10)

As stated above, these notions of the unity and equality of humanity were based upon such statements as those found in Gal 3:28 and Acts 10:34. The black Christian tradition enabled African Americans to critique racism and classism in American society and culture in both thought and practice. Moreover this fundamental principle was also a means of justifying and motivating African Americans' endeavors for survival and the transformation of American society. Moreover, the discovery of this principle revealed to African Americans the contradictions implicit in the religion of those white Americans whose practice of racism and oppression upon their fellow human beings contradicted this biblical understanding of humanity. In this way, "the black Christian tradition has exercised both priestly and prophetic functions, the former aiding and abetting the race in its capacity to endure the effects of racism, the latter utilizing all available means to effect religious and moral reform in the society at large" (Paris 1985: 11).

Enslaved African Americans and subsequent generations appropriated this understanding of God and humanity as a revolutionary hermeneutic for understanding scripture. This African American hermeneutic was based on their existential reality: even if the scripture said, "slaves obey your masters," it could not be the "word of God" because it justified the suffering of human beings, which challenged the very essence of the Divine as righteous and just. As far as African

Americans were concerned, race and class oppression were evil and against the will of God. In terms of the baptismal saying, then, the most important aspects for African Americans historically (notwithstanding Foote and Bethune) have been "no longer Jew or Greek, no longer slave or free"—that is, issues related to race and class. This has been evident in African American religious and political history. For it was out of the crucible of racial injustice and class oppression that the interpretive tradition arose to institutionalize a nonracist and nonclassist appropriation of the Christian faith. What the African American religious tradition has never done is to apply this very same principle to a consistent analysis of sexism. This is where the African American religious tradition has failed in the actualization of Gal 3:28, for again, like Paul, it too has had a limited agenda, which has neglected to address fully the concerns of women (that is, the "no longer male and female" aspect of the saying).

African American Scholarly Assessments of Paul and Galatians 3:28

Like their forebears, African American liberation/Womanist theologians and biblical scholars have also been compelled to assess Paul's legacy. Some have perceived almost unequivocal liberating potential in Paul's thought (Amos Jones), while some have taken a *via media* with respect to the liberating potential of Paul's thought, recognizing his ambivalence and ambiguity in the matters of class and sex (Callahan; Martin 1989; 1991; 1998; A. Smith 1998; Felder 1989a; 1989b). Others have viewed Paul's thought as conservative and useless to the cause of human freedom and, hence, to be dispensed without further adieu (Cleage; Cone 1975; Thurman 1981; D. Williams). This modern assessment of Paul is similar to that in the earlier African American interpretive tradition. In both cases, one has to confront Paul's ambivalence on the important matters of human freedom and oppression.

On this point, Delores Williams wonders how biblically derived messages of liberation, especially from the exodus and Paul, "can be taken seriously by today's masses of poor, homeless African Americans, female and male, who consider themselves to be experiencing a form of slavery—economic enslavement by the capitalistic American economy" (146–47). For Williams Paul's ambiguity is insurmountable for those today in oppressive situations who need to hear a clear and unequivocal voice for liberation. While her point is well taken, the suggestion of Cain Felder must also be considered:

> Does this mean that we simply ignore today those many New Testament passages that are patently conservative or, by modern standards, repressive on the status of women? Does the Christian in our time seek only to ascertain the probable stance of Jesus and Paul, discarding the

rest of the New Testament? To both questions, the response must be in the negative. (1989b: 147)

Felder raises a fundamental conceptual issue for our concerns: even if the position of Paul on various issues is unascertainable or unacceptable, his position alone does not determine a particular reading, hearing, or appropriation (regardless of authorial intent). Just like women and slaves in the early church, enslaved Africans gleaned liberating potential from Paul's gospel message, coined especially in Gal 3:28. To be sure, Paul had an ambiguous stance with respect to Gal 3:28. But his position alone does not limit the liberating potential of the paradigm. Contemporary African American interpreters of Paul who anguish about Paul's ambiguity may well take note of Callahan's reflections:

> In the modulation of activism and accommodation African Americans appreciated with ambivalence, and, rarely, with hostility, Paul's canonical ambiguity.... It is this profound ambiguity that black folks have not only appreciated in Paul, but, perhaps, have shared with him. (249)

GALATIANS 3:28—A POTENTIAL MODEL FOR CHALLENGING AND CRITIQUING SEXISM IN AFRICAN AMERICAN RELIGIOUS INSTITUTIONS

Although some contemporary African American biblical scholars and theologians have begun to advance critiques of sexist ideologies in African American religious traditions, Gal 3:28 has not been fully excavated. While the task cannot be taken up here,[2] I will briefly outline some of the problematic and beneficial aspects of appropriating Gal 3:28 as a liberative paradigm. I suggested above that in order for Gal 3:28 to serve as an appropriate and effective paradigm it has to be inclusive of the multiple struggles of the African American experience, fully embrace the concerns of African American women, and counter (especially biblically derived) sexist ideologies.

Problems with the Paradigm

The appropriation of Gal 3:28 as a liberating paradigm is not without its difficulties. Just as with the earlier classical biblical paradigms, there is always a need to assess and reassess them. Simply because the paradigm was used in the early African American religious tradition does not mean

---

2 I hope to take up this issue in a forthcoming work, *The Politics of Gender in African American Churches: An Interpretation of African American Experience through the Paradigm of Galatians 3:28.*

that it can be indiscriminately applied to our modern situation. Therefore, I will address, first, the various problems related to the appropriation of the paradigm in general: (1) the issue of authorial intent (i.e., Paul's understanding and use of the saying) and (2) the gap between ancient and modern understandings of equality. Second, I will address the issues particular to the African American situation: (1) fear of the loss of ethnic/cultural identity (and the lack of an Afrocentric focus), and (2) fear of this paradigm being appropriated by gay and lesbian Christians.

Problems of general interpretation and appropriation:[3] *(1) The issue of authorial intent.* It was noted above that Paul did not intend to eliminate social roles and differences but to relativize those roles in relation to Christ. Baptism into Christ, therefore, means the creation of a new unity of humanity that includes all people indiscriminately, but that unity does not entail an elimination of social hierarchy or one's former status. When Paul addresses the baptismal confession in 1 Cor 7 and 12, there is no hint of equality but only unity. Furthermore, in the context of chapter 12 he not only excludes the final pair of opposites related to sex/gender but also uses the image of the body. In this analogy some parts of the body have lesser honor and other parts have greater honor. In this same chapter on Christian unity, Paul provides an ordered list of "offices" in the assembly to emphasize difference within a hierarchical unity (Stowers: 303–4). It appears, then, that for Paul and others in the ancient Mediterranean area, "[u]nity ... does not seem to deny hierarchy, even in the assembly. Indeed, appeal to interdependent hierarchy is the ubiquitous ancient Mediterranean and Medieval European way of conceiving any sort of social unity. Unity in antiquity almost never implied equality" (304).

(2) The divide between ancient and modern understandings of equality. The preceding point brings forth the issue of ancient and modern understandings of equality. Of the three texts that deal with unity using the baptismal confession (1 Cor 7:14–24; 12:13; Gal 3:28), only Gal 3:28 is amenable to modern notions of egalitarianism (Stowers: 303). However, even with Gal 3:28 there are two options for understanding equality: (1) equality in terms of having the same fundamental capacity as moral agents; and (2) equality in terms of having the same social and economic power, status, and economic benefits in an unchanging arrangement. While the first has been common throughout history and does not conflict with social hierarchy,

---

[3] This section has benefited greatly from Stowers's critique of Gal 3:28 (302–10).

the second has never been realized. Therefore, Paul may have held to some version of the first view, holding that all people have the same moral capacity to approach God (303–4).

Problems particular to African American appropriation: (3) Loss of cultural/ethnic identity. Some African Americans fear that the phrase "no longer ... but all are one" will lead to the loss of cultural/ethnic identity and uniqueness. In a nation where blacks (and other people of color) have had to contend with the loss of cultural heritage through the slave trade and racist notions of black inferiority, some feel that having reclaimed a positive sense of "blackness" and a heritage as people of African descent, the use of such a paradigm will make them "invisible." African Americans should, therefore, seek paradigms that can reclaim a black/African heritage (Felder 1989a), since there is already evidence of black presence in the Bible but even here black presence has been made invisible in white biblical scholarship (R. Bailey 1991; 1995; Martin 1989).

(4) Use of the saying by gay and lesbian Christians. If the African American churches and religious institutions have been sexist, they have also been homophobic. In many traditional black churches, same-sex love is viewed as incompatible with Christian life and ethics. Therefore, any biblical appropriation that would lend itself to the cause is suspect and rejected. The statement by Irene Monroe in a sermon delivered on Gay Pride Day at Riverside Church in New York confirms this anxiety for some:

> I am reminded of Paul's letter to the Galatians (3:28) where he wrote, "there is neither Jew or Greek, neither male or female..."—and yes it also means neither straight nor gay—for "we are all one in Christ Jesus." Heretofore, the Jews had been known as the people of God and had been accepted into the family of God. Now all people had been accepted into the family of God and had been known as the people of God. (67)

With respect to the first two general points above it is important to note that authorial intent does not always guide what an audience hears or reads. Even in the New Testament itself there is evidence of later Christian communities reshaping the image and legacy of Paul to meet new and challenging situations within their communities (hence the Deutero-Pauline and Pastoral Epistles). This is an unavoidable (and necessary) process in order for the message to remain meaningful. This applies also, then, to the second point.

Given the last two particular concerns (3 and 4), it would be improper to view the Gal 3:28 paradigm as suggesting the dissolution of race, class, and sex or of the distinctiveness of these categories. African

Americans in the early tradition were able to use the paradigm to argue for the equality and unity of humanity, while at the same time establishing independent black churches. Thus within the African American interpretive tradition, this paradigm was not used to argue that cultural and ethnic distinctiveness should be removed but that such distinctiveness should not be used as a basis for the oppression of another human being. This principle must also apply to the last point, despite the uneasiness with it.

Potential of the Paradigm

Galatians 3:28 is compatible with black women's early and recent critiques of sexism in the African American religious tradition. The fruition of recent Womanist theology, biblical interpretation, and ethics has supplied the tradition with a foundation for a vision of wholeness and has raised the consciousness of many to the concerns of black women and all who are oppressed. In this vein, Gal 3:28 has the potential to serve as a liberatory paradigm because it meets the criteria established above.

(1) It is inclusive of the multiple struggles of the African American experience. Galatians 3:28 should be considered because it can avoid some of the pitfalls of the earlier biblical models. First, it is paradigmatic of the historical struggles of African Americans. It does not focus only on race and class but also on sex/gender. In this way, it is compatible with the historical religious-political struggles against oppression. In its political-religious usage the element "in Christ" has never limited it to the religious realm.

(2) It is inclusive of the concerns of women. A paradigm based on Gal 3:28 is not conceptually limited by biblical narrative traditions, nor is it in competition with the classical biblical paradigms or current paradigms and with work that black women are doing—it is complementary. Since it is not limited to a narrative framework (or by Paul's use and understanding of it), it is open-ended and applicable to black women's stories and traditions of struggle and survival. Not having a narrative framework, then, is one of its advantages. It can incorporate the stories of women (and indeed all blacks) who have had to contend with the tridimensional reality of race, class, and sex/gender.

(3) It provides a counter to biblically derived sexist notions. It was noted in the exegetical section of this essay (p. 47) that Gal 3:28 counters the order of the creation story in Gen 2, in which woman derives from man. On the one hand, the Genesis narrative has been used to accuse woman of

responsibility for the "fall" of humanity, for which she is "cursed" to bring forth children in pain and to submit to her husband (Gen 3:16). This story was perfect for supporting patriarchy. On the other hand, Gal 3:28 envisions a new order of creation that challenges the pattern of the old. In the new creation social roles are no longer vertical but horizontal. The activity of the Spirit in the Christian communities, empowering all indiscriminately (for the Spirit democratizes: Acts 2:17–21; cf. Joel 2:28–32), is evidence of this new order. Thus since the household codes use the order of the old creation to understand social roles, they can be directly challenged by Gal 3:28 as incompatible with the order of the new creation.

(4) Its theo-ethical use allows self-critical evaluation. The paradigm could be used to affirm the tridimensional concerns of Womanist scholars. Such a paradigm could serve as a wake-up call to African Americans (especially male pastors, preachers, bishops, and presidents of religious institutions) to consider liberation in holistic categories in both thought and practice. Consider Emilie Townes's statement on a Womanist ethics:

> Womanist ethics begins with the traditional role and place assigned Black women. An African-American woman contends with race, sex, class, and other sources of fragmentation. The challenge of a womanist social ethic is to create and articulate a positive moral standard, which critiques the arrogance and deadly elitism of dominance and is so bold as to name it as a systemic evil. (1993a: 78)

CONCLUSION

The use of Gal 3:28 as a liberative paradigm is not without its problems, but it does, however, provide a paradigm that can include in its orbit a vision of equality regardless of race, class, and sex/gender. Such a paradigm is needed, especially in African American churches and religious institutions where sexism continues. If things continue like "business as usual," we must take note of Francis Wood's warning:

> As long as men continue to define themselves by using the masters' tools of dominance and subordination, whether by commission or omission, as their measure of manhood, there will be no justice in the church. Until there is a new understanding and regard for the full personhood of all women with their gifts and talents in the church, we will not bear the yoke of Jesus. Instead, we will continue to bear the yoke of preserving patriarchal privilege. (46)

The Sorrow Songs: Laments From Ancient Israel and the African American Diaspora

Wilma Ann Bailey
Christian Theological Seminary

The ancient Israelites and the enslaved Africans of the United States, two communities of disparate time and place, found a connection in a common experience of slavery, loss of a homeland, exile, and assaults on their sense of identity and dignity. Beyond the shared experience, Blacks and Jews created a similar way of responding to the experiences that traumatized their communities. Both produced poetry and set it to music. In both communities, the laments, as we call them in the ancient Israelite corpus, and the spirituals or sorrow songs, as they are known in the African American community, functioned as a catharsis, a mnemonic device, and an affirmation of the intrinsic hopefulness that nurtures life in the most difficult of situations. The structure of the laments of the two communities was not identical, but the sentiments were the same. "Look and see if there is any sorrow like my sorrow" wrote the ancient Jewish poet (Lam 1:12b NRSV). "Nobody knows the trouble I've seen; nobody knows my sorrow" the African counterpart sang. African Americans identifying with the Ancient Israelites adopted imagery from their stories to express their own pain and longing. Both communities hoped to move the heart of God as they poured out their grief.

Connecting these two diverse groups, James Weldon Johnson wrote in 1925,

> It is not possible to estimate the sustaining influence that the story of the trials and tribulations of the Jews as related in the Old Testament exerted upon the Negro. This story at once caught and fired the imaginations of the Negro bards, and they sang, sang their hungry listeners into a firm faith that as God saved Daniel in the lion's [sic] den, so would He save them; as God preserved the Hebrew children in the fiery furnace, so would He preserve them; as God delivered Israel out of bondage in Egypt, so would He deliver them. (1985: 20–21)

LAMENTS IN THE HEBREW BIBLE

The Hebrew word for *lament* is *qînâ*. *Qînâ* is the descriptive term for both the dirge and the lament genres. A dirge is a funeral song. A lament is a song of mourning or wailing. The difference between the two is that a lament contains a complaint about the situation and appeals to God to remedy it. The word *qînâ* appears in some form about eighteen times in the Hebrew Bible, primarily in the prophetic books of Ezekiel (2:10; 19:1, 14 [bis]; 26:17; 27:2, 32; 28:12; 32:2, 16) Jeremiah (7:29; 9:9 [ET 10], 19 [ET 20]), and Amos (5:1; 8:10), in addition to one verse in 2 Samuel (1:17) and one verse in 2 Chronicles (35:25 [bis]). Ironically, the word does not appear in the book of Psalms or Lamentations. Hermann Gunkel noted the close connection between the lament form and prophecy (96). The lament is used within prophecy to describe a situation in metaphorical or realistic language that has not yet occurred. In one particularly interesting text because it deviates from the majority, Ezekiel is told to raise a lamentation in order to prevent *himself* from being seduced into rebelliousness and to give *himself* courage to continue in his difficult prophetic task (Ezek 2:10–3:10). Moreover, the prophet is given a scroll containing words of lamentation and is told to eat it. When he does, he comments that the taste of the scroll is as sweet as honey. This seems to be an affirmation of the ultimately positive role that laments played in the ancient Israelite community.

Gunkel understood the function of the lament, which he refers to as the complaint, to be to appeal to the Deity for assistance by describing the situation, typically political misfortunes (88) and petitioning for help or expressing a wish for relief (86, 91). He thought that the purpose of the lament was to influence the Deity, to seek divine assistance, to remedy the situation in which the community finds itself (86). Moreover, he insists that the laments were not used for situations that were deemed hopeless. Laments were found only in situations that could change for the better with divine assistance.

Paul Wayne Ferris Jr. defines a communal lament as one

> [w]hose, verbal content indicates that it was composed to be used by
> and/or on behalf of a community to express both complaint, and sorrow
> and grief over some perceived calamity, physical or cultural, which had
> befallen or was about to befall them and to appeal to God for deliver-
> ance. (10)

Mowinckel in his attempt to reconstruct the *Sitz im Leben* of the communal laments conjectured that the setting was a public fast day where penitential rites were carried out in order to "temper [God's] wrath and rouse his compassion" (1:193). Based upon his study of Assyro-Babylonian precedents, Mowinckel concluded that, of the communal laments that appear in the Hebrew Bible, the "I" form—where the king or a leader speaks on behalf of the people—and the "we" form, the "I" form is earlier (1:194) because it represents less of a consciousness of the individual. Mowinckel did concede that there were truly individual laments, but those, he believed, were primarily connected to illness. In the case of both the communal and individual laments, he understands sin to be the underlying cause of whatever disaster occurred according to the self-understanding of the ancient Israelites (1:195, 2:2). However, at times the confessions of sin may represent the ritual rather than the reality of their thought. This is particularly evident in the book of Lamentations, where confessions of sin are vague and general. One has the impression that they are not convinced that they sinned to such an extant as to merit the disaster that was rained upon them.

The laments that appear in the Hebrew Bible are the lyrics of songs that were sung in the cultic life of ancient Israel. The book of Lamentations is chanted on the ninth of Ab every year in the synagogue. Etan Levine notes that the musical scale of the chant "has no parallel in traditional Jewish repertoire, but it is found among Syrian Christians ... and among the Copts in Egypt. In ascending order, it progresses g sharp, A, B natural, C, D, E-flat; all internal cadential movements end on A, and the final endings are on G sharp" (13). It is generally thought that the melodies to the songs are no longer extant, though in 1976 musicologist Suzanne Haik-Vantoura published a controversial book in which she argued that the music of the Psalms of the Hebrew Bible are recoverable from cantillation signs that appear particularly below but also secondarily above the words in the text (70, 90).[1] She thinks that these signs are older than previously dated, arguing that the Masoretes of Tiberias (seventh to eighth centuries C.E.) preserved an ancient system in addition to more recent ones. Daniel Meir Weil insists that Haik-Vantoura's method is flawed in his book, *The Masoretic Chant of the Bible.* Whether or not one comes to the same conclusion, it is clear that there are ample references to musical instruments that were used in worship (Ferris: 84; Isa 16:11; Jer 48:36; Amos 5:23) and, most likely, musical notations of some sort (though not necessarily in the accent marks) or instructions to the musicians, choir, or congregation.

Toni Craven indicates that laments are the largest single category of psalm in the Hebrew Bible (26). The psalms are notoriously difficult to date and therefore to connect with particular events. Psalm 137 is a

---

[1] Haik-Vantoura notes that chironomy, the use of hand gestures to represent music, was practiced in ancient Israel. She finds an oblique reference in 1 Chr 25:2–4, 7. See Haik-Vantoura: 70, 90.

notable exception. The setting is Babylon following the destruction of Jerusalem in 587 B.C.E. The psalmist reports that the disheartened Judahite expatriates cannot sing the Lord's songs in the land of exile. They pronounce a curse upon themselves if they forget Jerusalem and call for retribution. The psalm ends with the disquieting image of infants being smashed against rocks. However, more typically the psalms of lament end on a more pleasant note.

Gunkel, Mowinckel (195–246), Ferris (91, 93), Craven (27), and other scholars who have worked on the laments list similar characteristics. It is generally agreed that there is no metrical structure that is common to biblical laments. According to Craven, the laments are characterized by the following elements: an address to God (or invocation), a statement of complaint (or description of the situation), a confession of trust, a petition, words of assurance, and a vow of praise (27). Needless to say, all of these elements do not appear in every lament. She (22) identifies the following psalms as communal laments: 12; 14 (= 53); 44; 53 (= 14); 58; 60; 74; 79; 80; 83; 85; 90; 123; 126; 129; 137. Ferris (14) labels the following psalms as laments, in addition to the book of Lamentations: 31; 35; 42; 43; 44; 56; 59; 60; 69; 74; 77; 79; 80; 83; 85; 89; 94; 102; 109; 137; 142. Ferris (16) also compares the communal-lament lists of eight leading scholars and indicates that only four make all of the lists: 60; 74; 79; 80. Despite general agreement as to how to define a lament, there is disagreement as to which psalms fall in that category largely because individual psalms too often exhibit characteristics of more than one genre and few psalms contain all of the characteristics as listed.

The four psalms that are generally agreed to be communal laments are nationalistic in content. They express the idea that God has rejected Israel and has been angry with the people. A description of the state of the kingdom is given. A request is made to God for help. A statement of confidence that God can help is expressed.

Shocking to modern sensibilities are the graphic descriptions of the situations that give rise to the laments and the calls for vengeance upon the perpetrators of the violence inflicted upon the psalmist and the visioning of pain and suffering in their house. Examples are found in Pss 3:7; 5:10; 6:10; 10:15; 28:4; 63:9–10; 69:28; 79:6; 139:19; 140:10. One cries out,

> The righteous will rejoice when they see vengeance done;
>> they will bathe their feet in the blood of the wicked. (Ps 58:11 [ET 58:10])[2]

---

2 All biblical quotations are from the New Revised Standard Version unless otherwise noted.

And from time to time, in the laments of ancient Israel, the Deity is directly accused of either causing the suffering or standing silent in the face of it. One declares,

> The Lord has destroyed without mercy
>> all the dwellings of Jacob;
> in his wrath he has broken down
>> the strongholds of daughter Judah. (Lam 2:2)

Yet another queries,

> Why do you sleep, O Lord? . . .
> Why do you hide your face?
>> Why do you forget our affliction and oppression? (Ps 44:23–24)

But in the same psalm where the poet demands

> Let burning coals fall on them!
>> Let them be flung into pits, no more to rise! (Ps 140:10)

an assurance of faith is heard:

> I know that the LORD maintains the cause of the needy,
>> and executes justice for the poor.
> Surely the righteous shall give thanks to your name;
>> the upright shall live in your presence. (Ps 140:12–13)

The venting of anger and grief in this way functioned not only as a catharsis but as a recognition that there was a fundamental dichotomy between the life experience of the community at that particular time and their theology, a theology that paradoxically affirmed the goodness of God and God's desire to bring blessing to all the people of the earth (Gen 12:3). Therefore with utmost confidence, they call upon God to act according to the divine mores.

NEGRO SPIRITUALS AS LAMENTS

Persons of African descent were enslaved in North America for a period of nearly 250 years. Africans were first brought to what would become the United States in 1619, a year before the Mayflower arrived at Plymouth Rock. After 1808, it was illegal to import enslaved persons into the United States, though Africans continued to be imported for that purpose illegally until the Civil War, and they continued to be bred and sold internally. Some Northern states abolished slavery as early as 1804, though there were some Africans enslaved in the North until emancipation. Slavery continued in the South because of the need for slaves to work on the cotton and sugar plantations. The thirteenth amendment to the Constitution, passed in 1865, abolished involuntary servitude throughout the United States except for those incarcerated for crimes committed.

John Lovell Jr., in his article "The Social Implications of the Negro Spiritual," records that the genre of spiritual emerged about one hundred years before the end of slavery in the U.S. and that its "heyday" spanned from 1830–1865 (129). Bernard Katz notes that in 1845 Frederick Douglass wrote, "The songs of the slave represent the sorrows of his heart" (xiii). Perhaps it is from this statement that Du Bois coined the phrase "sorrow songs" (Du Bois 1907: viii)." Not all of the spirituals are laments. But many are. The term "spiritual" derives from Eph 5:18b–19, where the church is encouraged to "be filled with the Spirit, as you sing psalms and hymns and spiritual songs." The term "spiritual songs" in the early nineteenth century was applied to the songs that were sung at the camp meetings as opposed to the hymns that were sung in standard church services. African Americans who were enslaved in the South called their songs "spirituals." Those spirituals that express sorrow, grief, or complaint, directly or indirectly, form the very large subgenre of "sorrow songs."

The laments that appear among the spirituals in the earliest collections are characterized by two- to six-line phrases that are repeated over and over with substitutions for key words or names. "I" or "my" language frequently appears in these songs. From time to time, there is a "call" to someone else to, for example, join in or watch out or be encouraged. (The "call" is also found in the laments of the book of Lamentations, where the personified Jerusalem calls to others to "look and see" in 1:12, but a call is not a characteristic feature of the laments in the Psalms.) A call-and-response pattern is very common in African American spirituals. These were folk songs that were easily remembered, passed on, and changed to reflect changing realities.

The "I" language in these songs is not semantically similar to the "I" songs of the Hebrew corpus and may bear a closer resemblance to the "we" laments of that corpus. Mowinckel conjectured that the "we" language was used later in ancient Israel, when there was a greater consciousness of the individual. Thus he writes, "The we-form witnesses to the fact that the people as a fellowship of personal individuals is more prominent in the religion of Israel than in the despotisms of Babylonia and Assyria" (1:94). Although the slave songs often appear to be personal laments, they were sung in groups, as the call-and-response pattern indicates. The entire group experienced the pain and trauma directly and vicariously. The collection of individual voices formed the "we." The "I" joined in with the shifting "Is" (plural) that were present.[3]

In the earliest collection of slave songs, three themes appear very frequently. The first is a *desire to go home or to have a home*, often expressed as "home in heaven." Examples are found in "Brother, Guide Me Home" and "Blow Your Trumpet, Gabriel," where a line reads, "And I hope dat trump might blow me home. To de new Jerusalem" (Allen, Ware, and Garrison: 3). In "Poor Rosy" the response line is "Heaven shall-a be my home" (Allen, Ware, and Garrison: 7). And "O'er the Crossing" contains the following lines:

> Bendin' knees a-achin', Body racked with pain,
> I wish I was a child of God,
> I'd git home bimeby. (Allen, Ware, and Garrison: 3)

A second prominent theme is a *call to persevere* with the hope that the current situation will change for the better. "O Brothers, Don't Get Weary," "No Man Can Hinder Me," and "Hold Out to the End" are titles and refrains in three such songs.

The third theme is *complaints often expressed vaguely as trouble, pain, or weariness.* Sometimes there are more specific references to being out in the hot sun and rain all day or "massa hollerin" and "missis scolding" ("Hail Mary" in Allen, Ware, and Garrison: 45), or being ill or confused. Long lists of complaints such as the list found in "No More Peck Of Corn" appear around the Civil War era. More typical is "I'm a rollin, I'm a rollin, I'm a rollin through an unfriendly world." Unfriendly! The lack of specific and graphic complaints is striking and quite in contrast to the laments of ancient Israel, where the graphic descriptions are the defining characteristic of the lament. The slave narratives and autobiographies mention beatings, maimings, rape, torture, and murder, yet these do not appear in the first spirituals. They rather make vague references to trouble or weariness that could be understood in a variety of ways, and it may be that it was simply safer not to be specific. The slaves could be overheard at any time. By contrast, the ancient Israelites were in their own communities or in foreign contexts where they had their own space. Confidence that God will remedy the situation is ubiquitous. This confidence, this trust, in the ultimate desire of God to remedy a bad situation was shared by the people of ancient Israel.

The April 28, 1848, edition of *The North Star*, a weekly abolitionist newspaper published by Frederick Douglass in Rochester, New York, contains the following anecdote:

---

[3] Enslaved persons were bought and sold. A community could be completely split up without notice.

I once passed a colored woman at work on a plantation, who was singing, apparently, with animation, and whose general manners would have led me to set her down as the happiest of the gang. I said to her, "Your work seems pleasant to you." She replied, "No massa." Supposing she referred to something particularly disagreeable in her immediate occupation, I said to her, "Tell me then what part of your work is most pleasant." She answered with much emphasis, "No part pleasant. We forced to do it."

The celebrated Dr. Rush of Philadelphia, in one of his published medical papers, entitled "An account of the diseases peculiar to the negroes in the West Indies, and which are produced by their slavery," says:

We are told by their masters that they are the happiest people in the world, because they are 'merry."—Mirth and a heavy heart, I believe, often meet together, and hence the propriety of Solomon's observation, "In the midst of laughter the heart is sad." Instead of considering the songs and dances as marks of their happiness, I have long considered them as physical symptoms of melancholy, and as certain proofs of their misery.[4]

This observation by Dr. Rush should cause a rethinking of the entire notion of what constitutes a lament. Craven describes the biblical lament genre as "prayers of complaint" that reflect experiences in the depths of loneliness, frustration and fearfulness" (26). However, it may be that particularly in the African American community, in addition to the classic lament or complaint form, there are laments that are more covert in their expressions of complaint, sorrow, grief, and loss. For example, the spiritual "I Got Shoes" is happy in its tune and lyrics. Underlying the lyric, however, is the complaint that at the present time, I do not have shoes, robes, and other necessities of life. Henry George Spaulding, a Union official during the Civil War, writing in 1863, records that except for the boat shanties, all of the songs of the Negroes have a "tinge of sadness." Further, he states that the Negroes consider the happy songs that had come to be associated with them through their use in minstrel shows to be "improper." He specifically mentions by name the Stephen Foster tunes, "O Susanna" and "Uncle Ned" (Katz: 8).

As is well known, the laments of Africans in Diaspora in the United States were brought to the attention of the world initially by a group of

---

4 No page number. No author given. Benjamin Rush was chief physician of the Continental Army, a scholar, and a signer of the Declaration of Independence. The quote dates back to 1778.

students from Fisk School (now Fisk University). Eight of the nine students, who ranged in age from fifteen to twenty-five, were persons who either had been enslaved or were the immediate descendants of enslaved Africans. In 1871, they started out on concert tours to raise money for the school. Their popularity increased when they changed their repertoire from classical European music to the songs of the folk tradition of the American Negro. Other African American schools followed suit, and those teenagers and young adults are to be credited with saving a vast collection of traditional music that would have been lost.

The Jubilee Singers sang primarily for European American audiences because their purpose was to raise money for Fisk. The songs that they chose to sing, therefore, represented those spirituals that would please a European American audience, rather than those songs and the versions of those songs that were perhaps most significant in the African American community. In addition, the songs were sung in choral arrangements or as art songs in order to entertain.

How were these songs originally sung? The anonymous author of *Methodist Error* writing in 1819 described the singing of the enslaved Africans in the following manner, "[They] sing ... short scraps of disjointed affirmations, pledges, or prayers, lengthened out with long repetition [*sic*] *choruses*" (Wesleyan Methodist: 30).

Frances Ann Kemble, a Philadephia socialite who spent several months among the enslaved Africans on a Sea Island plantation in the winter of 1838–1839, wrote in a journal that she kept at the time,

> they all sing in unison.... Their voices seem oftener tenor than any other quality, and the tune and time they keep, something quite wonderful; such truth of intonation and accent would make almost any music agreeable.... The way in which the chorus strikes in with the burden, between each phrase of the melody chanted by a single voice, is very curious and effective. (163, 259)

Kemble does not describe tunes or lyrics of religious songs. She does note that the enslaved Africans were forbidden to attend church services on the island. Some of them, however, were permitted to go to a church service, once per month, elsewhere (261–62).

Lucy McKim, a young woman who accompanied her father on a trip to the Southern plantations in 1862 for the explicit purpose of collecting the songs of the enslaved Africans, noted that the songs

> were sung at every sort of work, of course the tempo is not always alike. On the water, the oars dip "Poor Rosy" to an even andante: a stout boy and girl at the hominy mill will make the same "Poor Rosy" fly, to keep up with the whirling stone; and in the evening, after the day's work is

done, "Heab'n shall-a be my home" peals up slowly and mournfully from the distant quarters. One woman, a respectable house-servant, who had lost all but one of her twenty-two children, said to me: "Pshaw! Don't har to dese yer chil'en, missee. Dey just rattles it off—dey don't know how for sing it. I likes 'Poor Rosy' better dan all de songs, but it can't be sung widout *a full heart and a troubled sperrit*" (Allen, Ware, and Garrison: xxii–xxiii)

Thomas P. Fenner, who published a volume titled *Cabin and Plantation Songs As Sung by the Hampton Students* in 1874, noted in the preface that it was difficult to collect the song of the slave because "the freemen have an unfortunate inclination to despise it as a vestige of slavery; those who learned it in the old time, when it was the natural outpouring of their sorrows and longings, are dying off" (quoted in Dett: vi).

Indeed, the Jubilee Singers were at first reluctant to sing the plantation songs in concerts but for another reason, the songs were being used in minstrel shows to caricature African Americans. Therefore, George L. White, the Caucasian choir director of the first Jubilee Singers, was careful to create a way of singing that would distance the plantation songs from the minstrel representations. John W. Work, a successor of White at Fisk, writes:

Mr. White decided on a style of singing the spiritual which eliminated every element that detracted from the pure emotion of the song. Harmony was diatonic and limited very largely to the primary triads and the dominant seventh. Dialect was not stressed but was used only where it was vital to the spirit of the song. Finish, precision, and sincerity were demanded by this leader. Mr. White strove for an art presentation, not a caricature of atmosphere. (15)

Fenner, in his 1874 preface to the first edition of *Cabin and Plantation Songs As Sung by the Hampton Students,* notes that he (Fenner) did change the songs because there were elements of the way the songs were sung that, to use his own words, "cannot be transported to the boards of public performance" (Dett: v). Further, he wrote "that tones are frequently employed which we have no musical characters to represent" (Dett: 5). The changing of the social context in which the songs were sung, the rearrangements of the tunes, the redirected purpose of the songs, and the new audience all influenced which of the spirituals are remembered today and how they are remembered. Therefore, it is difficult to make generalized statements particularly about the content of the lyrics, since those that later generations may have deemed inappropriate may have dropped out.

In 1925, James Weldon Johnson and his brother, Rosamund, published a collection of popular spirituals. They included "Go Down Moses," "Swing Low, Sweet Chariot," "Deep River," "Roll Jordan Roll,"

"Joshua Fit the Battle of Jericho," "Little David, Play on Yo' Harp," and "Steal Away to Jesus." Except for "Steal Away," all of these use themes and imagery from ancient Israel. The next year, the brothers published a collection that included some lesser known spirituals. Among them were "I Want to Die Easy When I Die," "God's A-Gwineter Trouble de Water," "Mary Had a Baby," and "In That Great Gittin' Up Morning." All of these are spirituals that are well known today. But the earlier *Slave Songs of the United States* published in 1867 has quite a few songs that are not well known today. This may be because a disproportionate number of the songs stem from the Port Royal Islands off the Carolina coast and therefore represent an isolated community, or because they do not represent the concerns of a nonslave society or because they were less appealing to European American audiences.

Particularly intriguing are those songs called spirituals that have little or no religious content or where the religious content is vague and there is a lack of closure. Examples include "Motherless Child," "Hush, Hush, Somebody's Callin My Name," "Freedom Train A-Comin," and "I Didn't Hear Nobody Pray." Consider the last of these:

I didn't hear nobody pray.
I didn't hear nobody pray.
Way down yonder, by myself,
and I didn't hear nobody pray.

There is no grace in the lyrics of that song. There is no denouement. There is no comfort. It is sung because it permits an expression of grief.

In 1937, Sterling Brown wrote, "Down in the slave-quarters there grew up side by side with the spirituals, secular folk rhymes" (1937: 21). He provides the following examples:

I don't want to ride in no golden chariot,
I don't want to wear no golden crown,
I want to stay down here and be,
Just as I am without one plea.

Our Father who are in heaven
White man owe me 'leven, pay me seven,
They kingdom come, thy will be done
And ef I hadn't tuck that, I wouldn't get none. (21–22)[5]

Brown does not list either a source or a date for these lyrics.

---

[5] Charles Bell does recall that the enslaved Africans in South Carolina (circa 1805) were permitted to work on Sunday for pay (271–72).

Contrary to popular belief, the majority of Africans in America were not explicitly Christian until the Civil War era (Fisher: 34–35), when they began to enter the Black churches, mostly Baptist and Methodist, in droves. The earliest of the spirituals of the African American community can only be traced back to the 1840s because that is when people started collecting them, though there are references to slaves singing mournful songs much earlier. Is it possible, then, that this vast repertoire of spirituals with Christian or biblical themes had its origins in the slave period? Certainly many of them did. In addition to the songs themselves, there are collections of conversion stories, autobiographies, and poems that affirm Christianity's presence in the African American community. But some of the spirituals were certainly Christianized later on. In his 1901 autobiography, *Up from Slavery*, Booker T. Washington writes:

> Most of the verses of the plantation songs had some reference to freedom. True, they had sung those same verses before, but they had been careful to explain that the "freedom" in these songs referred to the next world, and had no connection with life in this world. Now they gradually threw off the mask, and were not afraid to let it be known that the "freedom" in their songs meant freedom of the body in this world. (19–20)

One of the earliest collections of plantation songs, the aforementioned *Slave Songs of the United States,* was published in 1867, two years after emancipation, but the songs were collected in 1861–1862 or earlier (Allen, Ware, and Garrison). It published songs collected by William Francis Allen, Charles Pickard Ware, and Lucy McKim Garrison. They were careful to include songs that had long been sung in the community of enslaved Africans, though a couple of postemancipation songs appear in that book and their late date of composition is noted. The editors indicated that secular songs or secular tunes had been appropriated by the church. Most of the songs that they collected were in religious gatherings, and they rued the fact that it was difficult to collect secular songs.

Frances Kemble, citing lyrics of a song sung by Negro boatmen, relates that the enslaved Africans frequently sang "an extremely spirited war song, beginning 'The trumpets blow, the bugles sound—Oh, stand your ground!'" (260). The slaves referred to this as "Caesar's Song," and Kemble was intrigued by what she thought may be an allusion to Julius Caesar. She did not comment on the meaning or implications of the words. Although it is widely known that the spirituals functioned as coded messages, sometimes, for example, to send information about a planned escape, the implications of that are not widely recognized. These were not necessarily songs of piety. Some *were* coded messages using the language of the church in order to appear harmless. Arthur C. Jones writes that the use of Christian stories and symbols does not mean that the slaves themselves were believers (8–9). Thomas Higginson, who collected spirituals during the Civil War, wrote that Negroes were whipped in South Carolina for singing the spiritual "We'll Soon Be Free," which has the recurring phrase "When de Lord will call us home." Although this song is filled with heavenly imagery, Southerners thought that "the Lord" was a euphemism for the Northern army. Higginson adds that "No More Peck O' Corn For Me," a secular song listing those things from the life of slavery that they soon expected to be over, was never sung in the open (692). John Lovell Jr., an African American scholar, wrote in 1939 that the slaves were obsessed with three things— freedom, justice, and a strategy to obtain freedom—and that these three appear in the spirituals (134–35).

It is very likely that the oldest of the spirituals were not specifically Christian in their original form, religious, at times, but not necessarily Christian. In his 1936 dissertation titled *The Evolution of the Slave Songs,* Fisher, for example, refers to a song the original title of which was "Run, Nigger, Run." It informed slaves of the presence of patrols in the area that were on the lookout for secret meetings. This song morphed into "Run, Mary, Run," recalling Mary at the tomb of Jesus who runs to tell the disciples that he has risen (155, 155 n. 38). The spiritual "Steal Away" signaled an impending escape attempt. Because the church preserved the spirituals, it is safe to conjecture that those songs that were explicitly Christian or that could be easily Christianized were kept, while others were lost.

The origin of the slave songs is a matter of much contention. Helen W. Ludlow, in the preface to the 1891 edition of *Cabin and Plantation Songs As Sung by the Hampton Students,* quotes one old "aunty" who attributed the songs to a divine origin. She is quoted as having said "When Mass'r Jesus walked de earth, when He feel tired He dit a-restin' on Jacob's well and make up dese yer spirituals for His people" (Dett: vii). Higginson relates that when asked the origin of the spirituals a South Carolinian man stated that he composed a particular one and related a particular happening in his life that caused him to do so (692).

Clearly there is a dependence upon stories and motifs that appear in the Hebrew Bible and the Christian Scriptures. Specific Hebrew Bible references in the early spirituals are almost always to narrative texts, prophecy, or apocalyptic literature. The Psalms themselves and other poetry, the wisdom literature, and legal materials are neither quoted nor alluded to in these songs with one exception. Lovell quotes a portion of a song that might allude to Ps 137. The lyrics are "Going to hang my harp on the willow tree. It'll sound way over in Galilee" (258). Notice that the first line is taken from the Hebrew Bible and the second from the New

Testament.[6] Biblical material was introduced to the enslaved Africans by way of sermons, scripture, or songs that were either preached to them or overheard by them. The preachers most often were Baptist or Methodist evangelists. The absence of sermon material from the psalms of communal lament and the book of Lamentations may be explained in part by their absence in the lectionary of the Methodist Church at the time. (The Baptist Church does not use lectionaries.) John Wesley, one of the founders of Methodism, excised one-third of the Psalter from the Methodist lectionary that he developed specifically for use in North America. He omitted those psalms that he deemed "highly improper for the mouths of a Christian Congregation" (White: 1) and eliminated material from others. These include most of the psalms of communal lament, including Ps 137. The book of Lamentations does not appear in Wesley's lectionary (Ruth).[7] A Russian visitor to Richard Allen's African Methodist congregation in Philadelphia in 1811 noted that psalms were read in the church (Southern: 91). The enslaved Africans in the South, however, rarely went to any church. Congregating of slaves was prohibited because of the general fear of revolts. Enslaved Africans were known to hold secret meetings at night. Some of these were for religious purposes, though not necessarily Christian worship. The Methodists and Baptists, as well, were primarily concerned with "saving souls," not teaching scripture (Ruth: 45).

Is it possible that enslaved Africans could have heard material from the Hebrew Scriptures directly from Jews? There were Jews in the South in the eighteenth and nineteenth centuries when slavery flourished. The first organized Jewish congregation in the south was Mickve Israel, formed by Sephardic Jews in 1733 in Savannah, Georgia. Interestingly enough, local legislation prohibited slavery in Savannah at that time (Mickve Israel). Jews made up only a small portion of the population of the antebellum South. Some did own slaves (Marcus: 2:703ff.), and they followed the patterns of their Gentile neighbors in their treatment of slaves. Jews, however, did not proselytize enslaved Africans in the United States (though there are guidelines for circumcising and therefore converting slaves in Jewish law). Jacob R. Marcus notes in his three-volume work, *The Colonial American Jew: 1492–1776,* that "unlike the Surinamese Jews and some of their coreligionists in the islands, North

---

6 See Randall C. Bailey's article titled "The Danger of Ignoring One's Own Cultural Bias in Interpreting the Text," for a discussion of the conflation of texts from the Hebrew Scriptures and the New Testament (1998: 71).

7 Ruth indicates that early on, few American Methodists were following the guidelines from the prayer book (50). They were focused on "saving souls."

American Jews made no attempt to convert Negro slaves to Judaism" (2:963). Because of the Jews' small numbers and the lack of proselytizing activity, it is unlikely that slaves would have picked up much in the way of biblical material directly from them, except informally.[8]

What biblical material would the enslaved Africans have picked up from the sermons of the period? The early Methodist preachers did not read chapter-long selections of scripture but two to four carefully chosen verses (Ruth: 56). The vast majority of enslaved persons were illiterate because it was illegal to teach them to read and write, so they had to depend upon the oral recitation of biblical texts. An analysis of the content, themes, and characters of the Hebrew Bible that appeared in the spirituals during the preemancipation period is not easy because even the earliest collectors often combined verses from diverse sources, geographic regions, and time periods to fill out songs. Lovell points out that the Bible of the spirituals is a "thin Bible with some names and events recurring quite often, others mentioned but rarely, and still others of alleged importance never mentioned" (262). (Similarly, the biblical psalms of lament rarely contain references to specific persons or events mentioned elsewhere in the Hebrew Bible.) From the Allen, Ware, and Garrison collection, one finds references to biblical figures such as Moses in "There's a Meeting Here Tonight" (9), "Join the Angel Band" (39), "Brother Moses Gone" (49), "Let God's Saints Come In" (76), which describes the exodus story, and "Come Along, Moses" (104). Two versions of "Join the Angel Band" are present in the Allen, Ware, and Garrison collection. One has Moses as the central figure: "If you look up de road you see fader Mosey, Join the angel band" (39). The other version sung in Charleston is Christocentric: "O join 'em all, join for Jesus" (39).

Abraham appears in "Rock o' My Soul in the Bosom of Abraham" (Allen, Ware, and Garrison: 73), and Adam in "What a Trying Time," which briefly tells the story of Adam in the garden eating the apple (114). Daniel is a favorite and anchors "O Daniel" (96). One line reads "O my Lord delivered Daniel, O why not deliver me too?" Other references to Daniel appear in "Lean on the Lord's Side" (117) and "Daniel Saw the Stone" (54). Noah figures in "De Ole Ark a Moverin' Along" (Dett: 58), and Ezekiel in "Ezekiel Saw de Wheel." (60). David is the central figure in "Little David, Play on Your Harp" (64). Jacob wrestling is mentioned

---

8 In a fellowship announcement regarding his dissertation, Jonathan Schorsch writes, "the decline of the circumcision of slaves in the 17th and 18th centuries among the western Sephardim, a decline reflective of an increasing discomfort with the religious absorption of slaves, now mostly Black, and the Sephardim uneasy themselves about their own status vis a vis Whiteness."

in "Wrestle On, Jacob" with the statement, "I will not let you go, My Lord" (Allen, Ware, and Garrison: 4). The recurring phrase has other people that the singer will not let go, such as the brother, sister, and so on (4). There is also a reference to the "tree of life" in "Roll Jordan Roll" (1). In "Trouble of the World," the phrase "I wish I was in Jubilee" is repeated (10). Gabriel is blowing a trumpet in "Blow Your Trumpet, Gabriel" (3).

In "Hold Your Light," the singer asks,

What make ole Satan da follow me so?
Satan hain't nottin' at all for to do wid me. (12)[9]

In "I Know When I'm Going Home," the first line reads "Old Satan told me to my face, O yes, Lord, De God I seek I never find" (41). Satan appears fairly frequently in the spirituals but more as a trickster figure than an evil being. This also is similar to the figure of the *satan* in the book of Job. Occasionally it is difficult to tell whether the reference is indeed to a biblical figure or to a member of their own community who shares the same name. Sometimes the names appear in isolation without a fragment of the story to indicate whether the singer was knowledgeable about the context and themes that surround the figure in the biblical text, but at other times the biblical story is told verse by verse.[10]

In contrast to the laments of ancient Israel, the extant spirituals of Africans in the United States never understood God to be responsible for their suffering, nor did they blame themselves. Like the ancient Israelites, the enslaved Africans envisioned God as the one who could remedy their situation in this world or the world to come. They believed that ultimately God was on their side. The religion of their oppressors would turn against them in the end. As a line in the spiritual "I Got Shoes" proclaims, "Everybody talkin' bout heaven ain't agoin there!"

Why is there an absence of God blaming in the spirituals as is found in some of the laments from ancient Israel? James Cone writes that the absence in assigning blame to God in the spirituals does not indicate silence on this subject. He argues that there existed what are referred to as "seculars" that did just that. He refers to some of the parody songs that were mentioned earlier. He also quotes Daniel Payne, a free, preemancipation, African Methodist Episcopal bishop, who wrote that he knew of enslaved Africans who "sneer and laugh" (Cone 1972: 63) when called to

---

9 See also Allen, Ware, and Garrison: 11, 16, 36, 49, 51, 57, 97, 128, and 107–8.
10 For discussions of biblical content in spirituals beyond those included in *Slave Songs of the United States,* see R. Bailey 1998; Copher: 79–93; and Lovell: 255–62.

prayer. However, what Payne goes on to describe is the enslaved Africans' ridiculing the hypocrisy of masters and mistresses who preached a partial gospel of "slaves obeying your master" while ignoring texts that speak of breaking the yoke of oppression. He further heard enslaved Africans denying the existence of God (ibid.). Charles Bell, an African American who was enslaved for fifty years, in an account of his life published originally in 1837 said:

> Many of them believed there were several gods, some of whom were good, and others evil, and they prayed as much to the latter as to the former.... There is, in general, very little sense of religious obligation, or duty amongst the slaves on the cotton plantations; and Christianity cannot be, with propriety, called the religion of these people. (164–65)

It is possible that songs that blamed a god or expressed disbelief were excised from their oral traditions before they could be written down? Such songs may have been among the ones that the first Jubilee Singers considered to be "improper." Moreover, most of the spirituals were collected by Christian ministers and Christian lay persons and most in the context of religious gatherings. Frances Kemble wrote in her journal that she heard enslaved men singing a song that she considered offensive (260–61).[11] The song was about women. She expressed her displeasure, and they did not again sing the song in her presence. The incident raises the question of whether the silencing of the enslaved Africans may have contributed to an absence of certain types of songs in the collections. The absence of "blaming god language" or "god is punishing us" language may also reflect the changing theological understandings of the slaves. If they were to blame god, which god would they blame: the gods of their ancestors who failed them in Africa or the god of this new world preached to them by Christian evangelists or the gods that they themselves formed in the new world? Perhaps they never associated any god with the plight that they were in. Except for Muslims and perhaps a few Christians, enslaved sub-Saharan Africans did not have to deal with the theological difficulties posed by monotheism.

COMPARISON OF SPIRITUALS WITH OTHER CHURCH MUSIC

Ethnomusicologists have tried to determine how much of the content, tunes, and rhythms of spirituals are to be attributed to African

---

11 Kemble quotes the lyrics of several secular songs (163–64).

roots and how much to the hymns and gospel songs of the church. James Weldon Johnson, weighing heavily on the former side, wrote, "by sheer spiritual forces ... African chants were metamorphosed into the Spirituals" (1985: 21). Bessie Mayle in an unpublished thesis notes similarities in style between African songs and those of Africans in America, particularly in what we call the "call and response" (61–68). The anonymous author of *Methodist Error,* a diatribe against physical and emotional excesses in worship, complained that Methodists had adopted songs that were "most frequently composed and first sung by the illiterate *blacks* of the society" (Wesleyan Methodist: 28–29). This would indicate that in the opinion of a person who lived during the period of slavery, some of the spiritual songs of the European American camp meetings were borrowed from the Africans and not the other way around.

To be sure, European American gospel songs did have an influence on a few of the spirituals, as George Pullen Jackson demonstrates in his seminal study titled *White Spirituals in the Southern Uplands,* originally published in 1933, and his second volume published a decade later titled *White and Negro Spirituals.* Jackson believed that the majority of Negro spirituals, at least the tunes,[12] had a European-American origin (1975: 266–67). This estimate is far too high. Jackson starts with the proposition that whenever similarities are found between a Negro spiritual and a European American spiritual or hymn, the latter was the original version. He even does this by comparing European American spirituals sung in the 1930s with Negro spirituals sung a century earlier. John W. Work, a contemporary of Jackson, argued very effectively against his premise and his conclusions in an article that appeared in 1935 (Lovell: 94). Jackson's method was to pair spirituals with what he believed to be precedents in the European American church. For example, he paired "O for a Thousand Tongues to Sing My Great Redeemer's Praise," sung to the tune Gaines rather than the more popular Azman, with "Swing Low, Sweet Chariot" (Jackson 1975: 182–83), and "Jesus, Thou Art the Sinner's Friend" with "Do Lord Remember Me" (164–65). While the former pairing is unconvincing because neither the tune nor the lyrics is similar, the latter has some merit because there is a similarity in tune and lyrics. If these are two versions of the same song, the theological differences are striking. In the European American version, the singer appeals to Jesus, placing himself or herself in the "bowels of [Jesus'] love" and refers to

---

12 Ted Gibbonney, Assistant Professor of Church Music at Christian Theological Seminary, tells me that folk tunes often share similarities as a result of their characteristic singability.

himself or herself as a sinner. In the African American version, the more general term "Lord" rather than the specific "Jesus" is used. There is no reference to the singer being a sinner. No location is given for the singer. Even in the spirituals that clearly derive from gospel songs of the period, there is a notable difference in theology and worldview. Another example is found in "Go in the Wilderness," which the editors of *Slave Songs of the United States* indicate combines an African American spiritual with a standard Methodist hymn. The African American song has the following words:

> I wait upon de Lord,
> I wait upon de Lord,
> I wait upon de Lord, my God,
> who take away de sin of the world.

The Methodist hymn addition reads:

> If you want to find Jesus, go in the wilderness,
> Go in de wilderness, go in the wilderness,
> Mournin' brudder, go in de wilderness. (Allen, Ware, and Garrison: 14)

John Work argues against Jackson that two-thirds of the Negro spirituals are of the call-and-response type, a form not found in European American spirituals or hymns, figures of speech are different in the Negro and European American spirituals, and the use of scales is different. Work estimated that fifteen or twenty of the six hundred to seven hundred songs that Jackson worked with may bear a resemblance (Lovell: 94). An interesting anecdote appears in the 1867 collection, *Slave Songs of the United States.* The editors of that book record that it was brought to their attention that the Negro spiritual "Praise Member" appears in a standard church hymnal of the time period titled *Choral Hymns.* The editors contacted the editor of that hymnal, who told them that "many of his songs were learned from Negroes in Philadelphia," then added, "Lt. Col. Trowbridge tells us that he heard this hymn before the war [the Civil War] among the colored people of Brooklyn" (Allen, Ware, and Garrison: ix). Therefore, the presence of a hymn in a standard church hymnal of the period does not mean that the hymn had its origins in the European American church.

Higginson reports that he requested his quartermaster to teach the Negroes a popular camp song titled "Marching Along." The words "gird on the armor" appear in the song, and the Negroes found that to be a difficult phrase. They probably had no idea what armor was. They immediately emended the phrase to "guide on the army," and that continued to be the way that it was sung in South Carolina (Higginson: ix–x).

The spirituals were folk songs. As with all folk songs, there is borrowing back and forth and emending to fit the desires of the community in which they are sung.

Miles Mark Fisher asserts,

> the so-called "Slave Songs" of the United States are best understood when they are considered as expressions of the experiences of individual Negroes, which can be dated and assigned to a geographical locale. They are, in brief, historical documents. Further, the writer has come to agree with Frederick Law Olmsted, who, in 1863, concluded that the religion the Negroes sang about was not derived primarily from the American Christianity of the nineteenth century. This is to emphasize the African Background patterns. (i)

Fisher records that Lucy McKim, a European American woman who collected slave songs from the Sea Islands off the coast of South Carolina in 1862, also thought the spirituals to be historical in nature, although "characterized as otherworldly" (Fisher: 37). He recalls that Talley believed that Nat Turner, who led an aborted slave revolt in 1831, wrote "Steal 'Wa'" on the eve of his execution because there was a thunderstorm the night before his execution and the song refers to thunder and lightening. One verse reads

> My Lord, calls me. He calls me by the thunder.
> The trumpet sounds within my soul. I ain't got long to stay here.

Moreover, the earliest references to hearing this song indicated that it was first sung around that time and in that place. Fisher cites a spiritual that sings about joining a band moving toward Jerusalem. Jerusalem is specifically identified with Courtland, Virginia, the destination of Nat Turner's band (Fisher: 163–65). Moreover, he notes that Earl Conrad attributed spiritual composition to Harriet Tubman (56). If Fisher is correct, then at least some of the preemancipation spirituals should be understood as describing historical events and situations, giving them something in common with the collection of laments in the biblical book of Lamentations as well as Ps 137. While it is unlikely that most of the spirituals are truly historical in nature, since spirituals rarely relate historical events, it is likely that a few of them are or, to be more specific, were historical in nature. Even those that were tied to a specific historical event (Thrower: 18)[13] were sung

---

13 Thrower notes that, when asked, Sea Islanders indicated that the songs that they sung were connected to happenings in their lives.

in other contexts, changed and spiritualized to the point where the origin was lost.[14]

The laments of ancient Israel were more fully developed than the African American spirituals, likely because those that did spring from the heart of the common people were appropriated for formal worship and made more complex, even as the simple two-line praise song of Exod 15:21 expanded into the victory hymn of Exod 15:1–18.

COMPARISON OF PSALM 79 AND "POOR ROSY"

The following comparison between Ps 79 and "Poor Rosy" will illustrate the similarities and differences between the laments of the two communities. Psalm 79 was chosen because it appears on all lists of biblical laments. "Poor Rosy" was chosen because the life situation in which this song was sung is known and its placement within the period of slavery is assured.

The lyrics to Ps 79 are:

A Psalm of Asaph

[1] O God, the nations have come into your inheritance;
    they have defiled your holy temple;
    they have laid Jerusalem in ruins.
[2] They have given the bodies of your servants
    to the birds of the air for food,
    the flesh of your faithful to the wild animals of the earth.
[3] They have poured out their blood like water
    all around Jerusalem,
    and there was no one to bury them.
[4] We have become a taunt to our neighbors,
    mocked and derided by those around us.
[5] How long, O LORD? Will you be angry forever?
    Will your jealous wrath burn like fire?
[6] Pour out your anger on the nations
    that do not know you,
  and on the kingdoms
    that do not call on your name.
[7] For they have devoured Jacob
    and laid waste his habitation.

---

14 Richard Allen, one of the founders of the African Methodist Episcopal Church, created a hymnbook in 1801 composed of standard European American hymns and hymns of his own creation.

[8] Do not remember against us the iniquities of our ancestors;
　　　let your compassion come speedily to meet us,
　　　　for we are brought very low.
[9] Help us, O God of our salvation,
　　　for the glory of your name;
　　deliver us, and forgive our sins
　　　for your name's sake.
[10] Why should the nations say,
　　　"Where is their God?"
　　Let the avenging of the outpoured blood of your servants
　　　be known among the nations before our eyes.
[11] Let the groans of the prisoners come before you;
　　　according to your great power preserve those doomed to die.
[12] Return sevenfold into the bosom of our neighbors
　　　the taunts with which they taunted you, O Lord!
[13] Then we your people, the flock of your pasture,
　　　will give thanks to you forever;
　　　from generation to generation we will recount your praise.

Psalm 79 centers on a specific complaint: the city of Jerusalem has been assaulted. This may suggest an exilic date for the psalm, though Jerusalem was attacked a number of times and another occasion may be envisioned. Anderson notes that 79:4 is nearly identical to Ps 44:14 (579). The psalm contains four of the six structural elements listed by Craven (27): address to God (79:1, 5, 9, 12), complaint (79:1–4, 7), petition (79:6, 8–12), and the vow (79:13). A cry for help appears in 79:9. A call for vengeance issues forth in 79:12. The only elements missing are the confession of trust and words of assurance. In addition, the cry of lament "How long?" appears in 79:5.

The lyrics to "Poor Rosy" are"

1. Poor Rosy, poor gal; Poor Rosy, poor gal
   Rosy break my poor heart, Heav'n shall-a be my home.
   I cannot stay in hell one day, Heaven shall-a be my home;
   I'll sing and pray my soul away, Heaven shall-a be my home.

2. Got hard trial in my way, Heav'n shall-a be my home.
   O when I talk, I talk wid God, Heav'n shall-a be my home.

3. I dunno what de people want of me, Heav'n shall-a be my home.
   (Allen, Ware, and Garrison: 7)

"Poor Caesar, poor boy" substitutes for "Poor Rosy, poor gal." "Massa" substitutes for "people," and "walk" for "talk (Allen: 7)." "Before I stay in hell one day" is a variation on the third verse.

"Poor Rosy" is illustrative of the semantic difficulties encountered in the spirituals. The first three lines could reflect a lover's longings for a lover who has spurned his love. But the next phrase, "Heav'n shall-a be my home," transforms the song into a spiritual. Rosy can be a spouse, a lover, a friend, or a child. The name "Caesar" substitutes for Rosy in this song when it reflects on a male. Allen notes that "This song ranks with 'Roll, Jordan,' in dignity and favor"(Allen, Ware, and Garrison: 7). There is no direct address to the deity. The phrase "hard trial" is typical of the vague complaint type that is found in the spirituals. The phrase "when I talk, I talk wid God" expresses a confession of trust that God hears and keeps confidences. The last stanza where "massa" can substitute for "people" also raises a complaint. Heaven and hell appear in the text, but it is unclear whether a transcendent heaven and hell are envisioned or whether this is code language for the current situation expressing a desire to be out of the hell that is their existence on earth and to enter into a safe and happy place, heaven, here on earth.

Conclusion

The enslaved Africans and ancient Israel shared a history of slavery, exile from their homeland, and being caricatured and abused, and they adopted the same method of expressing their grief, laments set to music. Elements common to both were statements of complaint and expressions of confidence that God would remedy their situation. The Africans in the United States identified with the Israelites and used some of their imagery, theological ideas, and person references in their own laments. Both communities used song to record particular historical events or life situations, though in many cases the historical contexts were forgotten as the songs were molded and shaped in the folk tradition. For both, the laments function as an aid to grief, to help people to grieve, to encourage them to grieve. Both communities appealed to God to bring an end to their suffering. In spite of this, there are laments that lack closure in the ancient Israelite and enslaved African communities, an indication that the grief process must not be cut short. The grieving could not come to an end until they were free to live as whole human beings.

TEXTUAL HARASSMENT? A HERMENEUTICAL PERSPECTIVE ON AFRICAN AMERICAN PREACHING

Ronald N. Liburd
Florida A&M University

INTRODUCTION

Inasmuch as two African American legal professionals have contributed to an astonishing degree to the currency that the word *harassment* has had in the American social and political lexicon,[1] I find it quite appropriate to tease out its meaning in the title of our discussion of the African American use of the Bible in preaching. The article is divided into three sections, the first of which examines the method biblical authors use to interpret their scriptures. The second analyzes the text of a sermon preached by a prominent African American theologian in order to demonstrate how preaching in the black church in America can be said to follow a method similar to that of biblical authors. The third section draws on hermeneutical theory in order to postulate a reason for this similarity, a similarity that is found to be grounded in both the nature of religious experience and the hermeneutical task itself. In light of this inquiry, the conclusion offers a challenge for black preachers to extend the liberation hermeneutical project if they are to remain committed to the task of eradicating all kinds of oppression.

Before I proceed, I think it is necessary for me to provide a context for this analysis. My social location is that of a West Indian brought up in the Anglican tradition, and for a time I knew of nothing else in the form of religion beyond that religious horizon. During my teen years—that vulnerable period—I converted to an evangelical Christian community of a very conservative variety. So today, I usually represent myself as a once-upon-a-time evangelical pastor who practiced Johannine evangelism of

---

[1] I suspect that it should be obvious I am referring to the events that surrounded the United States Senate confirmation hearings for the now Justice Clarence Thomas.

the classic type that holds there is no salvation apart from my variety. Both my liturgical and kerygmatic expressions of Christianity had been tuned in an Anglo-American key, so to speak, due to the colonizing activities of first British and then American missionaries in the English-speaking Caribbean. The American activity was particularly deleterious in that it was designed to uproot me from the cultural habits that defined my West Indianness: calypso music and carnival, for example, became religious taboos.[2] To be sure, I had always known that I was a descendant of slaves, for the anecdotes of dehumanization meted out to my ancestors were part of the folklore. But a certain irony always plagued my consciousness in that I lacked the technical equipment to handle the pervasive presence of slavery as an institution in a text whose divine authority I had come to accept. Happily, all this would change with my second sojourn in graduate school, where I was introduced to theologies, hermeneutics, and biblical studies in a "new key,"[3] that of liberation.

From this social location, then, I confess my inadequacy to respond with appropriateness when I attend a black church in worship and hear, for example, "Can I get a witness?" It should be fairly common knowledge that a West Indian who ventures to discuss such a topic as the one before us brings much baggage, such as ignorance and naïveté, that must be disposed of if any semblance of authenticity is to emerge from the discussion. The following anecdote should be illustrative of the kind of baggage to which I refer.

A pastor colleague from the island of Antigua, whose experience could have easily been my own embarrassment had I been similarly naïve, was invited to preach in a black church somewhere in Chicago.

---

2 I do not lay this charge without warrant. In the Caribbean, the leadership of the Seventh-day Adventist Church to which I converted regards the indigenous music genres and festivals as degenerate, and many pastors would move to have disciplinary action taken against any member thought to be thus miscreant. The basis for such views is the following paragraph in the church's official manual of polity and discipline, which is revised and published every five years by the General Conference of Seventh-day Adventists, headquartered in Washington, D.C.: "Great care should be exercised with the choice of music. Any melody partaking of the nature of jazz, rock, or related hybrid forms, or any language expressing foolish or trivial sentiments, will be shunned by persons of true culture. Let us use only good music in the house, in the social gathering, in the school, and in the church" (General Conference: 153).

Note the explicit declaration in this paragraph that music such as jazz, blues, rock, and, one can infer, perhaps calypso, reggae, merengue, and the like are not truly cultured art forms. And even in this modern epoch of increased multicultural awareness, this view is held "without apology," as one highly placed white Adventist pastor declared to me recently in a telephone conversation.

3 Here I am borrowing from the title of Robert McAfee Brown's 1978 work.

After delivering his sermon, he sat down, whereupon the dismayed host who had introduced him with much extravagance nudged him in a frantic whisper, "You need to 'open the doors of the church' now!" My friend promptly got up, sped to the back of the church like a mustang, and opened the doors of the church wide for the congregation to empty it. It seems he did not understand that the phrase "to open the doors of the church" meant to offer a verbal invitation to those in the congregation who were so disposed to come down the aisle and join the church.

That might suffice as an example of how West Indians can often be quite textually wooden and dense. None the less, the inadequacy of my social location aside, my understanding of the nature of biblical hermeneutics prompts me to venture into the following analysis of preaching as it is generally performed in the African American context with my disclaimer regarding its completeness.

Preaching, as most Christians have come to understand it, is an apologetical and sometimes polemical exercise. The preacher's primary goal in this task is to persuade a given audience of the correctness and urgency of the message proclaimed. It is a curious fact, for me at least, that the Scriptures from which Christians preach present us with no precise method as to how one preaches. Moreover, there is not, to my knowledge, a single specimen of a sermon[4] in the entire Bible. For this reason I conclude that preaching, as it is known and performed today, evolved as a postbiblical phenomenon, and there are as many variations of the art as there are theories about how to persuade people to become believers.

The theology department of the college where I was trained to be a pastor had a professor who reinforced the need to memorize biblical verses so as to be able to bring them together to prove a given doctrine. After his class, I would go to another class where the professor berated the proof-text method with the old adage: "A text taken out of its context is nothing more than a pretext for preaching." This latter teacher was putting to work the tools of historical criticism, which had shaped his own graduate education. It was in this latter class that I first encountered what he described as textual violation—what I am calling harassment—within

---

4 We should be mindful, however, of the anachronistic labeling as sermons Jeremiah's denunciation of Judah's leadership at Shiloh (26:1–24) and Jesus' ethical admonitions (Matt 5–7). The speeches of Peter and Paul that are recorded in Acts of the Apostles must be considered the author's own literary compositions done in the tradition of the Greco-Roman authors such as Thucydides, Plutarch, and Tacitus, who, as historians and biographers, wrote in the rhetorical tradition that required them to reproduce a discourse based on their conception of a speaker's character.

the Bible itself. To illustrate his point, this teacher had us read Hos 11:1 and then asked us to explain its meaning in that context. That done, he had us read Matt 2:14–15 to discover how the Evangelist interprets Hosea's reflection on Israel's ingratitude to God.

Following that teacher's insight, I have argued for a long time that Matthew's proof-text hermeneutics, his preaching so to speak, does violence to the integrity of the Hebrew text. This must be precisely the view advanced by John Reumann in this fitting protestation: "No one would propose Matthew's development of 'formula quotations' . . . as the way to do exegesis today" (12). Were I using contemporary American language in the 1970s to refer to Matthew's interpretation, I would have declared him guilty of textual harassment,[5] but the question mark in the title of this article suggests that I now have doubts about that judgment. A new understanding of the science of hermeneutics has forced me to see Matthew's use of the Hebrew text in an entirely different light, namely, the use of an ancient traumatic experience in Israel as a type for an equally traumatic experience in the Jesus Movement. I find in African American preaching something analogous to Matthew's use of Scripture and undertake in what follows an examination of the former in light of the latter.

I

Let us first look briefly at the biblical passages to which I have just referred and try to ascertain what role experience plays in assigning new meaning to biblical texts. At Hos 11:1–2 we read, "When Israel was a child, I loved him, and out of Egypt I called my son. The more I called them, the more they went from me; they kept sacrificing to the Baals, and offering incense to idols."[6] The context of the prophet's discourse is God's gracious love for Israel displayed in both the gracious act of delivering this people from Egyptian slavery and God's continued lovingkindness (ḥesed) despite Israel's unfaithfulness to its covenant with God. We note here that Hosea reinterprets the exodus event in metaphorical terms using the family imagery: child (and by implication),

---

5 Recently, I accidentally came upon Lloyd Bailey's work in which he discusses the problem of transmitting the ancient manuscripts and uses -the concept of harassment to underscore the peril of the potential interpreter. Note, however, that his use reverses the object of harassment: "Yet another problem lurks to harass the modern interpreter who would become attuned to what the 'author' said" (174).

6 All Bible citations are from the New Revised Standard Version (NRSV) unless otherwise indicated.

parent, and love. What seems to surface in this highly affective language is the pain that the prophet experiences for having a wife who has been unfaithful to him; therefore he employs the exodus and Israel's subsequent experiment with idolatry so as to keep his moorings to God. I refer to it as Hosea's familial and experiential reinterpretation of the exodus to mitigate his pain.[7]

Some seven centuries later, the author of Matthew, reflecting on the meaning of Jesus' miraculous flight from Herod, writes: "Then Joseph got up, took the child and his mother by night, and went to Egypt, and remained there until the death of Herod. This was to fulfill what had been spoken by the Lord through his prophet, 'Out of Egypt I have called my son'" (Matt 2:14–15). Once again, if we are guided by the canons of historical-critical exegesis, we are obliged to conclude that the Evangelist is taking liberties with the text of Hosea by making the eighth-century prophet a visionary to an experience that he clearly could not have had in mind. But if one were a first-century Jew convinced that Israel's existence is predicated on a messianic hope, then it is conceivable how the first Evangelist's rabbinic exegesis of Hosea is quite persuasive. As Dennis Duling notes regarding this passage, "Escape to and return from Egypt echo the stories of Joseph (Gen 37), Moses, and Israel.... The massacre echoes Pharaoh's act at the birth of Moses (Ex 1:15–22)" (1861). Moreover, if "Son of God" is a key messianic title in the Gospel of Matthew, then the "son" of Hos 11:1, which refers to Israel, is not, after all, a farfetched reference to Jesus.

The extent to which this type of interpretation pervades the writings of Jewish sects of the period in general, and the New Testament in particular, makes Matthew's exegesis look like a minor chord in an A-major symphony of Jewish interpretation.[8] The Essenes, for example, whose writings were discovered among the Dead Sea Scrolls, used the pesher to interpret Num 24:17–19 as a prophecy pointing to their community (Segal:

---

7 For a similar understanding of Hosea's use of his family circumstances to delineate God's loving relationship to Israel, see, for example, Gottwald (358–63); Soggin (248–54); and more recently, Weems's thought-provoking study from a womanist perspective (1995).

8 By the first century C.E., Jewish interpretation fell into four categories as follows: midrash, pesher, allegory, and verbal or literalistic. A note about the first two is in order at this point in light of our analysis of black preaching and its hermeneutics. In the first type (the midrash), the interpreter pays attention to the original context of the passage while at the same time makes a contemporary appropriation of the text. In the second type (the pesher), the interpreter relates the passage exclusively to the place and events of his time, and the author of Matthew, like the Essenes, seems most comfortable with this approach. This latter method of interpretation was generally regarded by Jews of the period as providing God's revealed solution.

49–50). Neither were the Essenes the only Jewish community to have employed this method of interpretation. Philo, a contemporary interpreter, used the allegory as a way to analogize Torah within his Jewish experience in the first century, while the Pharisees of the same and later period used the midrash[9] as their tool to interpret Torah. With every new situation, occasioned by the emergence of a new community of believers that felt itself constrained by the authority of the writings of Israelite religion, there was a corresponding hermeneutical device specifically crafted to accord self-definition to that new community of faith. Bloch states the situation precisely: "So long as there is a people of God who regard the Bible as the living Word of God, there will be midrash; only the name might change. Nothing is more characteristic in this regard than the use of the OT in the NT; it always involves midrashic actualization itself, in the present situation to which the ancient texts are applied and adapted" (33). Indeed it has been customary among some modern interpreters of the Hebrew Bible to use a similar method they label typology.

We shall see, later, how the nature of hermeneutics chastises against any notion of regarding such approaches to reading the biblical text as less than a faithful interpretation. David Lawton, in assessing the function of typology in biblical interpretation, thinks that it displaces the literal meaning of the original text, to be sure, but then goes on to make this cogent observation: "Implicit in this typological approach is the historical understanding that the commentator knows more than the individual human writer of each particular book" (Lawton: 21).[10]

At this point, the crucial question for the modern interpreter of the Bible is, How does one understand the use that these early tradents made of the traditions they received? I have not been able to find any serious New Testament scholar who dismisses the New Testament authors' interpretation of the Hebrew Scriptures as eisegesis in the way they most certainly have dismissed, for example, Augustine's allegorical interpretation of the parable of the Good Samaritan. What I have found, instead, is a careful and serious attempt to rehabilitate every single New Testament reinterpretation of Torah.

---

9 For a precise definition and informed understanding of the use of midrash, see the work of Renée Bloch. After making clear its homiletical purpose and its attentiveness to the text, Bloch then notes that midrashic exegesis had a practical goal in view, which "practical concern led midrash to reinterpret Scripture, [that is] to 'actualize it'" (32).

10 The remark is in reference to the church fathers' use of the Bible but is none the less equally applicable to the earlier periods of biblical interpretation, as many New Testament texts exhibit.

An example that typifies this approach is that of C. F. D. Moule's contribution to the Earle Ellis Festschrift, *Tradition and Interpretation in the New Testament*. In his article, "Jesus, Judaism, and Paul," Moule thinks that Paul in Rom 11 is using the principle of analogy to do serious interpretation of the Hebrew concept of Israel as a tree with authentic branches. Accordingly, Jesus is in fact Israel, since he epitomizes it: Israel is the elect people, and Jesus is the elect one. But since Paul uses the text of Jeremiah (31:31–34) to argue his case, Moule reluctantly concedes: "An observer may be forgiven for seeing Paul's use of Scripture as a tour de force...; and his opponents must have been quick to retort that, when the circumcision law is given (Gen 17), it is stringently enjoined on all Abraham's posterity." Then to end any notion of apparent equivocation on his part regarding the legitimacy of Paul's hermeneutical appropriation of Jeremiah, Moule, in the very next sentence, gives this sublime defense of the archapostle: "But, however little his case may be 'proved' from Scripture, the fact remains that he is convinced by *his experiences* that entry into the destiny of Israel at its fullest and most developed is now through the new covenant inaugurated by the death and resurrection of Jesus Christ" (45; my emphasis). Here one notes Moule's appeal to experience as the key ingredient in Paul's hermeneutics, and since he does not fault the apostle with the eisegesis epithet, this analysis obliges me to use experience as the central component to an appreciation of the nature of African American preaching.

II

We now turn to preaching in the African American context, which in shorthand we shall call black preaching. A certain degree of peril attends the task of selecting a single sermon to illustrate the parallel between the hermeneutics that undergirds black preaching and that which informs the biblical authors. With much trepidation, therefore, I have selected a sermon, preached in the mid-1970s by Gayraud S. Wilmore, entitled "Blackness As Sign and Assignment." My source does not give a venue, but I aver that it could have been preached anywhere in black America.[11]

---

11 The twenty-one sermons in Newbold's collection are the edited versions of the oral presentations by both lay and clergy black preachers in the United Presbyterian Church tradition. My selection has to overcome yet another complication—whether a black Presbyterian preacher is an authentic representation of black preaching—as this quotation demonstrates: "Black Presbyterian preachers often find themselves in the middle of a controversy. Some of the white preachers within the denomination question their homiletical ability. Many black clergy, colleagues outside the denomination, feel that black preachers stand out as scholars, Biblical interpreters, and lecturers, but not necessarily

After the birth of the black-consciousness movement, Wilmore became one of the clearest voices in the articulation of liberation theology in black America, and this sermon illustrates the importance of the black experience in American religion. His text is from the prophet Ezekiel: "Son of man, you dwell in the midst of a rebellious house.... Therefore, ... prepare for yourself an exile's baggage, ... for I have made you a sign for the house of Israel" (12:2–3, 6). The sermon begins with the statement, "Many people are confused about blackness." Then Wilmore lists the code words of the period—black power, black pride, black studies, black theology—to raise, what is for him, the momentous question: Is there a profound religious meaning in the idea of being a black people? Note how the question is rhetorically framed in order for him to posit his conviction thus: "I believe that black Christians—the black church in Africa and America—should articulate the theological meaning of blackness that arises from our religious experience as a people. I believe that we need to understand blackness both as a sign and as an assignment for God" (Wilmore 1977: 166).

With this assertion, Wilmore leads his audience to ponder on the strange pantomime Ezekiel enacts, that of Judah's exile in Babylon. God tells the prophet to dress himself up like an exile, to put an exile's baggage on his shoulders, and to go out through the city walls in the darkness of night, as one going sadly under great burden into captivity. Wilmore shows how Ezekiel portrays himself as a sign of God's people humiliated, uprooted from their land of comfort and safety, and made captive as a consequence of their rejection of God. He asserts that Ezekiel, with his exile's clothing and baggage, is God's message: "for I have made you," God said, "a sign for the house of Israel." And now he is ready for the hermeneutical leap. Let us substitute, Wilmore continues, the color of blackness for the exile's clothing and baggage that Ezekiel carried by God's command.

From here on in the sermon blackness becomes the rallying point. In a country where every member of the audience has experienced the humiliation and indignity of racism, color becomes critical in the decipherment of religious meaning, and for Wilmore and his congregation blackness is that cipher. He would have them know, for example, that whereas white men, by the sheer power of their culture, money, guns, and Bibles (he actually said Bibles!), have made the white/black symbolism the *modus*

---

as preachers. Such judgments were primarily occasioned by the fact that white questioners insisted on judging black preaching by white standards. Further, a number of brothers and sisters concluded that no authentic black preaching occurs outside the black church" (Newbold: 11).

operandi "first in Europe and America, later in South Africa, and now all over the world" (1977: 168), by the same token black people can use the Bible to change that meaning. For Wilmore, this is a serious matter, and note how he foils the racial cliché of a popular white preacher:

> Colors convey powerful religious meanings, as the history of liturgics shows. And if a white preacher like the Rev. Buchner Payne can say that God chose whiteness because there is no darkness in him and that there can be no darkness in heaven, a black preacher can say that God chose blackness because God is mystery and cosmic fecundity, for there can be no white, lifeless sterility in heaven! (168)

Then he concludes that "black people have a right, even a responsibility, to interpret the Christian faith in such a way as to make blackness a profound expression of our religious experience" (168).

I find it significant that Wilmore does not say "interpret the Bible" but rather "interpret the Christian faith," for he must be well aware that the biblical text does not allow him to indict the system of slavery and its concomitant racial prejudice in America. I am not suggesting that his approach dispenses with the Bible. To the contrary, the biblical warrants for his Christian faith force him, in what must be the crescendo of his sermon, to indict slavery and its pernicious results in America:

> Jesus Christ is crucial to black Christianity because darkness was his experience, and we know something about darkness. The Good Friday spiritual asks the question, "Were you there?" And the unspoken answer is, "Yes, we were all there when the Nigger of Galilee was lynched in Jerusalem." Is there any wonder that we can identify with him? (171).

What Wilmore does here is to draw a parallel between the humiliation of black people in America (and the rest of the world, for that matter!) and the humiliation of Jesus' crucifixion. Notice his conclusion to the parallel he draws: "But as Jesus stood the test, we too stood the test, singing our blues and gospel, finger-popping all the while. As his strength was made perfect in weakness, so was ours" (171).

I have excerpted a few passages from his sermon so as to highlight what Wilmore understands his role is as an interpreter and preacher in the black church tradition. What comes through again and again is the primary role of experience in the hermeneutical task, an aspect repeatedly emphasized by modern hermeneuticians in the liberationist tradition in general, and black interpreters in particular.[12] We note that

---

12 See note 20 below for a representative list of African American interpreters.

while Ezekiel's pantomime of the Babylonian exile serves as the launch pad, it is the prophet's clothing and baggage that become the touchstone for Wilmore's message, for he translates them into the symbols that have the greatest emotional appeal for his audience: color and blackness. These symbols are the constants in the experience of black people on this side of the Atlantic, and Wilmore, like all other black preachers in America before and after him, knows how to exact maximum capital from these circumstances. The manner in which the black preacher uses experience to explicate the biblical text has a striking correspondence to the New Testament author's use of experience as a window to enter the Hebrew Bible. This similarity is what should force one to rethink the nature of religious experience in the practice of hermeneutics. It is to this matter that we now finally turn.

III

It has been generally accepted that Friedrich Schleiermacher gave us a different theory of hermeneutics by relocating the emphasis away from the strict interpretation of biblical texts toward a theory of interpretation and understanding that takes as essential the role of human existence.[13] That is to say, he initiated the paradigm shift from an emphasis on the primacy of the biblical text toward an accent on human existence—indeed human experience—as central to the hermeneutical task in understanding religion.[14] "Understanding," since Schleiermacher therefore, "has become the cornerstone of hermeneutical theory" (Mueller-Vollmer: 9). Schleiermacher, we must keep in mind, has written at length on this matter of hermeneutics, which makes it impossible for me to exhaust his program here. I simply wish to highlight what I find distinctive and important in his hermeneutical theory for our purposes here. For him, understanding and speech utterance involve a double aspect, the coalescence of two

---

13 Anthony Thiselton, in noting that the "decisive foundation of theoretical hermeneutics as a modern discipline occurred with the work of Friedrich Schleiermacher"(95), and that he "established hermeneutics as a modern discipline in its own right" (97), has correctly lamented the fact that the "sophistication of his work is widely underrated" (98).

14 In the summer of 1799 an anonymous author published in Göttingen a book entitled *Über die Religion: Reden an die Gebildeten unter ihren Verächtern* (English translation: *On Religion: Speeches to Its Cultured Despisers*), which, according to its title, aimed at addressing a German intellectual climate deeply affected by the Enlightenment. In that climate, intellectuals generally thought that religion was either irrelevant or irrational. That unknown author turned out to be Schleiermacher, who, as a young scholar, aimed in this work to write a defense for religion as a necessary human exercise, but in the process he signaled the influence that his work in hermeneutics was to have throughout the nineteenth century.

entirely different planes, the first of which has the utterance limited to its linguistic system, while the second links the utterance to an understanding of the speaker's life process, namely, his or her internal or mental history. Understanding, to use his own words,

> takes place only in the coinherence of these two moments:
> 1. An act of speaking cannot even be understood as a moment in a person's development unless it is understood in relation to the language. . . .
> 2. Nor can an act of speaking be understood as a modification of the language unless it is understood as a moment in the development of the person. (Cited in Mueller-Vollmer: 10–11; see Schleiermacher in Mueller-Vollmer: 75)

Schleiermacher's students worked on his lecture notes, to which they added explanations, and for their teacher's second assertion we get this explanation:[15] "because an individual is able to influence a language by speaking, which is how a language develops" (Mueller-Vollmer 1989, 75).

A procession of German scholars pursued biblical interpretation along the lines suggested by Schleiermacher. Harnack and Troeltsch come to mind as typifying this approach. Rudolf Bultmann, in his introduction to Harnack's book, says something about the task of appropriating tradition critically and, although his context and purpose are somewhat different from ours, and without raiding his work for our purposes, his insight is worth noting:

> We will remain true to Harnack only if we appropriate his legacy critically. True loyalty is never an "archaizing repetition," but only a critical appropriation which makes the legitimate impulses of tradition its very own and endows these emphases with validity in a new form. (Harnack: xvii)[16]

---

15 Schleiermacher's lecture notes, now translated (Schleiermacher 1971), are in fragmentary state and at several points do not make coherent prose. We are therefore dependent on his students, who made judgments as to what precisely could have been meant by a vague or ambiguous statement, phrase, or concept.

16 Appropriately, we remind ourselves at this point that Bultmann's insight drawn from existentialism, the philosophical idea that is grounded in the nature of human existence, allowed the New Testament scholar to embark on his radical program of demythologization of the fantastic stories of Jesus' birth and demise. His reminder to interpreters, that there can be no presuppositionless hermeneutics, has served to caution scholars against positing the fallacy of doing objective interpretation of the biblical text, since this approach would necessarily mean the search for and preservation of a single interpretation. For his explication of these ideas, see Bultmann 1956: 175–208; 1958; 1960: 289–96.

This admonition from Bultmann informs, to a great degree, my understanding of black preaching as a hermeneutical exercise in which the sociopolitical (and economic!) experience of African Americans becomes the bench mark for sermon performance. The preacher, as interpreter therefore, relies less on the language and context of the text or passage being preached,[17] and more on the experience of an oppressed people as the event that generates religious meaning and evokes worshipful response. Indeed, the idea that one's experience is decisive for credible biblical interpretation has been recognized by no less a sociologist of religion than Ernst Troeltsch, who is represented as having written emphatically on the use of analogy

> because it embraces all present and past historical occurrence in a single context of events, allows no arbitrary establishment of occurrences or revelatory texts without analogy, and enables the interpreter to make contemporary historical phenomena which are directly known and familiar to him the interpretive framework and criterion for comparable events in the past. (Stuhlmacher: 45)

Here again we should note, for example, that Wilmore, who lives in a country where the lynching of innocent black men was accorded tacit legitimacy, appropriates the text of Ezekiel in a manner that allows him to substitute blackness as the "baggage," and in doing so, leads his congregants to realize a fitting correspondence between their experience of human suffering as a group and that of Jesus, whose execution they have already come to regard as a miscarriage of justice. The derisive epithet, "nigger," is deliberately recast as the most potent emotional instrument for the actualization of a religious experience—black religion—to which both preacher and worshiper can relate. A comment on Christian faith and the interpretive experience is apropos here: "Interpretation is the demand made by faith insofar as the object of faith is not a dead, but living truth which is always transmitted in an historical mediation and which has to be constantly actualized" (Geffré: 165).

I refer to Bultmann once more because he followed his own admonition (earlier mentioned in Harnack's work) in his interpretation of the New Testament, particularly the Gospel traditions about Jesus, with his

---

17 I do not wish to convey the idea that black preaching, the kind I examine here, pays no attention to context. That would be mischievous. Indeed, the importance of context for the black preacher becomes evident from the way she or he draws correspondence between her or his circumstance and that of the characters found in the text being preached, and it is precisely in this connection that we find the previously mentioned definition for midrash appropriate (see notes 8 and 9 above).

radical and challenging project of demythologization (1958[18]). The critical issue for Bultmann was not so much the proclamation of the gospel as the New Testament writers had come to fashion it, but rather how he, as a child of the Enlightenment and product of its mind-altering concepts of the universe, could come to embrace a cosmology of the first-century religionists that vastly differed from his.[19] Indeed, a different view of science (with the discoveries of Galileo, Copernicus, Newton, and Kepler) and epistemology (with the work of Descartes, Hume, and Kant), and a different understanding of history resulted in a radically changed view of the world (*Weltanschauung*) that preceded Bultmann by a century. Since he was not prepared to negotiate away the epistemological posits that resulted in new ways of experiencing reality, Bultmann simply had to devise a method of interpreting the New Testament that reflected what he experienced as both a Lutheran pastor deeply committed to the kerygmatic function of the New Testament and an existentialist theologian giving meaning to the calamitous results of Nazism and World War II.

From a sociology of religion standpoint, ethical reflection and the preaching that eventuates are the fruits of experience, and it is the social location of both preacher and congregants that validates their experience and gives it plausibility over other experiences alien to them (Berger 1992: 86). The black experience in North America is pertinent in this regard, for it provides the warrant for a peculiar type of biblical exposition. This results in a plenitude of African American scholars of religion who have from time to time called attention to the experiential character of black interpretation of the Bible. The list of scholars runs the gamut of the field: biblical studies, theology, ethics, phenomenology and history of religion, philosophy of religion, church history, sociology of religion, homiletics,

---

18 This work represents Bultmann's clearest articulation of his demythologizing project, because in it he was able (1) to restate and clarify his position after the storm of protest that followed the initial lecture he gave in 1941 to a group of German pastors, and (2) to answer his critics both in Europe and North America.

19 Hans Schwartz, writing about the personification of evil, has correctly sharpened the problem as Bultmann conceived it: "At least since Rudolf Bultmann's essay on demythologization it has become clear that we cannot believe in the New Testament world of spirits and demons and at the same time enjoy all the technological 'achievements' of the thoroughly enlightened twentieth century that have been made possible by human inventiveness and rational planning" (205).

20 The following is a representative list of African American scholars from several fields in religion whose primary concern is to place the black experience at the center of hermeneutics: Cannon (1988), Cone (1969; 1990a; 1990b), G. Davis, Felder (1989a; 1989b; 1991), Grant (1989a; 1989b), Hood, Long (1986), Mitchell, Raboteau, Reid, Townes (1993b), West, D. Williams, Wilmore (1983), and Wimbush (1989). The work of Gerald Davis, a folklorist, is

and so forth.[20] We are struck by the fact that in all of these fields African American scholars display an awareness of the inadequacy or, as one scholar has put it, "the detriment" (Wimbush 1989: 44) of the traditional historical-critical methods to assemble a hermeneutics of liberation that is so cardinal to black religious experience in America. In this regard, I mention the book by Theophus Smith, *Conjuring Culture*. One of the many things he notes that becomes pertinent to our discussion is the way that typology functions as a hermeneutical tool to link biblical types or figures to postbiblical persons, places, and events. Following Sacvan Bercovitch's description of the Puritans' use of the Bible, Smith provides us with this insight: "Going beyond orthodox exegesis of Scripture, the Puritans rendered their *own experience as a coequal source* of theological reflection. Their ostensible biblicism ... functioned as a mask which veiled or disguised their 'inversion' of the traditional relationship between Scripture and experience" (73, my emphasis). This process, which I have already described as actualization, lies at the heart of biblical hermeneutics, and, to use Edgar McKnight's apt description, I propose it to be "the creation and recreation of the world of the reader in the process of reading" (McKnight: 255).[21] To state it another way, we might say that biblical hermeneutics concedes that the primal text is limited in its formal (traditional) explanation and accepts that true understanding lies in the reading/hearing community's experiential appropriation of the meaning of the text, which can neither be regimented nor formalized (Lategan and Vorster: 13).

It is now appropriate, therefore, for me to declare that my motive for invoking Bultmann is really to situate black preaching of the type I have analyzed within the Bultmannian tradition in the following sense. These insights suggest to me that there is a history of biblical interpretation in which hermeneuticians of the past, who were all affected by both a commitment to their religious heritage and the experiences of their contemporary existence, were able to forge divergent paths of interpretation from the traditional ones. Black preaching, with its parallel commitment to religious heritage and its experience of oppression, stands squarely within that history. Ironically, however, the vast majority of black preachers may be guilty of ignoring, and are therefore unwilling to

---

listed here because it represents, to my knowledge, the most methodologically thorough analysis of the typical sermon preached in the black church in America.

21 For fuller treatments of how the reader brings contemporary significance to the interpretation and appropriation of biblical texts, see McKnight's book, especially ch. 2 ("Toward the Postmodern: Historical-Hermeneutic Approaches") and ch. 5 ("The Role of the Reader: Actualizing of Biblical Discourse").

take the risk of admitting, the far-reaching liberating consequences of their hermeneutical craft.[22]

What the black preacher does in the pulpit, therefore, should be viewed not as textual harassment but rather as an act of interpretation that parallels the ancient rabbinic tradition of creating Scripture. This is indeed a complex phenomenon that has far-reaching implications for modern biblical hermeneutics in general and for that of the African American variety in particular. In addressing this complexity of the Bible and its interpretation, James Kugel positively describes the midrashic approach as "the ongoing canonization of Scripture" (1981: 234), and following Kugel's insight, McKnight has suggested that just such an "ongoing canonization" can be actualized by a radical reader-oriented view of the role and nature of biblical texts (173).

CONCLUSION

When I originally conceived this article, I did not envision a detailed discussion of canon, but its mention here merits further deliberation in light of the pervasiveness among most African American preachers to idolize the Bible.[23] Black preaching in the liberative tradition has created a

---

22 See Geffré (11, 165–66) for a fine exposition of the ramifications for contemporary interpretation of ancient texts. On the problems that hermeneuticians in France face, Geffré argues (1) for a multiplicity of interpretations of events—the event of Jesus Christ, for example—within the religious community, and (2) that no one interpretation should be accorded absolute value. The following two paragraphs are relevant to our discussion and warrant reproducing them in full: "Even in the New Testament, theology is contemporary with faith, in other words, faith is of necessity expressed in constant confrontation with culture. The whole of the New Testament can in fact be regarded as an act of interpretation of the event of Jesus Christ carried out by the early Church. And, far from being an obstacle, the distance that separates us from the New Testament is the very condition of a new act of interpretation for us today. It is the closing of the text that is the condition of a creative taking over of the text. We have to speak of an analogy or a fundamental homology between the biblical statements and their socio-cultural environment on the one hand and, on the other, the discourse of faith that we should have today and our present social situation" (165). "Having a critical and responsible faith today means producing a new interpretation of the Christian message by taking our historical situation into account while at the same time taking our place within the same tradition that produced the original text. There is an analogy between the New Testament and the function that it performed in the early Church on the one hand and, on the other, the production of a new text today and function that that text fulfills in the Church and society" (165–66).

23 The obvious exceptions, of course, are those preachers who, because of their academic training, are able to deal with the various human problems that the Bible presents the modern reader without losing sight of its capacity to engender religious faith among the faithful. These, regrettably, represent a very small minority.

paradox in that, despite its hermeneutics of liberation, it runs the risk of being left far behind as the last bastion of oppression, judged by its appeal to biblical authority in its systematic marginalization of people on such contemporary social issues as the role of women in church (and society) and sexual orientation. Like most Christian churches committed to the idea of biblical authority, the black church has not generally taken an affirmative stand on women's ordination and is intolerant of homosexuality. Yet on the matter of slavery, an institution that has tacit biblical warrant, the black church finds it necessary to dispense with the notion of biblical authority, preferring rather to make its case a moral one by arguing for the liberation of blacks on the basis of human equality.

It seems to me that it is in the area of contemporary social issues that the black preacher should become alert to the need for a different approach to the Bible. And surely, no other issue ought to be more important in bringing about this new attentiveness than the issue of slavery in America and the devastating consequences of a social ethos that continues to bedevil the American body politic even more than a century after its demise. But that issue should actually sensitize and nettle the preacher's understanding to the malignant nature of oppression. To put the matter another way, if black preaching is to live up to its reputation as an exercise in liberation, then it must broaden its agenda to include in its preachments any and all issues that negatively affect those in society who are marginalized simply because they fail to meet a preferential test that the religious powers of society impose on them. For since both black and white preachers and interpreters were able to defy the majority view on slavery despite its biblical warrants, then it seems all the more reasonable that the black preacher is eminently positioned to defy the majority on such equally oppressive views on gender roles and homosexuality, ostensibly based on the authority of the Bible.

If the sermon analyzed here can be said to be paradigmatic of black preaching in America—and I think it is!—then its defining character is that which is constant in its reminder that African Americans, despite their playing fair, have been cheated in the game of life, so to speak, in these shores. It is to this reminder that the black preacher returns constantly to "holla" and "whoop" in order to evoke the corresponding response from a sympathetic audience. A nagging problem remains, however, in that black preaching needs to correct what is perceived as its singular, narrow focus on racial injustice, a focus that tends to blind its preacher to other aspects of oppression—that of women, for example—ostensibly predicated on the notion of biblical authority.

Since black preaching, by its very nature, purports to be an exercise in liberation hermeneutics, it must therefore be as equally aggressive in its rejection of positions, ostensibly based on the authority of the Bible, that result in oppression and marginalization of other people. A people who experienced dehumanization and marginalization, again based on biblical authority, and who now are able to proclaim a gospel of liberation, must not be seen to be silent, indifferent, or insensitive to equally oppressive and tribalistic structures of religion. If it does not lift its voice in similar denunciation, then its preaching is self-serving and anything but liberating. This weakness in black preaching has been recently recognized and given apt and excellent exposition by none other than James Cone as he apologizes for his neglect of this issue in his earlier works on black theology:

> Contrary to what many black men say (especially preachers), sexism is not merely a problem for white women. Rather it is a problem of the human condition. It destroys the family and society, and makes it impossible for persons to create a society defined according to God's intention for humanity. Any black male theologian or preacher who ignores sexism as a central problem in our society and church (as important as racism, because they are interconnected), is just as guilty of distorting the gospel as is a white theologian who does the same with racism. If we black male theologians do not take seriously the need to incorporate into our theology a critique of our sexist practices in the black community, then we have no right to complain when white theologians snob black theology. (Cone 1990a: xvi)

The pervasive nature of racial oppression in America is no doubt the reason that black preaching has emerged as a somewhat single-issue hermeneutics of liberation. However, in order for black preaching to maximize its potential for becoming truly committed to the basic principles of human liberation, it must also renounce other areas of oppression that affect members of the black community. This, it appears, can only be accomplished if the preachers overcome the strictures inherent in what has been described in the postcanonization epoch as a faithful commitment to biblical authority, an authority of the kind that impedes the rich process of actualization that we see evident in the scriptures themselves. The irony is that African American preaching of the variety analyzed here already participates precisely in this process of actualization that keeps the scriptural canon open-ended. But alas, with the authority of the biblical canon hovering for many an African American preacher, how last would she or he be to discern the very process of open-endedness that informs and sustains the hermeneutics of liberation that has nourished and sustained black preaching!

A Case Study in Eighteenth-Century Afro-Diasporan Biblical Hermeneutics and Historiography: The Masonic Charges of Prince Hall[1]

Hugh Rowland Page
University of Notre Dame

1. Introduction and Rationale

The examination of biblical interpretation from a historical perspective and the study of interpretive constructs in the writing of history have long been established disciplines within the larger academy. In recent years, the importance of Afrodiasporan contributions to biblical interpretation and the historiography of the ancient world has come to be appreciated by an ever-widening circle of humanists and social scientists (see, e.g., the studies edited by Felder 1991; Wimbush 2000b). While certain aspects of this dual hermeneutical tradition have been explored,[2] many remain unexamined. Black Freemasonry is one such aspect in need of additional study. Its hermeneutical and historiographic norms are integral parts of both the Euro-American and the Afrodiasporan interpretive traditions and deserving of careful analysis.

This paper will examine the interpretive methods employed by Prince Hall (1748–1807), the founder of the first Black Masonic lodge, as evidenced in two charges delivered in 1792 and 1797 respectively. It will also assess Hall's historiographic praxis, particular attention being given

---

1 I wish to thank Dr. Cheryl T. Gilkes, Dr. John D. Saillant, and Dr. Randall C. Bailey, each of whom provided valuable input at various stages in the writing of this essay. A special word of gratitude is due as well to Ms. Emily K. Arndt, who painstakingly transcribed the text of Hall's charges for me from microtext format.

2 Afrodiasporan biblical interpretation has been the subject of critical inquiry for some time. For an overview of key contributions in this area, see R. Bailey 2000. To date, widespread interest in the process by which Afrodiasporan peoples within and beyond the Americas have appropriated, narrated, and constructed the history of Africa and the ancient Near East has yet to develop.

to the way in which he presents an Afrodiasporan perspective on the history of Egypt, Syro-Palestine, Mesopotamia, Greece, and Rome.

It is hoped that this paper will contribute to our understanding of early African American biblical interpretation, the development of historiographic traditions within the Afro-Caribbean and African American communities, the possible role of secret societies like the First African Lodge of Boston as clandestine centers for worship and learning, and the emergence of various forms of Afrocentric hermeneutics in institutions other than the Black church. As an initial study, its agenda will be confined to an overview of Black Freemasonry and its founder, a description of the charges and their thematic content, a survey of the biblical texts cited by the charges and the historical events cited by the author, and a brief analysis of the interpretive model employed by the author. It will also test a preliminary template for assessing the interpretive and historiographic norms of Hall's charges and other Afrodiasporan texts.[3]

The information used in preparation of this paper is readily available in the public domain. It does not breach the confidentiality of Prince Hall Masonry or the protocols of other Masonic bodies.[4]

2. FREEMASONRY: A SYSTEMIC SKETCH

Freemasonry is perhaps best described as an initiatic system that uses the tools of the medieval stonemason's trade as allegorized implements through which life's mysteries are revealed.[5] For this reason,

---

[3] I consider the present treatment little more than a critical note intended to lay the groundwork for additional study of Hall and African American Freemasonry. Such foundational research is needed to set the stage for more detailed analyses of the charges and other texts produced by Hall. For example, his letter book and the charter of First African Lodge should be studied individually and as part of a larger corpus of work. On Hall's letter book, see Upton. It could be argued that these documents provided the raw materials from which Hall and other Black Masons made Freemasonry a coherent Afrodiasporan symbolic universe. As such, it would be a particularly good subject for the kind of semiotic analysis modeled by Geertz (1973b). Like religion, ideology, common sense, and art—all of which Geertz (1973a; 2000) has treated as cultural systems—it can be similarly construed.

[4] My goal is to focus attention on Prince Hall's work as exegete, and to do so in a manner that does not violate the integrity of the Masonic organization that he founded. Though this study focuses on his public discourse, I have not made use of information restricted to initiated members of the fraternity to illumine any of the allusions found in his charges. This course of action is in keeping with the spirit of those guidelines for ethnographic research proposed by LeCompte and Schensul (203–4).

[5] Stemper has noted that by the eighteenth century, European Freemasonry incorporated no less than seven distinct ideological strains with the lore of operative stonemasons: (1) biblical motifs; (2) the philosophy of the Elizabethan court; (3) German Rosicrucianism; (4) Neoplatonism; (5) Hermeticism; (6) Renaissance humanism; and (7)

contemporary Masons are often referred to as speculative Masons to distinguish them from their operative counterparts (Mackey 1927: 704–5). Its origins are debated, but there is general consensus that speculative Masonry formally begins with the organization of the first Grand Lodge in England on 24 June 1717 and with James Anderson's publication of his book of Masonic Constitutions in 1723 (Coil: 70–71; Newton: 162–63; Piatigorsky: 38–39; Whalen 1966: 47).

The language of the modern Freemason is highly specialized, much of it understandable only after one has undergone initiation into the society (for an overview of Masonic symbolism, see Mackey 1955). The ritual and descriptions of other aspects of lodge life are accessible to the public in a number of books and articles dedicated to this purpose, the result of continuing scholarly interest in the fraternity and tensions between anti-Masonic and pro-Masonic forces in the United States and elsewhere.[6]

The traditional origin of the fraternity is traced to the construction of the Solomonic temple in Jerusalem and its chief Phoenician architect and engineer, Hiram, though at least one scholar has traced what he terms its "real foundations" to the human "creative impulse" as such is manifest in the very earliest artistic and architectural achievements discovered in Egypt, Europe, and South America (Newton: 5–14; for an

---

the chivalric tradition. He has also noted that from a global perspective the organization has been perceived as both supportive of and antagonistic toward existing institutions both governmental and religious. One wonders if early African American civic and religious leaders such as Hall, Absalom Jones, Richard Allen, and others recognized and appreciated the opportunity that these transgressive and liminalizing elements afforded for individual and communal identity construction. This issue needs further examination. Moreover, the extent to which these trajectories are understood and utilized by current Black Masons within and outside of the Prince Hall family is also deserving of additional study.

6 A concise treatment of Masonic ritual is found in Piatigorsky (79–86, 233–66). Perkins offers a good popular interpretation of Masonic philosophy. For differing perspectives on the complex relationship between Christianity and Freemasonry, see Newton; Whalen 1998. See M. Johnson for data on the origins of Masonry in America, and Heaton on the lodge affiliation of selected early American political luminaries. For a probing study of the early history and political impact of anti-Masonic sentiment in this country, see Vaughn. See Leazer for an analysis of recent Southern Baptist resistance to Freemasonry. Paucity of primary sources makes it virtually impossible to give a precise description of the ritual life and inner workings of an eighteenth-century lodge in England or America. Fortunately, a study of early Masonic public discourse, of which Hall's charges are exemplars, necessitates only general familiarity with a core of Masonic symbols whose semantic range has remained consistent over time. It should be noted that some Masonic organizations donate works to public and university libraries that describe their worldview and ideas. Such collections should be the subject of sociohistorical and other forms of analysis to get a clearer picture of the myriad forces that have shaped perceptions of the fraternity (Masonic, ecclesial, and public) over time.

introduction to Masonic historiography, see Coil: 7–26). While the merits of the aforementioned interpretations might be subject to debate, few would disagree with the assertion that the Christian Bible is the foundational document for Freemasonry, insofar as it is the repository for the most essential components of the fraternity's generative myth.[7]

Definitions of Freemasonry are quite varied. A survey of extant literature on the subject supports Coil's assertion that while "different persons may agree upon some phases or points of the subject, few will be able to agree upon all" (214). Taken as a whole, however, the set of core teachings that constitute the curriculum of Blue Lodge Masonry (that which embraces the first three degrees), the various higher degrees offered through ancillary organizations (e.g., the Royal Arch, Scottish Rite, and York Rite), and several well-known adoptive organizations (e.g., Eastern Star and Shrine) can be understood as a comprehensive educational system whose scope embraces biblical study, ethics, chivalry, religion, and other subjects deemed necessary for the formation of character.[8]

3. Prince Hall and the Origins of African American Freemasonry

Even after years of critical inquiry, Prince Hall is a historical enigma. More than a few questions remain about his birth, ancestry, and early life. According to one account, Hall was born on 12 September 1748 in Bridgetown, Barbados, to an English father and a French mother. His father was a leather worker, and at a young age Hall was made an apprentice in this trade. He came to Boston in 1765. In subsequent years

---

7 For a selective list of biblical passages significant to Freemasons, see Mackey 1927: vi–x.

8 A survey of characters and events referenced in the ritual initiations and discourses of the various degrees reveals the enormous breadth of the Masonic *Weltanschauung*. Scores of biblical characters and historical figures (ancient and modern) are cited in these sources. Even more remarkable is the fact that numerous deities from the Roman, Greek, Mesopotamian, Persian, Hindu, and Syro-Palestinian pantheons are present as well. For a list of these figures and their significance within the Masonic ritual system, see Van Gorden (1980; 1985; 1986). No simple answer can be offered to the long-standing question of whether Freemasonry should be construed as a religion. However, as a system that offers a program of pragmatic, moral, and spiritual (though avowedly nonsectarian) character formation, it might be said to advocate a particular approach to living and being in the world. If one adopts McGrath's definition of spirituality as "what a person does with what they believe," then Freemasonry can be understood as a body of liturgical rites and lore that gives rise to and supports a Masonic spirituality. Given the pluriformity that obtains in scholarly conceptions of spirituality and the range of phenomena currently viewed as expressions thereof, there is little reason to exclude Freemasonry from the list. For a recent discussion of some contemporary spiritualities, see Brown, Farr, and Hoffman 1997.

he worked, educated himself, and fought in the Revolutionary War on the side of the American colonies. He also became a preacher and a civic leader in the Boston community. After being made a Mason in a British military lodge (British Lodge number 58),[9] Hall and other African American Masons received a dispensation from this body to organize an independent lodge until such time as they were able to secure a charter from the Provincial Grand Master (for Massachusetts) that would empower them to function as a fully autonomous body. Unable to obtain this document, Hall petitioned the Grand Lodge of England for a charter in 1784. A charter to form African Lodge number 459 was granted in 1787. In January of 1791, Hall was made Provincial Grand Master for North America by the Grand Lodge of England. In June of the same year, African Lodge constituted itself as the African Grand Lodge with authority to establish subsidiary lodges. Hall died on 7 December 1807. On 24 June 1808 the officers of African Grand Lodge changed the name to Prince Hall Grand Lodge to honor the legendary Masonic pioneer (Grimshaw: 67–96).[10] This institution continues to flourish and is the most prominent of several independent Afro-Masonic organizations in America today (Coil: 204; Gilkes 2000: 392, 396).[11]

Questions have been raised about Hall's parents, occupation, and activities before 1775 (see, e.g., the critique of Grimshaw by Sherman). Furthermore, events surrounding the chartering of African Lodge number 459 and the creation of the African Grand Lodge have been subject to debate. For example, Kaplan and Kaplan (203) state that Hall's parents and place of birth are unknown and that he was a slave living in Boston who was manumitted by his owner, William Hall, in 1770. Similarly, Coil questions the veracity of Hall's purported appointment as Provincial Grand Master in 1791 (206). Though much of Hall's early life is likely to stay a mystery, there is unambiguous evidence of his activities as community organizer, spokesperson, and Masonic innovator. Among the more important documents bearing his name are two charges delivered in 1792 and 1797 respectively, both of which witness to Hall's genius as exegete, apologist, and rhetorician.

---

9 According to Greene, this lodge (number 441) belonged to an Irish regiment and was under the jurisdiction of the Grand Lodge of Ireland (248–49).

10 The accounts of Hall's early years narrated by Crawford (14) and Greene (238–39) parallel that of Grimshaw closely. Both add that Hall was ultimately ordained as a Methodist minister.

11 Muraskin and L. Williams 1975 provide important insight into the sociological and sociohistorical contexts of Prince Hall Freemasonry in the U.S.

4. The Charges

4.1. St. John's Day 1792

In his first charge (1792), delivered on the occasion of the St. John's Day celebration at the Hall of Brother William Smith in Charlestown on 25 June 1792, Hall's expressed purpose is to delineate for his audience the duties of a Mason. His parameters include:

1. Belief in one Supreme Being and obedience to civil laws and authorities (including refusal to participate in—materially or by means of moral support—plots against the same).
2. Love and benevolence for the human family in its entirety (including enemies) regardless of color.
3. Regular attendance at lodge meetings and willingness to help a fellow Mason in distress with substantive assistance.

He illustrates the second of these points (the importance of love and benevolence) with biblical references to the story of Abraham and Lot (Gen 13:7–12), the account of Ebedmelech—whom Hall designates "a black man" (1792: 4)—and his assistance of Jeremiah (Jer 38:7–13), Elisha's benevolence toward the Aramean army (2 Kgs 6:22–23), and the story of the good Samaritan (Luke 10:30–37). He illustrates the third (willingness to offer substantial assistance to one in distress) with historical allusions to African church leaders such as Tertullian—who, he indicates, "was born in Carthage in Africa, and died in Anno Christi 202" (8)—and his defense of Christianity against the false accusations of Roman authorities; Cyprian—who Hall says "was not only Bishop of Carthage, but of Spain and the east, west, and northern churches" (ibid.)—and his heroic faith, even to martyrdom; Augustine—with particular reference to his observations concerning charity, prayer, and love; and Fulgentius—special attention being directed to his reflections on the importance of following Christian precepts and helping the servants of Christ who are in distress.

Hall states his reason for citing these figures from the history of the church:

> Thus my brethren I have quoted a few of your revered fathers, for your imitation, which I hope you will endeavor to follow, so far as your abilities will permit in your present situation and the disadvantages you labor under on account of your being deprived of the means of education in your younger days, as you see it is at this day with our children, for we see notwithstanding we are rated for that, and other Town charges, we are deprived of that blessing. (1792: 9–10)

He encourages his audience to be patient and exhorts them to look ahead to better days in the future, using Ps 68:31 as referential text. "Hear what the Great Architect of the universal world saith, *Ethiopia shall stretch forth her hands unto me*" (10). He also challenges his audience to lay aside those matters that are unimportant and work toward securing for themselves an education—an effort that may yet be aided by the patronage of some group of beneficent individuals as was the case in Philadelphia.

Then follows a historical sketch of Masonic progress that begins with the destruction of Jerusalem by Titus Vespasian in 70 C.E. He traces the evolution and heroic deeds of the Order of St. John, describing their defense of the remains of the Jerusalem temple against Turkish assault, their 104-year stay in "the Cyrean city of Ptolemy" (11), their eighteen-year sojourn in Cyprus, their siege and 213-year reign in Rhodes (whence they came to be known as the Knights of Rhodes), and their move to Malta in 1530, where they remained until Hall's time (and from which move they came to be known as Knights of Malta).

Hall then ponders what is, for him, a historical question with significant contemporary import:

> Query, Whether at that day, when there was an African church, and perhaps the largest Christian church on earth, whether there was no African of that order; or whether, if they were all whites, they would refuse to accept them as their fellow Christians and brother Masons; or whether there were any so weak, or rather so foolish, as to say, because they were Blacks, that would make their lodge or army too common or too cheap? (11–12)

Hall appears to be making reference here to ecclesiastical, Masonic, and political powers in late eighteenth-century New England who denied him and his associates equal status in church, lodge, and state. He also draws an associative connection between the valor of the early Christian orders of knights whose history he has just outlined and the Black soldiers who fought in the war for colonial independence:

> Sure, this was not our conduct in the late war; for then they marched shoulder to shoulder, brother soldier and brother soldier, to the field of battle; let who will answer; he that despises a black man for the sake of his color, reproacheth his Maker, and he hath resented it, in the case of Aaron and Miriam. See for this Numbers 12. (12)

He concludes his historical sketch by mentioning the date of the founding of his lodge in 1787—at which time the Duke of Cumberland, who was technically overseer of all lodges (who issued the charter for African Lodge), had under his charge 489 lodges.

Hall closes his charge by reminding his audience that they are members of an honorable fraternity—one whose precepts they must uphold. Their obligations to God and one another are to be kept constantly in mind. In a concluding paragraph rich in Masonic and Christian allusions, he dismisses them with these reflections on the expected yield of their earthly labors:

> If thus, we by the grace of God, live up to this our Profession; we may cheerfully go the rounds of the compass of this life. Having lived according to the plumb line of righteousness, the square of justice, the level of truth and sincerity. And when we are come to the end of time, we may then bid farewell to that delightful Sun and Moon, and the other planets, that move so beautiful round her in their orbits, and all things, here below, and ascend to that new Jerusalem, where we shall not want these tapers, for God is the Light thereof; where the Wicked cease from troubling, and where the weary are at rest. (13)

Hall juxtaposes allegorized images of the mason's tools (compass, plumb line, square, and level) with references to the harmony of the cosmos, the eschatological vision of the divinely illumined New Jerusalem (Rev 3:12; 21:2, 24), and a Joban quote that alludes to the cessation of toil and trouble that accompanies death's embrace (Job 3:17). The impact of this hermeneutical move is difficult to assess. Eschatological trajectories pointing to both the present and the future seem to be held in equilibrium. The Mason is cast as one who works to construct a social and moral edifice within which humanity might thrive while awaiting the advent of a more perfect domicile built by ineffable hands. Hall's tone is, therefore, bittersweet and mutedly optimistic.

4.2. St. John's Day 1797

In the second charge (1797) delivered on the occasion of the St. John's Day celebration to the African Lodge at Menotomy on 24 June 1797, Hall begins by describing the importance of a Mason's accepting responsibility not only for the social well-being of fellow brethren in the craft and their families but also for all humans who suffer. These are for Hall (who uses Job 19:21 as a referential text) "crying out with holy Job, 'have pity on me, O my friends, for the hand of the Lord hath touched me'" (1797: 4). His justification for this comprehensive concern is that all in distress are under the dominion of Christ, who is "head and grand master" of all humankind (ibid.).

He then discusses in greater detail those in need of assistance, beginning with the people of the African Diaspora, and likens those who trade in human flesh to the merchants encountered in Rev 18:11–13.

> Among these numerous sons and daughters of distress, I shall begin with our friends and brethren; and first let us see them dragg'd from their native country, by the iron hand of tyranny and oppression from their dear friends and connections, with weeping eyes and aching hearts, to a strange land and strange people, whose tender mercies are cruel; and there to bear the iron yoke of slavery and cruelty till death as a friend shall relieve them. And must not the unhappy condition of these our fellow men draw forth our hearty prayer and wishes for their deliverance from the merchants and traders, whose characters you have in the 18th chap. of the Revelations, 11, 12, and 13 verses, and who knows but these same sort of traders may in a short time, in like manner, bewail the loss of the African traffick, to their shame and confusion. (4–5)

He notes, as a contemporary indicator of sociopolitical change related to the cessation of the slave trade, recent events in the West Indies—no doubt a reference to slave uprisings that began in Haiti during 1791 (Franklin and Moss: 101). In connection with this, he makes reference to Jer 13:23 and either Rom 2:11, Eph 6:9, or Col 3:25.

> if I mistake not, it now begins to dawn in some of the West-India islands; which puts me in mind of a nation (that I have somewhere read of) called Ethiopians, that cannot change their skin: But God can and will change their conditions, and their hearts too; and let Boston and the world know that He hath no respect of persons; and that the bulwark of envy, pride, scorn, and contempt; which is so visible to be seen in some and felt, shall fall, to rise no more. (Hall 1797: 5)

Hall issues a stern reminder that divine initiative is the source of that which has taken place in the West Indies and implies that the same shall be true in Boston and elsewhere in the world. This is an interesting alteration in perspective from his earlier charge in which he counsels a more conservative approach to social change.

A brief digression follows in which Hall describes the warfare and political upheaval existing throughout the world. He cites Rom 12:15 in encouraging his readers to "sympathize with them in their troubles, and mingle a tear of sorrow with them, and do as we are exhorted to—'weep with those that weep'" (5). This for him is a sign of the general nature of human life. It is characterized by periodic highs and lows: "So in the common affairs of life we sometimes enjoy health and prosperity; at another time sickness and adversity, crosses and disappointments" (6). He concludes that all that he has mentioned to this point is evidence that human independence is a fiction and that all—despite social station—are dependent upon one another: "there is not an independent mortal on earth; but dependent one upon the other, from the king to the beggar (ibid.).

Hall then comments upon several biblical texts and derives from them moral lessons that he deems of value to his audience. He begins with Jethro's instructions to Moses (Exod 18:22–24) regarding the establishment of courts and the selection of leaders. Casting Jethro as Ethiopian and archetypal Mason—that is, one who understood "geometry as well as laws" (7)—he remarks that this was the most important piece of advice that Moses ever received from another mortal. His second (2 Kgs 5:3–14) deals with the healing of Naaman the Syrian. The narrative is important for Hall because it illustrates how a woman held captive suspended concern with her own state and empathized with her enemy to the point of securing a means for the healing of his leprosy. Moreover, she saved him from an inward leprosy that, in Hall's opinion, would have been far worse than his outer affliction. He then moves on to three texts that describe proper deference to those who minister the divine will. In the first (1 Kgs 18:7–16) Obadiah shows deference to the prophet Elijah. In the second (Acts 8:27–31), the story of the European (*sic*) eunuch and Philip is recounted. This second story is important for Hall because it was an indicator of the willingness of a Christian minister to ride with a Black man and of a wealthy monarch to ride with a poor servant of the Christian god. The third text, the story of Solomon's encounter with the Queen of Sheba (1 Kgs 10:1–10, 13), is related in a most interesting manner:

> So our Grand Master, Solomon, was not ashamed to take the Queen of Sheba by the hand, and lead her into his court, at the hour of high twelve, and there converse with her on points of Masonry (for if ever there was a female Mason in the world she was one) and other curious matters; and gratified her, by shewing her all his riches and curious pieces of architecture in the temple, and in his house. (9)

One expects the honorific treatment of Solomon. It is his temple that provides the backdrop against which the Masonic allegories are reenacted in the rituals of Freemasonry. The place accorded the Queen of Sheba is fascinating.[12] Hall casts her as peer of Solomon and a Mason—a most extraordinary datum. Moreover, he appears to be addressing

---

12 Hall's reading of the story differs markedly from that of R. Bailey (1991: 181–82), though a comparison of the two demonstrates the ways in which interpretive context influences the parameters of an interpreter's engagement with a text. It also raises the question of how Hall envisioned the charges. Did he see them as exhortations? Did he consider them to be brief scholarly tomes (according to the standards of his day)? One also wonders to what extent he ascribed historical veracity to certain biblical narratives and the events in Masonic lore. These issues require further reflection.

the issue of equal treatment for women as he says, in continuing this line of discourse:

> I hope that no one will dare openly (tho' in fact the behavior of some implies as much) to say, as our Lord said on another occasion. "Behold a greater than Solomon is here." But yet let them consider that our Grand Master Solomon did not divide the living child, whatever he might do with the dead one, neither did he pretend to make a law, to forbid the parties from having free intercourse with one another without the fear of censure, or be turned out of the synagogue. (9–10)

Hall once again alludes to the unpredictability of life and appeals to his listeners to focus their attention on acquiring those things that have a nonchanging character. He mentions specifically the importance of patience as that quality needed to endure the harsh realities faced by his brethren, particularly those living in Boston who are

> shamefully abused, and that at such a degree, that you may truly be said to carry your lives in your hands; and the arrows of death are flying about your heads; helpless old women have their clothes torn off their backs, even to the exposing of their nakedness; and by whom are these disgraceful and abusive actions committed, not by the men born and bred in Boston, for they are better bred; but by a mob or horde of shameless, low-lived, envious, spiteful persons, some of them not long since, servants in gentlemen's kitchings, scouring knives, tending horses, and driving chaise. (10–11)

This patience is crucial for him because in spite of the behavior of the mob, it is the duty of his audience to uphold the laws of the state in which they reside, even if this involves the tolerance of personal indignities. For Hall a change was coming, indicated by what transpired in the French West Indies—a social transmutation that alleviated the suffering of the Black populace. Here he paraphrases and expands Ps 68:31 as his conclusion: "Thus doth Ethiopia begin to stretch forth her hand, from the sink of slavery to freedom and equality" (12). Hall then bolsters the confidence of his audience by commenting upon their store of common wisdom, which has flourished in spite of their limited access to the means of formal education. Divine grace has bestowed on them the ability to reason and meditate. Moreover, in matters such as navigation, meteorology, and astronomy, the powers of human observation and reflection have provided the means through which his audience has beheld and (in some measure) understood the mysteries of nature. For Hall, even the most simple and unsophisticated of articulated observations made by one of his fellow Masons provided evidence of their possession of a kind of natural knowledge bestowed by the creator: "God can out of the mouth of babes and Africans shew forth his glory" (13).

Next follows a warning about enslavement to human fear, which, among other national and international problems, was in Hall's mind a principle cause of the beginning of the African slave trade:

> What was the reason that our African kings and princes have plunged themselves and their peaceable kingdoms into bloody wars, to the destroying of towns and kingdoms, but the fear of the report of a great gun or glittering of arms and swords, which struck these kings near the seaports with such a panic of fear, as not only to destroy the peace and happiness of their inland brethren, but plunged millions of their fellow countrymen into slavery and cruel bondage. (14)

For Hall, the destructive force of this fear is illustrated throughout the Bible from Genesis to Revelation. Even Jesus mentions it in the Sermon on the Mount. The only remedy for this fear is to replace it with the fear of God. Thus, Christians and Masons should heed those who are in positions of authority, but worship God alone. It is difficult to determine with any degree of precision the biblical texts that Hall had in mind, but there do seem to be allusions to Rom 13, 1 Tim 6:1, and Rev 22:9.[13]

> My brethren let us pay all due respect to all whom God hath put in places of honor over us: do justly and be faithful to them that hire you, and treat them with that respect they may deserve; but worship no man. Worship God, this much is your duty as Christians and as Masons. (15–16)

Hall reminds his audience how important empathy for those in distress is. He illustrates this with specific reference to Congressional action in the release of Algerian captives—an event in which he sees the hand of God working together with human agents to bring about God's glory for the good of humankind—and concludes that all should trust in God's ability to deliver from any distress. He seems to have in mind, at least initially, those forces in the larger society that threaten the physical well-being of the Afrodiasporan community in Boston. However, he is also providing counsel for dealing with the nonacceptance of members of the African Lodge by their Euro-American colonial counterparts. His concluding remarks con-

---

13 Here and elsewhere one is reminded of the degree to which Hall's universe of discourse is biblically saturated. Thus, it is no easy task to differentiate between quotations, allusions, etc. This is, of course, a problem encountered in the attempt to assess external source usage within the Hebrew Bible, Septuagint, and New Testament as well.

tain specific instructions for dealing with the inequities within the larger American Masonic brotherhood, which, while direct and powerful, illustrate the ambiguous position occupied by the members of his lodge:

> Live and act as Masons, that you may die as Masons; let those despisers see, altho' many of us cannot read, yet by our searches and researches into men and things, we have supplied that defect, and if they will let us we shall call ourselves a chartered lodge, of just and lawful Masons. (18)

5. The Hermeneutical Program of the Charges

Hall's use of biblical texts may be termed associative and anecdotal. Biblical paraphrases and adaptations are used occasionally along with brief exegeses of selected texts. His hermeneutical method combines sociopolitical commentary with Christian theological concerns and Masonic tradition. The Afrodiasporan experience in the larger Atlantic world and the Masonic symbolic universe are tools that Hall uses in his engagement with the Bible. One question that needs further consideration is the extent to which one or the other of these tools can be understood as primary. Hall's suggestion that Jethro and Christ are Masonic figures leads one to believe that the Masonic *Weltanschauung* is Hall's primary interpretive tool. Furthermore, the biblical characters and events selected by him for exposition are important for one or more of the following reasons: (1) they illustrate important moral and ethical lessons; (2) they are archetypal Masonic figures; or (3) they have an African connection.

6. The Historiographic Tendencies of the Charges

Hall's sweep of history is selective. It embraces elements associated with the traditional history of the Masonic fraternity (e.g., references to Solomon and the Order of St. John), key African figures in the sacred traditions of Judaism and Christianity (e.g., Moses, Jethro, Solomon, the Queen of Sheba, Tertullian, Cyprian, Augustine, and Fulgentius), and eighteenth-century sociopolitical developments in both the American colonies and the Caribbean. His choice and interpretation of biblical texts reflect an interest in African personages and locales in ancient Israelite tradition and early Christian lore, as well as a sensitivity to the role that socially marginal persons and Masonic figures play in mediating the divine will.[14]

---

14 Hall's personal textual canon (within the entirety of the biblical canon) needs to be examined further. However, it should be undertaken as part of a more extensive study of his

One of the distinctive markers of Hall's historiographic and hermeneutical efforts is seen in his fusion of three disparate streams of interpretation: Masonic, Afro-Christian, and Euro-Christian. One might do well to speak of Hall's interpretive paradigm as *Afro-Masonic with a decidedly Christian undertone.* This raises a related question: How did Hall self-designate? Did he see himself primarily as Mason, African American, citizen, Christian, Afro-Christian, or some combination thereof? The charges offer no single clear answer to this. At points Hall seems to privilege his identity as Mason. The inclusivity of this label, insofar as the fraternity's object of reverence is the Judeo-Christian god conceptualized as the artisan responsible for the creation of the known cosmos, makes Freemasonry—in some respects—a more significant vessel of divine grace than the Christian church. It also makes the Mason a mediator of that grace and a valued citizen. As member of a secret society whose tenets decree that all humans are equal and which requires for admission only the simple belief in God, his religio-political creed is consonant with the ideal of the founders of the American republic. As a Christian, his self-understanding is realized through Masonic ideals. Christ is, after all, Grand Master of the earthly lodge in Hall's opinion (1797: 4).

The inclusion of such a large number of biblical references to specific characters in these charges is an important structural feature. Comparison to other exempla of this genre need to be undertaken before any significant conclusions about their selection and placement can be drawn. Nevertheless, criteria for the inclusion of historical characters are similar to those for the inclusion of their biblical counterparts—they illustrate important moral and ethical lessons; they are archetypal Masonic figures; or they have an African connection.

Wimbush has noted that the eighteenth century is a foundational period in African American biblical interpretation and that attention needs to be paid to songs, sermons, addresses, and other genres from this period (1991: 88–89). A comparison of Hall's works with those of other civic and religious leaders at the time is now necessary. However, future scholars might do well to eschew methodologies that attempt to be totalizing and hegemonic. Our understanding of the African American sociocultural milieu is expanding as new artifacts are made available for study, the circle of researchers widens, and the questions posed to

---

entire corpus of writings. His public discourse, Masonic correspondence, as well as the charters and other official documents issued by his lodge should be analyzed holistically and from a variety of perspectives (e.g., Border Studies, Diasporan Studies, Womanist theory, etc.). This should be part of a larger effort to assemble and edit for scholarly perusal the full corpus of Hall's intellectual output.

extant materials increase. Furthermore, the threads that have long formed an interconnected Atlantic web linking disparate African and Afrodiasporan communities throughout history are being more clearly discerned. Thus, future efforts to understand the role of the Bible, as well as those to comprehend any aspect of African American life, must be fully interdisciplinary and reflect an awareness of their own historical and social "situatedness."

7. Conclusions and Suggestions for Future Research

As we begin to explore more fully the various modes of Afrodiasporan historiography and biblical interpretation, there is much to be gained from examining and reassessing the personal papers and official proclamations of key figures such as Prince Hall. The contribution that this would make, particularly to our understanding of early Black intellectual and political movements (e.g., Garveyism, Afrocentrism, etc.), would be invaluable. In addition, the role that institutions other than the Black church have played in the shaping of ethical systems, life philosophies, and interpretive norms— many of which contain religious themes—needs further exploration. Needless to say, the role that the aforementioned play in shaping conceptions of self and community also requires attention.

Black Freemasonry is quite important in this regard. Prince Hall's vision of speculative Masonry, for example, embraces Christianity—a fact that merits comment. When one considers this fact in light of the history of the Masonic movement as a whole, Hall emerges as reformer and innovator. According to one historical sketch of the evolution of Masonic ideas (Coil: 214–34), Freemasonry embraced a "nominally Trinitarian" version of Christianity before 1717. At this time, Christian adherence was replaced by a neutral religious posture. This changed in 1750 as theistic elements, some of which were Christian, became part of the Masonic mainstream. Since the mid-eighteenth century, Masonic attitudes toward religion have continued to change. At present, many Grand Lodges require new members simply to assert belief in a supreme being.

Hall's Christocentric leanings appear somewhat anomalous. It is not without significance, of course, that Hall (possibly) and many subsequent leading lights in Black Freemasonry have also been members of the Christian clergy. Thus, the infusion of Black Freemasonry with Christian elements can be accounted for on one level. However, the "fleshing out" of this pro-Christian apologia and the muting of the implicit deistic tendencies in speculative Masonry by Hall and others need to be given additional consideration. Is Hall's biblical hermeneutic a remnant of a preexisting Afro-colonial interpretive and historiographic tradition? Was Hall harking back to an earlier, perhaps more pristine, Masonic ideal? Was he attempting to create a kind of Masonic Christianity that would incorporate liberative elements of both traditions that would be empowering for African Americans? Is he displaying the moral virtue of improvisation that Paris has identified as part of African and Afrodiasporan spirituality (1995: 146)? Is he engaging in what Wimbush has termed "radical creolization" and "cultural bricolage" in these charges (2000a: 13)? All of these questions need further consideration.

I believe that the assertions made by Wimbush are correct. I would also suggest, following his lead, that what I call the Agglutino-Synthetic Impulse (ASI)—that is, the tendency to adopt, test, and selectively assimilate ideas—that is part of the theological, cosmological, anthropological, ontological, and teleological speculation of all human communities is a *measurable* cultural variable affected in an infinite variety of ways by the experiences of social marginalization, dispersion, and dislocation.[15] Thus, the work of Hall and other early Black Freemasons should be analyzed so as to chart the process by which new concepts and lore are incorporated and utilized in intellectual speculation and cultural construction.

Hall's charges need also to be compared with comparable pieces produced by other Masons (African American and Euro-American) to see if comparable interpretive and historiographic canons are employed. Hall's charges also raise some issues that should be considered from the perspective of Christian theology. For example, what are the ecclesial implications of asserting that Jesus is the earth's "Grand Master" (Hall 1797: 4)? What was the ecumenical scope of Hall's Masonic version of Christianity? What liberative potential did Hall's version of Freemasonry hold for the community of Black Bostonians (especially women) in the late eighteenth century? Was the lodge an exclusive enclave of privileged Black men? One is also led to speculate on the relationship between some contemporary Afrocentric hermeneutical

---

15 I have been influenced greatly in my thinking about this impulse in Afrodiasporan life by Wimbush's comments on the African American cultural "lag" (2000a: 9, cf. n. 20; 23–24, esp. n. 60). I do think, however, that at times the rate at which particular individuals and groups experience the various stages in the threefold life cycle is quite varied. Thus, to focus exclusively on the "lag" would be inappropriate. The statistical measurement called for by Wimbush (9 n. 20) will, one suspects, show great diversity in cyclic rate. In fact, his diagram of the process (24) suggests that the speed of the cycle is actually faster for African Americans than for humanity in general since the former represent a smaller ring in his series of concentric circles. The measurement of ASI within Wimbush's threefold paradigm would provide a way of assessing the ways that specific cultural elements are assimilated and/or rejected by African American social aggregates.

and historiographic paradigms and the method employed by Hall. Specifically, are there Afrocentric interpretive schools or themes whose origins may be traced to Black Freemasonry?

In the introductory essay to his recently edited collection of articles on the Bible and African Americans, Wimbush issues a call for the reconfiguration of both biblical and Afrodiasporan studies. The new orientation that he proposes is interdisciplinary, self-critical, crosscultural, and sensitive to the dominant organizational thrust of the biblical canon—one best embodied in the concept of dark reading and the threefold process of "world-making" that consists of flight (*marronage*), formation, and self-designation. For him, to "read darkness" is to encounter "the world in emergency mode, as through the individual and collective experience of trauma" (2000a: 21). The life cycle that begins with flight/*marronage* he characterizes as one experienced by the entirety of the human family, with the African American experience being a particularly compelling example thereof. Within it, he problematizes the reciprocal relationship between sacred texts and communities. With regard to African American engagement of the Bible, he poses the tantalizing questions—"Did the people (re-)create the text? Did the text create a people?" (15)—and suggests that in fact "African Americans became a people not exclusively so but to a great degree through creative identification with and creative engagement of the Bible" (18).

It can certainly be argued that the Black Masonic tradition emerged in response to social crisis and that Prince Hall's charges engage the Bible and Masonic lore in such light. One can detect therein elements of all three stages of the life cycle as outlined by Wimbush. Hall defines himself and his movement in response to external challenges that question his legitimacy as Mason and threaten the survival of his lodge. The establishment of an independent Afrodiasporan form of speculative Masonry can certainly be understood as a conscious act of defiance, a turning away (flight/*marronage*) from the colonial branch of the fraternity. His two charges can be said to offer an apologia for the African Lodge as ecumenical locus and a safe intellectual, ideological, political, and religious space in which a creative encounter between Afrodiasporan, Masonic, and Christian ideas could be negotiated (formation). Hall's establishment of the African Lodge as a Grand Lodge—with the power to authorize the formation of its own subsidiary lodges—is an example of Wimbush's third stage (self-making).

Wimbush also suggests two additional directions for biblical scholarship that have a bearing on the ways one might engage Hall and his charges. First, he posits that scholars should look at the psychological, social, and other dynamics that lead people to "create and continue to define themselves by, address each other through and on the basis of, sacred texts" (2000a: 16). Second, he proposes that biblical scholarship be "indigenized," have as its initial step the study of "the complex textu(r)alizations of society and culture," and pay particular attention to the Bible's role in creating one's own life setting (19).

In thinking about the first of these questions, one wonders what factors might account for Hall's interest in Freemasonry. Did he see it as a resource that would foster social equality for African Americans? It could not have escaped the attention of Hall that the head of the Continental army and future first president of the United States, as well as many of his associates, were in fact Masons—the philosophical lineage for a free republic originating to some degree in the revolutionary speculation of certain colonial Masons.[16] It is possible that Hall understood the need for independent organizations within the struggling Black community—that is, for centers of holistic learning that would be empowered to construct themselves within social and ideological parameters that were determined internally rather than externally. It is noteworthy in this regard that the founding of First African Lodge preceded the founding of the Free African Society of Philadelphia (spring 1787), the ordination of the first Black priest in the Episcopal Church (Absalom Jones, 1795), and the birth of the African Methodist Episcopal Church (with the construction of Bethel Church by Richard Allen in 1794; concerning these events see Kaplan and Kaplan).

It is also interesting that, in June 1797, Hall installed Absalom Jones and Richard Allen as officers of the first Afro-Masonic lodge in Philadelphia (Kaplan and Kaplan: 109). The debate between Jones and Allen over the direction that the Afro-Christian community in Philadelphia should take in the late 1700s is well-known. One wonders how Masonry figured into this later equation, particularly as a means for bridging the disciplinary and theological gap between the nascent Black Anglicanism and Black Methodism of which these two individuals were themselves progenitors?

Concerning the second of Wimbush's questions, a closer examination needs to be made of the current status of fraternal and sororal organizations in the life of the African American community. Work similar to that of Gilkes on the kinds of biblical usage that obtain in these groups is needed so that some sense can be had of the impact that such engagements have had and continue to have in forming the African American community. It is unwarranted to suggest that fraternities, sororities, lodges, and similar organizations are as central to the process

---

16 Washington was made a master Mason in 1753 (Heaton: 74).

of African American community formation as the Bible. However, Gilkes's astute observation that such organizations "constitute and construct dimensions of the ethnic distinctiveness of black Americans" (2000, 395) is an invitation to explore the impact of their respective myths, traditions, rituals, and authoritative texts on African American interpretive strategies and ethnogenesis.

In conclusion, Hall has left us an illuminating example of colonial biblical engagement that provides an important referent for understanding the evolution and varieties of Afrodiasporan biblical interpretation and historiography in the contemporary world. His homiletic work also calls attention to the important role that members of fraternal and sororal orders have played in the appropriation and exposition of sacred texts within the African American and Afrodiasporan communities.

APPENDIX

Biblical Characters, Historical Figures, and Events
Cited in Hall's Charges

Text/Figure(s) Code	Theme/Role	Reason for Citation	Inclusion
Gen 13:7–12	Abram and Lot separate	Illustrates value of acting to eliminate distress (internal - family)	Mo
Jer 38:7–13	Ebedmelech	Relief of prophet's distress by a Black man	Mo, Af
2 Kgs 6:22–23	Elisha's mercy to captives	Demonstrates beneficent behavior toward those in distress	Mo
Luke 10:30–37	Good Samaritan	Illustrates kind behavior; presents example for listeners to follow	Mo
Cyprian	African Christian leader	Fidelity to Christian gospel	Mo, Af
Augustine	African Christian leader	Comments upon charity, prayer, and love in his works	Mo, Af

Fulgentius	African Christian leader	Stresses following Christian precepts and relief of distressed Christians	Mo, Af
Order of St. John	Progress of Masonic organization	Establishes honorable lineage of Afro-Masonry	Mo, Ma
Rev 18:11–13	Merchants viewed as slavers	Slavers in contemporary colonies will soon regret their actions	Mo, Af
Exod 18:22–24	Jethro and Moses	Jethro as archetypal Mason; emphasis on human interdependence	Mo, Af, Ma
2 Kgs 5:3–14	Naaman's healing	Illustrates lowering of a proud spirit by a servant	Mo
1 Kgs 10:1–10	Solomon and Queen of Sheba	Queen is archetypal Mason; Solomon is important Masonic figure; Solomon not ashamed to have discourse with her	Mo, Af, Ma
1 Kgs 18:7–16	Obadiah's behavior	Deference to a prophet; illustrates proper behavior when juxtaposed to that of Naaman (above)	Mo
Acts 8:27–31	Philip and Ethiopian eunuch	Both are properly disposed to one another	Mo, Af

Key: Mo = moral reason for inclusion of reference
Ma = Masonic reason for inclusion of reference
Af = connection with Africa is reason for inclusion of reference

LET MY PEOPLE GO! THREADS OF EXODUS IN AFRICAN AMERICAN NARRATIVES

Cheryl A. Kirk-Duggan
Graduate Theological Union

Kicking back,
Busted out of bondage:
Many thousands gone:
Redeemed sanctified, holy people;
Enslaved by bullies and power brokers;
Witnessing to the ills
Of those who thirst control.

Kicking back,
Busted out of bondage:
The Symphony, the Concerto,
Of harmony and dissonance.
Thousands of Voices:
Many gone, some forgotten.
Fugues and Movements:
Of life, a quiet God, a speaking God,
Of Moses and Others,
Of murder and genocide,
Of promise and doubt,
Of drownings and law.

Kicking back,
Busted out of bondage:
Voices of Shiprah and Puah;
Of Anne Frank and Sojourner Truth;
Of Yochebed and Miriam;
Of Pharaoh's Daughter;
Tell the Whole Story:
When we sing the Exodus Song:
"Let my people go!"

Kicking back,
Busted out of bondage:
Talking and living
In the midst of Exodus.
Where is our Reed Sea?
Our Mount Sinai?
What are we free to do, to be?
Free not to be?
Who is our Moses? Our Pharaoh?
Our Yochebed and Miriam?
Who are: We? Them?
Is there an Us?
Who is our God?
Let my people go!

Certain themes of exodus, such as freedom from slavery, deliverance, and overcoming, exist in many African American cultural artifacts, due to the sociohistorical, theological, ethical, sociological, and

aesthetic history of African Americans in the United States. With vary-
ing kinds of exegesis, folk, artist, and scholar alike have used the
threads of exodus to weave their tapestries of proclamation and peda-
gogy. This essay explores the use of the exodus motif in selected works
by playwright Lorraine Hansberry, musicians Sweet Honey in the Rock,
and certain African American homileticists. After a critique of African
American biblical and theological interpretations of exodus themes and
hermeneutics, I explore (1) Hansberry's concept of bondage and deliverance; (2) Sweet Honey's notion of freedom from and freedom to; and
(3) the use of the exodus text and motif in the preaching drama of the
Black church.

THE TEXT OF EXODUS AND LIBERATION HERMENEUTICS

Exodus, a story of redemption and of fleeing from slavery and the
revelation of legal, covenantal, and cultic laws at Sinai, may be considered a process of physical and spiritual empowerment. Freedom
becomes a response to oppression and movement toward the sacred.
Freedom or liberation includes rebirth, death, joy and sorrow, creation
and destruction. The exodus story deals with God's sovereignty, the
story of the protagonist Moses, the covenant relationship between
Yahweh and the people of Israel, and the construction of the tabernacle.
The exodus motif has served as a key metaphor for many liberation theologies, particularly for African Americans, who have equated the Black
experience in America with the Israelite experience in Egypt (Felder
1989b: 5; Cone 1984: 99–121; Roberts 1983: 9–10). This reading of exodus
unfolds a divine preference for the persecuted, the disempowered as a
mode to expose, dialogue about, and then eliminate classism, sexism,
racism, anti-Semitism, homophobia, and other experiences of oppression
(Setel: 26–30). Pixley suggests that with the received exodus text, a new
classless society through Yahweh's laws of justice at Sinai now exists; the
community is no longer a class embedded within an Asian mode of production but a community based on primitive communism. He further
notes that Yahweh calls and sends forth Moses with prophetic voice,
champions the cause of liberation, and will not allow Moses or anyone to
stop revolutionary salvation. Yet, the Decalogue and Covenant Codes
are steeped in class/ master/slave/owner/poor categories, amid the
quest for liberation.

God's act of liberation—the drowning of Pharaoh's army in the
Reed Sea—witnesses the freeing of the lineage of Abraham, Isaac, and
Jacob. Before the emergence of a discipline of Black theology, African
Americans of faith saw their God in the God of those oppressed by
Pharaoh. Those in bondage to antebellum slavery and racism saw God

as one sensitive to the oppressed who destroyed the oppressor, making the exodus text "the critical text revelatory of God's action in history on behalf of the oppressed" (J. Young: 93–94).

For many who practiced the slave religions, exodus signifies resurrection. Jesus the Liberator and Yahweh the Liberator-Revealer depict a God of justice, a God who judges oppressors and elects the oppressed. Many Black theologians see in Jesus the existential reality of the Mosaic God of liberation (ibid., 97). Building on Black slave religion, these scholars locate the substance of their work in the faith of their ancestors, not in the patristics (ibid., 98). Central to the religious faith of the Diaspora, the biblical stories, metaphors, themes, and personalities inspire, provide meaning, and raise hopes of liberation. Biblical symbols of Egyptian bondage, exodus, Babylonian captivity, and the powers and principalities epitomize the oppressive life stories of Black folk (Felder 1989: 5–6).

As distinct from historical-critical biblical method, precritical biblical use informs a type of experiential, communal, biblical, and religious interpretation. Many Black churches follow the models of populist evangelical White churches, using vivid drama and innovative interpretations to illumine the biblical text. Despite the unlearned and precritical exegesis, the literal Bible is a Word of Life that ministers to the Black church. The spirituals of the United States, chants of collective exorcism, are an early, unique form that rereads the biblical text. These songs tailor biblical metaphors, ideas, and themes, particularly Israel's bondage and deliverance, to community use. Black churches tend to use the biblical text in three ways: (1) biblical literalism; (2) the leading or reading into or eisegesis model; and (3) the use of historical-critical exegesis to exposition (Felder 1989b: 79, 82, 85, 88–89, 104; R. Bailey 1998: 66). As a result, in exploring biblical images of liberation, freedom stands in juxtaposition to bondage.

The biblical text does not explicitly condemn bondage. The biblical text both reveals Israelite captivity by the Egyptians (Exod 3:7–9; 5:10–12) and sanctions institutional slavery (Exod 21:2–9, 20–21, 27, 32; Deut 15:12–15). This paradox implies that the Hebrew Bible focus on freedom was more religious than a sociopolitical, lived reality; that is, slavery was bad for them to experience but acceptable for them to initiate and practice. Even in the New Testament Hebrew-Greco-Roman world, slavery was normative. While Jesus embodied freedom, freedom itself was mired in religious, political, and social concerns. As a role model, Jesus employs both his freedom from evil and his freedom for service to God. Thus, Jesus was free to disregard tradition and free to identify with women (Matt 9:20–22; Luke 13:10–17; John 4:7–28), the poor (Matt 5:2–4; 11:4–6; Mark 10:20–22; 12:42–44; Luke 12:32–34), and outcasts (Matt 9:9–12;

21:30–33; Mark 1:39–41; Luke 3:11–14; 7:28–30; 14:12–14; 17:11–13) such as tax collectors and lepers (Felder 1989b: 104–6).

Black biblical religious experience embraces this Jesus and the religiosity of people who have ancestry, physical traits, and/or self-understanding and identity within the Black race. Involving a complex mix from ancient Africa, the Black Diaspora, and adaptations by Blacks of other religious faiths and rituals, diverse, complex Black religious experiences involve certain patterns of harmony and dissonance. These kinds of religious experience also see the divine and the supernatural as a part of natural order, take spirituality and eschatology seriously, and are shaped by the oppressions of colonialism, slavery, and racism (Pinn 1998: 1–10; T. Smith: 3–18).

The African American community has given Black women's experiences equal weight with that of Black men in its appropriation of biblical texts. Delores Williams sees two traditions of interpretation, which she names: (1) "the liberation tradition of African American biblical appropriation," which emphasizes God connecting with men in liberation battles and focusing on the oppressed; and (2) the survival/quality-of-life tradition of African American biblical appropriation or a female-centered interpretation, which de-emphasizes male authority and encounters the surrogacy, slave heritage, survival, personal, and salvific encounters by God of the woman Hagar. The first category, in large part, relies on the exodus traditions; the second on those in Genesis (D. Williams: 1, 6).

In South African liberation theology, several metaphors for freedom and hope maintain: the *imago dei,* the creation stories, and the Trinity, together with the exodus, are sources for divine grace and empowerment in dismantling apartheid (Hood: 84, 88). The exodus event serves as a metaphor for making sense of the ministry of Jesus Christ as ministry to the poor and the oppressed. In Jamaica, Rastafarianism, based on the teachings of Marcus Garvey (1887–1940), became the religion of liberation, a metamorphosis of the African Orthodox Church. Instead of primary reliance on exodus sources, the book of Revelation is the principal Rasta biblical source, particularly 5:1–5 and chapter 19 (T. Smith: 128–31). The biblical texts that served as liberationist motifs on both the American and African continents infuse the music created by the children born of both lands.

In slave music and consciousness, there were no distinct divisions between the sacred and allegedly secular. The Hebrew Bible and New Testament provided themes and role models, including Brother Jonah, Sister Mary, Brother Daniel, Brother Moses. Their music exuded change, transformation, ultimate justice, self-worth, not depravity or unworthiness. In their selective choosing of biblical texts, Jesus becomes a Hebrew Bible warrior, one who confronts the devil, African martyrdom, and a conquering King who rides a horse (L. Levine: 72–76). In our postmodernist world, theologians and biblical scholars, facing different types of bondage, offer commentary on the exodus paradigm from a liberationist context, notably in the works of Joseph A. Johnson Jr., Cain H. Felder, Randall Bailey, and Josiah Young.

In the paradox of the Black church and Black community, African Americans live under the guise of Black liberation, of exodus. Black theology, however, has often been located in predominantly White academia, dissociated from lived Black religion. Theologian James Cone argues that the emergence of Black power coupled with Black theology altered the relationship between the Black church and Black theology. When Black theology shifted away from the church, removing prophetic self-criticism from the church and removing a praxis context from the discipline, both institutions lost, and the language of liberation became opaque, fostering alienation between Black church leaders and Black theologians. Many Black churches and pastors aligned with the religious insights of White evangelicals and the racist Moral Majority. Both Black theology and a Black church that deigns to take the exodus event seriously must rethink and then alter its relationship with Black historical theological documents as the spirituals, blues, and signifying through oral sayings. True liberation requires the acknowledgment that Black religion and White evangelical religion are not synonymous. Black liberation theology and religion requires a critical use of Bible, social-science methodology, and listening to the voices of the poor (Cone 1984: 99–121), and, I suggest, the middle class, and the rich, in dialogue.

Liberationist theologians of many cultures, including those of African heritage, identify with the Hebrews' move from bondage to freedom in the exodus story (Weems 1991: 74). Central to Israel's identity and witness about the character of their God, this story illumines the voices of the Hebrews oppressed in their revolution against despotism and slavery. For many of the enslaved of the African Diaspora, exodus depicted a God who listened to the cries of those in bondage and subsequently delivered them from their oppression. That many of the despots were African was not at the focus of the enslaved Africans in the Americas (ibid., 74–75).

The enslaved of African descent understood the biblical God in the context of their traditional beliefs, in a God of power and of moral integrity. J. Deotis Roberts argues that slaves experienced the Hebrew Bible God like their own African Supreme Being and related to the exodus event politically and religiously. From their sacred cosmology, they sensed that their realities—earth and heaven—would be changed as they sang the spiritual, "Go down Moses.... Tell 'Ol' Pharaoh, to let my people go" (1983: 9–10). Along with the option for a theology from below, from the lived experience of Black folk, it is important to acknowledge that the "oppression-liberation" paradigm neither adequately informs Black believers, nor does it adequately open up the biblical comprehension of the Black experience (1983: 41). If interpreters remain selective in their use of biblical texts and do not deal with the two-edged nature of the texts, as a "library with many editors and authors," then it is up to us, as postliberationists, to examine the Bible and its ambiguities and paradoxes when exploring the possibilities of redemption and humanization, the transformation of society, and the call for justice. Central to the Black experience, the Bible's themes of deliverance and liberation, prophets, Jesus, justice, and the oppressed, resonate with the Black child, who reared in this country does not need a scholar to explain the concepts of justice and injustice to her or him. For Roberts, the enslavement and deliverance of Israel became and becomes the bondage and liberation of African Americans on an individual and existential plane (1983: 41, 59–60).

Bailey offers a cautionary tale about doing a focused liberationist reading of Exod 7–11, particularly given the contrast of the muted liberationist polemic of P versus the liberationist/oppressionist motifs of J and E. Bailey notes that the tone of the P materials in Exodus is quite different from their Deuteronomistic renderings and those in the prophetic materials. P mutes the tune for freedom and suggests that Pharaoh is really a pawn or a puppet of Yahweh; Pharaoh is not the problem. One of the issues at stake, then, is the lapse of faith by the Israelite children. The reshaping of P in Exodus signals the need for faith by Israel and the superiority of Yahweh to all other deities. Lastly, P taunts and teases the Egyptians regarding the Egyptians and their institutions. Thus, the central focus for P is recognizing and honoring Yahweh's preeminence, with liberation a modest secondary matter. The P tradition never says, "Let my people go!" (R. Bailey 1994: 12–17).

Similarly, many womanist scholars question the move to use the biblical exodus experience as a normative model for validating God's liberative acts for all oppressed peoples of the world. Delores Williams posits that the lives of non-Hebrews smell of nonliberation. Neither the Hebrew Bible nor the New Testament texts contains a "Thou Shalt Not" regarding slavery. Consequently, the biblical texts do not prohibit slavery. To the contrary, many passages legitimize and sanction slavery, particularly of non-Hebrews. In addition, the Holiness and Covenant Codes draw lines between female and male slave rights: males possess significant owner restrictions regarding their slave status, whereas female slaves remain a subhuman species of property. While the community as evidenced in the spirituals uses the exodus text against oppression, theologians and ethicists must analyze both the appropriation by the community and the text themselves to note any biases against women and non-Israelites in the exodus tradition through communal, objective, and subjective inquiry. Such inquiry shows with whom all related parties identify, from the canonical writers to the scholars and the community. Williams also warns us of the necessity of telling the entire exodus story, which includes the reparations from the Egyptians, God's acts of violence against the Egyptians, the genocide against the Canaanites, and the theft of the Canaanite land. Williams does not wish to negate the appropriation of the texts but admonishes Black scholars to let Black hearers know that this is a Black appropriation of the texts borne of American slavery and that Black scholars must not deny Black history prior to slavery. Williams argues that not only is the wilderness experience more inclusive of male/female/family, of sacred and secular, of intelligence and ingenuity in the middle of struggle, but that the wilderness experience attests the leadership role of Black mothers and women and that the wilderness tradition as part of the exodus story is often given short shrift by feminists and Black liberation theologians (147–52, 160–61).

While the book of Exodus begins with paying attention to women, it manages to distort and displace their power, finding them acceptable when they play within the boundaries and dangerous when they blur boundaries or step outside. A surface reading reflects powerful women, as the birth and nurture of Moses occurs through the collusion of the midwives, the resourcefulness of Moses' mother and sister, and the compassion of the Egyptian princess, as the liberation of Israel unfolds. J. Cheryl Exum shows us that the critical question, of how these women's stories affect our reading of the whole story, is fraught with role reversals, the diffusing of women's influence, and a retrenchment of oppression. Moses' story, a saga of a baby and five women, elevates Moses and presses the women deeply into the background. Aware of the androcentric interests in the text, an inquiring feminist/womanist/Mujerista/Latina biblical mind would ask, "Are the women being manipulated and shaped through male interpretation?" As we learn more about male hermeneutics as opposed to women's real lives, we encounter a well-honed practice of male hegemony or patriarchy. That is, by forcing women into traditional, domestic roles, nurturing women's complicity with patriarchy controls women's power because the use of such power both threatens patriarchy and subverts male authority. Thus the apparent power and place of women honored in Exod 1–2 virtually disappears, as the role reversal of applying female metaphors to God and Moses generally eradicates women's presence in Exodus. In addition, much can be made of the significant issues of class and race oppression within the text. So often, it is much easier to deal with the concept of a chosen people and to cheerfully disregard matters of manifest destiny, demonization based upon the Egyptians' race, and the vast complexities of how class and diversity plays out within the book of Exodus. These issues are not of great concern to the Exodus redactor, nor to many contemporary scholars.

Renita Weems, however, argues that because many of the biblical texts assume differences between categories of women and men, slave and free, these texts, cited by contemporary liberation movements, are contradictory and problematic. The exodus story does not challenge or question these differences but merely relates this ideology based upon difference. That is, since these biblical texts are social productions and come out of a particular material and social context, their use is problematic in debates about power when public policy is either challenged or defended. As Jesus learned, after a forty-day fast, even Satan can quote scripture (Matt 4:5–7). Though the Mosaic story becomes a women's story with the midwives' resistance and the narrator informs the audience about what happens to Pharaoh and caricatures him in the process, the narrator fails to challenge the differences. In fact, the story-teller argues for the religious superiority of the God of Israel. We are left with the realization that one must exercise caution in using these texts in the hope of transforming modern race, gender, and class issues (Weems 1992). For example, what difference does it make that the Egyptian princess "adopts" the slave boy, and he grows up in a royal family? What of the fact that Moses marries Zipporah, a foreign woman? How does ethnic identity and exposure to education shape a particular character? What of the boy child's Levitical lineage? And what of the privilege that comes of being a symbolic, venerated nation where the redactor uses women to debunk the men, particularly amid the irony and ridicule directed to the man-god Pharaoh. While space will not allow a full-blown discussion on these issues, suffice it to say that these are clearly questions of ethics and justice that arise from the book of Exodus (R. Bailey 1995: 25–35). We are also left with a picture of a God who is beyond one of love and promise.

Although the warrior-God tradition in Exodus and the prophetic traditions inspired social movements of liberation and freedom, they are themselves violent and antithetical to peace and social justice. To extol liberation is one thing, but to embody that liberation in the guise of a patriarchal, warfare-focused God is problematic. The Canaanites are dispossessed of their land, like present-day Palestinians, and the downfall of the Egyptians is celebrated in song (Exod 15); this seems antithetical to social justice. Carol Christ presses us to ask, "Can a God who uses violence against one people [the Egyptians or the Canaanites] to liberate another people [the Hebrews] be a liberator?" (202, 206, 212).

While many Black theologians see God as liberator in Exodus, God's absence in chapters 1 and 2, as in certain lament psalms, is not addressed. Nevertheless, the community did not give up, but cried out. Exodus 3 and 4 is the experience of the numinous, holy God, of theophany, with Moses' very human response being that of *tremendum*, of fear, of being overpowered by the divine, of urgency and energy—of Glory. Some motifs in the exodus story are not incorporated in the liberation models, including Moses' ambivalence, from "bold and profane curiosity" to being afraid to look upon God's presence, and the Passover tradition. One exception is how the pilgrimage feast for multiple families has been central to Black family ethos, especially family reunions (Gowan: 8, 26–34, 64, 152). Robert Allen Warrior reminds us that the received text of the exodus story provides an incongruous model of liberation for any people from any context, because not only does Yahweh the deliverer become Yahweh the conqueror, but the plight of the indigenous persons, the Canaanites, is totally disregarded. For the sake of the Abrahamic, covenantal Hebrew land acquisition, a land already inhabited by the indigenous Canaanites, Yahweh orders the merciless annihilation of the indigenous people. Irrespective of the text's historical accuracy, the scapegoated Canaanites are decimated in the narrative. For Jews and Christians who take this part of the canon seriously, this barbarism, injustice, and violation of innocent peoples needs to be examined critically: from its impact on American ideology and consciousness to its style of alleged leadership and social change.

Is the freedom paradigm, then, any less valid because most liberation motifs for Black religious traditions focus primarily on Exod 1–15, particularly in light of warrior's concerns? What does it mean for an indigenous people to be enslaved and transported to a land held sacred by another indigenous people, both decimated by the same conquering mentality? What impact does the covenant tradition have on Black liberation thought? The threads of the experience of theophany as God with us, the providence of God, and the acceptance of God as King occur with a great deal of frequency. How do such readings of Exodus affect personal and communal faith, interreligious dialogue, and ecumenical hermeneutics?

In a critique of liberation motifs based on the exodus story, Levingston notes that it is important to clarify the different appropriations of Exodus. A Jewish critique would question other liberation interpretations as relates to Judaism, Jews, and Israel. While both Judaism and liberation theologies rely on the moments of deliverance from Egypt, there are commonalities and dissonances. Both Jews and Christians use the bread and wine for a covenant meal, but for the former it concerns the Passover and exodus; for the latter, Jesus' Last Supper and the crucifixion. With concern for the poor, Jewish thought insists on giving charity and justice in concert with their covenant relationship with God, but not overcompensation or preference at the expense of others. Levingston argues that for

Michael Walzer, as a moment of God's revelation, exodus is rooted in the covenant status of Israel, which meant a life of responsibility, justice, and freedom, not in the drowning of Pharaoh's army. Black religious history locates modern liberation with the Emancipation Proclamation and the Civil Rights movements and legislation. For many Jews, the Holocaust and the founding the State of Israel is as central as the exodus, both challenging Jews to attain power and liberation and requiring a regulation of covenantal ethics and creating corrective tools. The dissonances occur when liberationist thought is anti-Judaic or denigrates Judaism. In addition, the Ten Commandments or *mitzvot,* basic to Hebrew society after exodus, have not been sufficiently explored or utilized by liberation theologians. For Jewish thought, the poor and those of the covenant are not synonymous. The liberating catalyst in exodus is the covenant, not just slavery or poverty. Levingston also notes that Jon Levenson cautions against creating a new type of supersessionism, where Jews are omitted out of their basic story and replaced by the oppressed, the poor. One must also be careful not to limit ethical concerns only to the poor. Interpretations must avoid triumphalism and making claims of being generic and universal when indeed they are particular. And one must guard against the support for the poor resulting in injustices toward others, particularly that such practices do not become totalitarian (Levingston: 1, 3–10).

And what of God's character in Exodus? God's role is not completely defined when using the term "liberator." God's liberation or deliverance of Israel occurs in concert with God's judgment against Egypt (especially the plagues and drowning of the Egyptians at the Reed Sea, a holy war). God's promises and revelation result in a mass genocide (Gowan: 67, 72, 76, 161). From a humanist perspective, Anthony Pinn (1995) argues that the use of exodus and Christ events as liberative moments does not adequately disprove or contradict William Jones's claim of divine racism, which is the lead question of Jones's seminal work, *Is God a White Racist?* Pinn presses Jones, particularly given that the exodus and Christ events mainly highlight God's racial or tribal preference for the Hebrews. Given that Jones avoids the divine racism charge by shifting divine responsibility to human onus and sees God as limited, how does one hold a limited God over against a providential God (94–96)? Ending with a question and backing off from the direct question of whether or not God is racist, sexist, classist, homophobic, or ageist echoes the inadequacy of arguments pertaining to theodicy to date. Taking another tack, does God's name give us any insight?

Where the English language has a verb "to be" in all tenses, Hebrew would not use a verb for the present tense of the verb "to be." Thus Yahweh expresses being, becoming in a manner meaning to take place, come to pass, become, be—present; whereas Western tradition, following the Septuagint rendering, sees Exod 3:14 as descriptive of God's essen-tial being;, namely, "I am that I am." The Yahweh who speaks is a God as active presence; that is, that person is present, ready to act. For Israel, Yahweh's presence is a saving act of grace. For Lerner, the Torah teaches those formerly enslaved not to re-create the bondage they just experienced, and they are a people of God, a people of the "I shall be who I shall be," following the Hebrew tex —a God whose name evokes the potential of "transcendence, freedom, and self- determination" (Gowan: 94; M. Lerner: 55–64). The "I shall be who I shall be" places God in the future, in process, if you will, which means humanity can never catch up with God, a sensibility that resonates with many African religious traditions. How, then, does God's beingness affect the slaves' understanding of who they are? Further, how do we theologically and ethically help contemporary persons relate to Moses as prophet, priest, and judge, as prototype for vessels of liberation and salvation, a Moses who never admits to, confesses to, or is prosecuted for murder (Exod 2:11–14)? Works from African American cultural production can lend a keen interpretative eye to a biblical conundrum.

Hansberry's *A Raisin in the Sun* Read through Exodus Illumines Tensions

Deliberating and exegeting exodus themes are critical both for assess-ing the hermeneutics of Black folk and formal discourse and in heightening the awareness of the different ways this profound metaphor of liberation has been interpreted by Black and Jewish constituencies. This overview of exegetical and hermeneutical issues surrounding exodus as a liberation paradigm gives the barest hint as to the complex issues surrounding the use of the second book of Torah as a Word of deliverance. This biblical theme has been adapted by popular culture artists, in the church, and in the most recent 1960s Civil Rights move-ment. Given the ongoing oppression and marginalization of many peoples of color, it becomes crucial that we wrestle with these texts, if we hope to use them to further the cause of liberation. The sociocultural and historical location of peoples of African descent in the United States has created an environment where many have directly or indirectly employed these motifs. In the world of drama and playwrights, Lorraine Hansberry (1930–1965), a noted Black playwright, artist, intellectual, rad-ical visionary, and critical thinker, attests to some of the tensions of exodus in her three-act play, *A Raisin in the Sun.* It is the story of two gen-erations whose "dream deferred" almost dries up like a grape left out in the sun. The "drama of despair" universalizes suffering without losing the ethos of Blackness, framed by complex levels of contradictions between the "exodus" from what was (order and comfort) to what is (fatigue, disorder, weariness within the physical space and furnishings), amidst oppression, questions of identity, longing for dreams, betrayal, and dreams recovered.

This is a drama about the daily pathos of a poor Black family living in a crowded apartment, struggling to change their lives. The cast includes the head of the household, Lena Younger, usually portrayed as a ruthlessly domineering, controlling force in the lives of her grown children—Beneatha, Walter Lee, and his wife Ruth—who saves her affection and unconditional love for her grandson, Travis. The death of Big Walter, Lena's husband, makes her the beneficiary of his life insurance, money that can signal change. Lena hopes to use the money for better housing and for Beneatha's college education. Walter Lee wants to use the money to buy a liquor store. In addition to the play, inspired by Langston Hughes's poem "Harlem," where he asks, "What happens to a dream deferred?. . . Does it dry up like a raisin [grape left] in the sun? . . . or does it explode?" (in Hughes 1969), Hansberry sold the movie rights to Columbia Pictures and worked on the screenplay. Her later additions to the script heightened her critique of segregation, expressed the increased militant spirit of Black America, exposed United States imperialism, African colonialism, and independence, and unveiled stereotypical images of matriarchal Black women and irresponsible Black men. Lena's understanding of reality is shaped by the loving marriage and the strength and compassion of life with Big Walter (Hine et al.: 524–28; hooks 1989: 21).

The exodus event in *Raisin in the Sun* is the move from a Southside Chicago tenement to a house in the suburbs. This exodus, this "transformation of a social situation from oppression to freedom" (Brueggemann: 1:678), involves a deliverance from cramped quarters, no vegetation, and dying hope, to space, gardens, possibilities. The particular catalyst is the delivery of the check from Big Walter's insurance company. The Moses is the grandson Travis, who "holds the envelop high above his head, like a little dancer, his face is radiant and he is breathless. He moves to his grandmother with sudden slow ceremony and puts the envelope into her hands. She accepts it, and then merely holds it and looks at it [saying] 'Come on! Open it ... Lord have mercy, I wish Walter Lee was here!'" (Hansberry: 54–55) The female characters often embody the attributes of the midwives, Moses' mother and sister, Pharaoh's daughter, and the divine in a fluid manner.

Most of the family appears to be in bondage to the check that's due to come and to the ethos that comes with daily fighting poverty and the need to make do. Latent oppression and poverty forced the Youngers into a situation that echoes the plight of the Hebrews when the Egyptians "made their lives bitter with hard service" (Exod 1:14). The shared bathroom with other tenants on the hall and the small window that provides the lone natural light for the entire apartment embody the constraints of imposed classism and racism. This bondage is part of the fiber of the family, often present in the quiet tension that exists in simple conversations. This spirit of being captive to something that may not be overcome (Exod 1:8–11) emerges as "sullen politeness," automatic complaints, "maximum indifference," affected interest, passive aggressive behavior, mechanical body movements, and defiance of fiscal reality refuted by disgust (Hansberry: 6–12).

Specifically, family members are in bondage to experiences and forces. Walter Lee is so obsessed with buying a liquor store that he gets involved in graft to get the license approved and is subsequently betrayed by a shady friend. Walter Lee dreams, but Ruth, his wife, is almost smothered by the day-to-day reality of lack, pain, and scrimping to make do. She is tired and bitter from her life experiences, and Ruth's fatigue impedes her ability to listen to Walter Lee. His "talk and no action ethos" produces her barbed tongue of hurtful retort. Walter Lee feels misunderstood and not heard and reacts by needing to control and/or demean Black women. His demeanor and actions, self-described as volcanic—echoing Moses' rage when he murdered the Egyptian for beating the Hebrew—are on the verge of full eruption, because Lena says "No" to his dream. He alienates everyone around him with his bitter attacks. Bitterness is a powerful visitor.

Both Walter Lee and Beneatha, like Aaron and Miriam (Num 12:1–12), have their own selfish and egalitarian views about the money. Beneatha struggles to shake loose the bondage of the mundane, as she searches for her own identity, to self-express in diverse ways. She refuses to be categorized or relegated to the stereotypical female role, has a great distaste for assimilationist Negroes, and represents both an emerging womanist who wants her autonomy and a woman who seeks to please men.

The dynamics between Lena and daughter Beneatha span a continuum: Lena is both supportive and overbearing; Beneatha perceives her mother as a tyrant but accords her respect. Lena's wisdom is the perspicacity of Black experience, borne of compassion and of understanding (hooks 1989: 21). Walter Lee is everyone, that is, "the most ordinary human being ... [with] elements of profundity, of profound anguish" (ibid.). Though Walter Lee sometimes acts foolishly, irresponsibly, and self-centeredly, he longs to live in a world of dreams fulfilled, not deferred. Hansberry's play is a prophetic vision of the life issues and struggles of African Americans, of those seeking to change their own social reality. Lena wanted a house in the suburban White neighborhood only because the house was better made and less expensive—her promised land. As an artist and activist, Hansberry also critiques the problems and obsessions with wealth, snobbishness, sexism, racism, classism, and the reality and necessity of God.

Beneatha, a pun on "lower class," contends that only human beings make miracles and thus the liberation needed in Africa is from British and French colonial rule, not salvation from heathenism. Lena counters that God still exists in her house. According to Steven Carter, Hansberry held that a belief in God was a temporary but necessary crutch. Hansberry affirmed the role of the church in the freedom struggle, did not attack folk who were religious, and admired their ability to make their own crutches as long as needed, but Hansberry believed that once one could walk, one could throw away these artificial supports. Hansberry appears to have a humanist stance rather than a particular religious belief, perhaps that of a skeptic. For Hansberry, the warp and woof of faith and skepticism together create a framework for bondage and a call for exodus.

The hopeful place of dreams has also become bondage (Exod 3:7, 9). Big Walter, a dreamer, like his son, could never catch up with his dreams. He said, "Seem like God didn't see fit to give the Black man nothing but dreams—but [God] did give us children to make them dreams seem worth while" (Hansberry: 29). Lena and Ruth come to realize that Walter Lee is in bondage to something, that he has deep needs, and that he must be delivered from pathos (Exod 3:8) to the chance of having this store, the opportunity to be in charge. The picture of deliverance and what is important in life varies from character to character.

The tension unfolds amid a cornucopia of desire. Walter Lee desires wealth and employment with dignity. Lena believes that they have existed with dignity, their children did not get lynched, and they had a roof over their heads. Beneatha dreams of being a doctor as she searches for identity. Ruth struggles over whether or not to terminate her pregnancy. When the check comes, Lena buys the house in the White neighborhood because it is built better, is less expensive, and because she sees her family falling apart. Walter Lee feels she butchered his dream. Lena acquiesces and gives him the remainder of the money, an act of love and trust, because "There ain't nothing worth holding on to, ... if it means it's going to destroy my boy" (Hansberry: 94). Walter's newfound exuberance is truncated when (1) Karl Lindner of their new neighborhood association offers to buy their house so they will not move in (99–105). Second, they find out that Willy has left town with all of the money, the "money made out of my father's flesh," including Beneatha's school money, *"money of the man who grew thin' before he was forty ... working and working and working like somebody's old horse ... killing himself ... and you—you give it all away in a day"* (117).

The family's wilderness experience (Exod 15:22–19:3) in the Canaan of despair, loss, disbelief, anguish, and horror occurs before they can ever cross the Reed Sea (Exod 14). While Hansberry does not explicitly use exodus materials, the themes weave in and out of her narrative. Initially, in the fallout reminiscent of the conflicts and frenzy at the foot of the mountain while Moses is delayed (Exod 32), Walter Lee lies on the bed listless, and Beneatha senses she has stopped caring about people. Asagai, her boyfriend, shouts that one should live the answer and not try to respond to people's stupid mistakes and the wrongs of the world. Asagai invites Beneatha to go to Africa with him. Lena thinks they have dreamed too big and need to remain on the Southside. Walter Lee contacts Linder and invites him to come and pay the family for not moving into the neighborhood, for he thinks there is nothing but taking in the world, regardless. Beneatha and Mama both sense that death has come to the house. Where Beneatha sees Walter as a toothless rat, Mama sees him as one needing love, for the pain he has been through and for what losing the money did to him. People need love when they are at their lowest and are burdened with self-doubt and self-loathing for being so persecuted by the world. The family experiences deliverance as Walter Lee experiences "the rainbow after the rain" before his entire family, when he tells Linder the family has decided to move into the house because they are proud people and because his father earned them that right.

In sum, the systemic oppression, decision making, and conflicts in Hansberry's *A Raisin in the Sun* echo the exodus text. The family prepares for deliverance when they receive Big Walter's check (Exod 1–4). Ruth must deal with the question of keeping or terminating her pregnancy, paralleling the conundrum for Shiprah and Puah (Exod 1:17–19). The family has been sustained by the dream of Lena and Big Walter, to "let my people/ family go," to flee from poverty and tenement life to a suburban setting that embodied more freedom (Exod 5–11). Specifically, they had to deal with the plagues of pain, grief, loss, betrayal, racism, classism, false perceptions, denial, and a certain fear of the unknown. The angst, need for transformation, and the ultimate celebration of *A Raisin in the Sun* resonate with the mosaics of the move toward salvific freedom in Black homiletics as a living performance of proclamation. The angst and celebration of *A Raisin in the Sun* are bits of the mosaics found in the music of Sweet Honey in the Rock.

Sweet Honey in the Rock's Exodus Mosaic

Sweet Honey in the Rock, an a capella all-women's group founded in 1973, sings traditional and original songs of protest and resistance against oppression. They perform at churches and in concerts and festivals throughout this country and in Ecuador, Mexico, Germany, Japan, England, Canada, Australia, Africa, and the Caribbean. Since Sweet Honey's founding by Bernice Johnson Reagon, former Curator for the American History Museum of the Smithsonian Institution and now professor at American University, their songs have been and continue to be a testament of commitment, faith, and perseverance to make a difference. In their moving performances, their audiences leave changed, converted toward social justice. In commenting on their twentieth-anniversary album, Reagon noted that, for Sweet Honey, it is important that they are "clearly visible for all to know that we do remember who we are and we act in our present charged by that memory. We cherish and celebrate the opportunity to make our mark on these shifting unstable sands. We are warriors.... We name through our singing the expanding community we sound. When you see our songs, you see the tip of the mountain upon which we stand and it is solid ground"(Sweet Honey in the Rock 1993).

Many of their songs embody the spirit of exodus as a process of "freedom from" and "freedom to." Sweet Honey believes, as celebrated in "Ella's Song," in a freedom that will not let one rest, a freedom from complacence and self-pity, and a freedom to demand that the killing of all mother's sons, of Black mothers and White mothers, be equally important; until then we cannot rest (Sweet Honey in the Rock 1988). Their music wants us to be free from a society that "accepts, builds and works from a foundation of obvious painful lies and untruths." They mourn the fact that every human being must survive in this kind of society ("Ballad of the Broken Word, "Sweet Honey in the Rock 1993). Sweet Honey also recites a powerful commentary on the freedom to appreciate beauty. In "Wanting Memories" (1993), Sweet Honey desires the freedom to appreciate personal and communal memories in a manner that allows everyone to see clearly through their own eyes, the freedom to offer comfort, to remember lessons from the past, to laugh and remember the truth of the beauty of healthy youthful experiences. When a loved one is gone, one is still free to remember that person's voice, to remember lessons taught of simple respect, of a please and a thank-you, to engage in a celebration of gratitude and blessing. In "No Mirrors in My Nana's House" (ibid.), Sweet Honey celebrates the freedom to experience the beauty reflected through the eyes of a loved one and to be free from being in bondage to commercialized standards set by the fashion district and Women's Wear Daily. Their music celebrates the freedom to take a stance against oppression ("Sojourner's Battle Hymn," ibid.) and freedom from loneliness ("Stay," ibid.). One has the freedom to build and nurture intimate relations, to be tender, to "stay a little bit longer."

Some songs celebrate the freedom of a woman to be, to "break down, sit down, like everybody else call it quits." We ought to be free to appreciate those women who have washed floors to send us to college, to make the world safe, to make sure their children survived, the women who were free to be, who helped make a way out of no way ("Oughta Be a Woman," Sweet Honey in the Rock 1988). "More Than a Paycheck" (ibid.) is an indictment against the freedom to bring environmental illnesses, disease, injury, and stress to our families in the name of money. "Battle for My Life" (ibid.) is a consciousness-raising song that invites humanity to be free enough to see the problems of the human condition. The price of not being free occurs when some dominant power spreads disease in the name of conquest, explodes neutron bombs to ascertain power, raises the budget for defense, chains people's bodies to dope, causing oppression through poverty. Conversely, people are not free to own, berate, or abuse children, because they "are not your children. They are the sons and daughters of life's longing for itself; they come through you but they are not from you" ("On Children," ibid.; lyrics from *The Prophet*, by Kahlil Gibran). Sweet Honey's songs of resistance and liberation are philosophical and practical, speaking of communities and individuals; they are songs about women. The songs, named for women and focusing on women, grow out of a freedom to self-express profoundly and provocatively: about friendships and struggles; about loneliness and bruises; about babies and singing; about the freedom to take names and air complaints; and about the freedom to dare the world to change. Sweet Honey's songs are a political cry for freedom in the ghetto, in South Africa ("Crying for Freedom in South Africa," Sweet Honey in the Rock 1998). Sweet Honey sings of the freedom to be "a gift of love," a freedom to be a "Fannie Lou Hamer" (ibid.), and to let our lights shine; about the freedom to experience beginnings and endings, to feel, to experience the divine ("Feel Something Drawing Me On," ibid). The music and drama and ritual that unfolds in Sweet Honey in the Rock's live performances often mirror the homiletic and liturgical drama that unfolds in Black pulpits.

Exodus As Seen through Black Preaching

Contemporary and historical Black preaching unfolds as a drama that addresses physical and spiritual liberation. Using theological and ethical models of Christian faith, Black proclamation addresses political, socio-economic, and religious issues in the hope of transforming individuals, communities, and social evils. Black preaching wrestles with problems of its own constituency and the ultimate redemption and freedom of all peoples. In much of Black preaching, the hermeneutics include God as the point of departure, scripture as resource and substance, the process of experiencing and incarnating the text, understandable communication, and experience as proclaimed dialogue. This Black preaching drama is not escapism or singularly other-worldly and eschatological pie in the sky in the sweet by-and-by. These sermons speak of change **now!**, of overturning oppression **now!**, and of a **now!** and **not yet!** eschatology. While much of Black preaching focuses on liberation and salvation, out of a sample of a dozen volumes of sermons by African American female and male preachers, less than ten sermons were based on the exegesis of the book of Exodus. Some of the sermons in these anthologies did not cite a particular pericope, though some referred to a particular book of the Bible. The challenge was to analyze sermons based on the book of Exodus to discover the hermeneutics of these Black homileticists (H. Young; Stewart).

Using Exod 15:1–3; Luke 1:46–47, 51–53—yoking Moses' song of praise and deliverance framed by Miriam's song with Mary's exaltation or praise in the Magnificat—and the spirituals, James Cones extols, "What Does It Mean to Be Saved?" Cone argues that in part due to the influence of Greek philosophy, the doctrine of salvation has been distorted to remove salvation from history, separating civil from spiritual liberation. The exodus motif is the celebration of God's historical deliverance of people from bondage, a rescue event of redemption and healing. This revolutionary liberative act of God's kingdom or rule incarnated in Jesus Christ brings peace, justice, and holistic health, a call for existential and eschatological freedom (Cone 1976).

In critique of Cone's use of scripture, South African biblical scholar Itumeleng Mosala cautions pastors and philosophers alike in their broad sweeping liberationist readings of Luke 1 and 2. Mosala questions how historical-cultural foundations connect and shape Black theological-hermeneutical assumptions and argues for an ideological and theoretical break from dominant theologies and simple liberationist readings of the canon. Mosala does a materialist reading of Luke 1 and 2, giving particular attention to the economics, modes of production, and the complex class structure, which includes a ruling, a dominant (artisans, peasantry), and an under class (those exploited politically, economically, ideologically) within the colonial occupied Palestine by Rome.

In his sermon, "What Does It Mean to Be Saved?" J. Deotis Roberts (1976) reads Dostoevsky, Jean Paul Sartre, Richard Wright, stories from Japan and India, and the book of Exodus. He contends that writers throughout time speak of what is most universally human: the experience of pain, despair, persecution and the need for courage, hope, and to find meaning in life. Exodus as a story of God's deliverance is a call of faith, a call of righteousness for God's people to aid the afflicted, the poor, the oppressed. Exodus is a call to radicalize the church and to be a responsible people because God's deliverance occurs if God's people are willing to do their part for justice, freedom, and righteousness.

Dwight Clinton Jones uses Exod 1:8, "Now a new king arose over Egypt, who did not know Joseph," to proclaim "The Lord Is on Our Side." Jones claims that for the Israelites oppressed by Egyptians, the Jews annihilated by Germans, and for Blacks dehumanized by Whites, Emmanuel, God, was on their side. This God is on the side of all oppressed, but not against the rich. Like the Pharaohs of the world, the Marie Antoinettes, the Hitlers, the Richard Nixons, who forgot about the Josephs of the world, the persons who have elevated or served them, all persons are called to not forget or fear. One should not forget history nor forget those who have supported us, where we came from, who we used to be, the problems and challenges of the past. Nor should those in the majority fear those in the minority. The minority will always exist, those with a mind made up to make a difference, and those who have God on their side.

The story of exodus involves a call by Yahweh and responses by Pharaoh, the community, and Moses, says Edward Wheeler, in his sermon "Going beyond News from the Brickyard." In the face of God's call and command, "Let my people go," Pharaoh, like many in our contemporary world, totally ignores God. The community of faith begins by meeting the message of deliverance with enthusiasm but does not understand the cost that freedom requires; the community of faith fails to realize that by cowering to oppression it makes it that much more difficult to leave the role of victim. Moses was a hesitant leader but became upset at Pharaoh's resistance, so much so that at points Moses doubted God and Moses' own function as the people's deliverer. Pharaoh resisted, the people complained, and Moses had doubts. Ultimately God spoke deliverance and the Hebrews were liberated.

Alan Ragland, in his sermon, "From Heaven to Hell: What Went Wrong in Egypt," proclaims that exodus shows how turbulence creates oppression and how negative social status changes where those once respected become liabilities. These changes are not an opportunity to cry victim, since in many cases those who cry victim are usually "benign accomplices to these evil transformations" by those wielding a powerful, "complex conspiracy of social ill will." In Egypt and in the United States, institutionalized racism and classism produced a segregated society. Then the victims aided and abetted their plight through: (1) being complacent and comfortable within their present situation; (2) learning dominant value systems and merely assimilating; (3) being accountable to no one, where "an interim survival strategy" became a 430-year residency; (4) forgetting the "pilgrim instinct," of being nomads and sojourners; (5) losing their sense of ultimate destiny with God; and (6) losing their entrepreneurial esteem or getting by too long on someone else's territory. Ragland says the oppressed are called to confess and repent of their complicity and contributions toward their own bondage, to remember and reestablish their godly identity, to recover the relationship with God and the related values, to reorganize their communities, to rely on divine power for liberation, to resume their pilgrimage toward God's promises.

In sum, Black homileticians pursue a variety of tracks in their hermeneutical explorations of the book of Exodus. Of the five samples interrogated here, the topics included dogma, deliverance, and the complexities and responsibilities involved in existential and eschatological freedom. Cone critiques ahistorical salvation and posits divine, liberative revolution incarnated in Jesus Christ. Roberts universalizes pain, persecution, and despair, as he calls for responsible faith and divine deliverance. Dwight Clinton Jones reminds us that while God is on the side of the oppressed, one should not forget history or fear difference. Wheeler contends that not only do many ignore God's call to "Let my people go," but the oppressed community often fails to realize the cost of freedom, as they acquiesce by leaving all liberation to divine action. Ragland observes amid the reality of systemic oppression, turbulence causes subjugation and the oppressed are often complicit in their own demise. In these collections, only two sermons included pericopes Exod 1 and 15, the bookends for the journey from slavery to freedom. Interestingly, no sermons focused specifically on the plagues, on Moses' murder of the Egyptian, or the later Sinai experiences. None of the volumes of sermons by women preachers contained sermons on the book of Exodus, which is not to say they did not focus on liberation. These results indicate the limits of published works as opposed to a sample of preached sermons from a larger populace. At the same time, these sermons reflect a tendency to read the liberative themes in the book of Exodus without reckoning with the cost to innocent Egyptians, persons also presumably created by God, and the later cost to the indigenous persons already occupying the land. These sermons fail to explore or critique the depth and breadth of the divine ego, who must control the liberating process and harden Pharaoh's heart, even when the latter decided to no longer "play a game of chicken" and is willing to let the Hebrews go.

Conclusion

In line with the tenets of these sermons, several scholars contend that the exodus text gives Black clergy a way to denounce White hegemony, privilege, and supremacy, particularly that molded as Christianity, and to announce Black liberation, Black power. Both laity and clergy, in spirituals, political tracts, testimonies, and sermons, attest to the import of the exodus motif as central to lived theology and ethics. Historic voices of Henry Highland Garnet and David Walker agitated for freedom. Garnet used the exodus story to press the fight of freedom toward insurrection. He equated exodus with resistance. Their personal liberating God was the God who sanctioned revolt. Harriet Tubman (1820–1913) was a "Conductor"—a heroine of the Underground Railroad—nicknamed Black Moses, an abolitionist par excellence who led many an exodus to Canada, to Canaan. For many oppressed, exodus is a "familiar theo-political paradigm," a "revelation-liberation event," and a story that demonstrates how Israel knows God and how Israel knows herself within her dependent relationship with this liberator God (J. Young: 94–96; Cone 1986; King). Many of the Freedom Fighters of the 1960s Civil Rights movement (Kirk-Duggan), focused on the demise of evil, injustice, oppression, and exploitation, not on the death of the Egyptians; that is, the Freedom Fighters converged on divine justice, an essential component in Black folk's doctrine of God.

The exodus story is a complex, powerful story of deliverance, freedom, enslavement, and genocide as well as a story of powerful women, without whom the protagonist, Moses, could not have survived. The themes of exodus pervade African American religious and secular cultural narratives. A world at the beginning of the twenty-first century demands that we listen carefully to all the voices within the exodus story and to read the entire narrative, if we desire to transform the hardened hearts of the oppressors and make real the dreams deferred of the oppressed.

A Prodigal Sings the Blues:
The Characterization of Harriett Williams
in Langston Hughes's *Not without Laughter*

Abraham Smith
Perkins School of Theology

> *Read on down to chapter nine,*
> *women must learn to take their time*
> *Read on down to chapter ten,*
> *takin' other women men you are doin' a sin*
> *Sing 'em, sing 'em, sing them blues,*
> *let me convert your soul.*
> Bessie Smith, "Preaching the Blues" (A. Davis: 328)

Introduction

The princess who sings at the end of Langston Hughes's *Not without Laughter* is one of four women whose ways are imitated by young Sandy Rodgers, the male character around whom the novel appears to revolve (Hughes 1995b).[1] The "princess" is not Sandy's mother, Anjee, a passive

---

1 Ostensibly, *Not without Laughter* is about the coming of age of Sandy, the young character whose life is traced from age five to sixteen. In truth, the novel is about the travails and joys of a single black family, one led by Aunt Hager, a former slave and an old washerwoman in the small Kansas town of Stanton. The book traces the lives of this poor family from its "disintegration" to its "re-creation" (Miller: 369). The opening chapter, a depiction of a storm and its aftermath, not only reveals the six chief characters of the novel (Aunt Hager, her grandson [Sandy], her three daughters [Tempy, Anjee, and Harriett], and her son-in-law [Jimboy]), but it also reveals the indomitable spirit and the race-transcending care of Aunt Hager as she deals with the material losses caused by the storm on the one hand and the needs of black and white citizens hurt by the storm on the other. Chapters 2 through 6, characterization studies, reveal the crushing work experiences of some of the characters: from Hager's clothes-washing to eke out a living for her family, to Jimboy's day labor always cut short because of racial prejudice, to Anjee's domestic work for a white family, to Harriett's country-club work with wages that do not match the level of her intelligence. Each

acquiescent woman who accepts the world as it is. Nor is the princess Sandy's older aunt, Tempy, an assimilationist who apes bourgeois lifestyle and rarely goes to visit her own mother. Nor is the princess Sandy's grandmother, Aunt Hager, a woman whose heart is full of Christian forgiveness. Rather, the princess is the one who combines the best values of her mother and of Sandy's blues-singing father, Jimboy. The princess is the one who refuses to settle for mediocre wages and stereotypes of black people, the one who offers to help Sandy finance his way through school—the spirited, soulful, and sassy Harriett Williams.

George Kent (27) has shown the importance of Harriett Williams for Hughes's evocation of the blues singer as one deeply in touch with the harsh realities of rural and urban existence. Cheryl A. Wall (44), as well, contours the importance of Harriett's character in the novel's reconstruction of the evolution of the blues from the rural areas to the city. With this

---

character's different response to the work experience forms the seed for the family's disintegration: Hager suffers quietly with a stalwart faith in God; Jimboy travels from place to place; Anjee consumes herself with making Jimboy happy when he is at home or pitying herself when he is away. Harriett critiques white society as the cause of oppressive labor conditions for blacks. Chapter 7 is devoted to "White Folks," and it reveals the plights of blacks under the yoke of racial oppression, both in the past (slavery and loss of land because of racial prejudice) and in the present (the lowest wages and the most despised occupations). Chapters 8 and 9 reveal the growing conflict between Aunt Hager and her youngest daughter, Harriett. In 8, Harriett's trip to a dance hall with her young nephew and against her mother's wishes leads to a thrashing. In 9, she leaves Stanton to travel with a carnival. While she is away, time passes on in Stanton. Sandy is punished for lying about the use to which he put a nickel given to him for his Sunday school class (ch. 10). He and other black children are given seats in the back of a classroom, and his father, ever the rover, moves on yet again (ch. 11). In the "Hard Winter" (ch. 12), the absence of Jimboy leaves Anjee heartsick, and Harriett, penniless and hungry, seeks to return home. Following Christmas (ch. 13), Harriett makes her "Return" (ch. 14) to see her mother but not to live with her. Chapter 15 depicts the move of Anjee to Detroit to be with her husband Jimboy (though both will later move on to Chicago). In chapters 16 through 18, the story shifts to show the development of young Sandy: in 16, Aunt Hager, like a griot, teaches the value of love over hate; in 17, Sandy gets his first job as a shoeshine boy; and in 18, he faces the disappointment of not being able to enter an amusement park because of racism. In Chapter 19, young Sandy seeks to comfort his grandmother at the news that Harriett has been arrested for streetwalking, and in chapter 20 he quits a job as a bellhop when a white man orders him to dance. In chapter 21 his grandmother becomes deathly sick, and in chapter 22 she passes away. Several chapters follow (23–27) that trace the development of Sandy, who now lives with his elitist aunt Tempy because the whereabouts of his mother and father are unknown. In chapter 28, Sandy finally hears from his mother, who has moved on to Chicago. For a while there, he works as an elevator-boy without a chance to return to school (ch. 29). In the final chapter, Harriett, while on tour as a singer, is reunited with Anjee and Sandy in Chicago, and promises financial aid to help her nephew escape his treadmill labor and attain an education in preparation for leadership in the black community. Thus, the family is finally re-created in an effort not only to help themselves but the larger Black community as well.

essay, I commend these previous efforts and add another: her importance as a symbol of success in urban America, despite the plights of her life, which recall and roughly follow the trajectory of a well-known biblical figure within one of Luke's parables, the Prodigal Son (Luke 15:11–32).[2] As I will suggest, moreover, an analysis of the characterization of Harriett Williams will demonstrate that *Not without Laughter* is not a story with disparate threads, as some have asserted (Bone: 75–77; Dickinson: 53). Rather, the novel coheres well when read against the backdrop of the parable of the Prodigal Son.

To present this characterization study, three steps are necessary: (1) a reconstruction of the blues singer as a spiritual icon; (2) an examination of the blues singer as a prodigal son or daughter; and (3) an analysis of the novel's extended typological appropriation of the parable of the Prodigal Son.

1. The Blues Singer As a Spiritual Icon

Although some scholars initially made a distinction between the blues and religion (Work: 28), many scholars now suggest that the distinction is misleading and unfortunate (Oliver; Garon). While noting the chronological difference between the blues and the spirituals, James Cone calls the blues "secular spirituals" and suggests that the blues were "impelled by the same search for the truth of the black experience" as found in the spirituals (1972: 100). Furthermore, the blues, avers Cone, affirmed black "somebodiness" (105), responded to the incongruities of life (103), and expressed—through its "priests and priestesses"—"the Word of black existence, depicting its joy and sorrow, love and hate, and the awesome burden of being 'free' in a racist society when one is black" (102).

With acknowledgments to James Cone and Lawrence Levine for their insights on the spiritual elements in the blues, Jon Michael Spencer argues "that the Christian religion was the sacred history and the fate of blues people and that blues and blues life subsisted within larger spheres of Christianity" (1990: 109). Limiting the parameters of

---

2 While I acknowledge the title's bias in perhaps misrepresenting Luke's primary focus on the father (as opposed to the younger son), I am here treating the reception of the parable and its title in a more popular arena—an arena in which many persons have largely featured the younger son as the primary character in the parable. In music, see, e.g., Robert Wilkins's "Prodigal Son" song (A. Davis 1998: 114; cf. Spencer 1990: 107–31); in poetry and art, see this author's analysis of Aaron Douglas's "Prodigal Son" illustration for James Weldon Johnson's *God's Trombones* (A. Smith 2000).

his discussion to the blues to the pre–World War II blues, a notably "more segregated" form of the blues, Spencer notes that the theological basis for the blues is that the blues simply spoke the truth (109). The blues person constantly calls on God; takes on the character of a preacher of the gospel (esp. with the expression "Read on down in Chapter Ten"); laments about trouble (usually money or a lover); revolts in the protest tradition against hypocrisy, repressive sex, and Jim Crow ethics; and often uses the word "sin" in his or her lyrics (111–20). Furthermore, the blues often draws on the Bible (especially the Adam and Eve images, 120–24). In a later work, Spencer extends his analysis of the blues to a full-length monograph. He argues that the blues singers included "oh Lord" interpolations as fillers in their music (1993: 37–40), preached from a cultural bible that owed its cosmology to Jewish and Christian narratives (35, 40–42), drew from the content and titles of spirituals (43–46), and criticized the hypocrisy or self-righteousness of church folk (49–52). In addition, he notes the prominence of the Adamic myth in the ethics of the blues life (56–67). According to Spencer, the Adamic myth (a cluster of themes about the origin of humankind, of temptation and evil, and of humankind's posterity) explains the blues as punishment for eating from the "forbidden tree" (3).

In an extraordinary argument about the protofeminist social consciousness of three early blues women (Gertrude "Ma" Rainey, Bessie Smith, and Billie Holiday), Angela Y. Davis explains the rise of the blues and the deep spirituality of the blues. When postslavery religion lost the fluidity between religious practices and the rest of "everyday life—work, family, sabotage, escape," especially as seen in the replacement of the spirituals with gospel songs, the blues emerged as that music which continued the spirituals' tradition of a focus on the "everyday lives of black people" (5–6). Thus, for Davis, the rise of the blues was a necessary extenuation of the social consciousness already at work in the spirituals. Indeed, one can clearly see the social consciousness of the blues in Billie Holiday's "Strange Fruit" (1939), a blues song about lynching:

> Southern trees bear a strange fruit
> Blood on the leaves, blood on the root
> Black bodies swinging in the Southern breeze
> Strange fruit hanging from the poplar trees
> Pastoral scene of the gallant South. (A. Davis: 181)

Furthermore, for Davis, the spirituality of the blues is manifested in several ways: in the working-class's recognition of the blues singers as authorities on love, in the spiritual (biblical) diction of some blues songs, and in the self-consciousness of the blues singer who sought to oppose the "Christian monopolization of black spirituality" (120–37).

As for the recognition of blues singers as authorities on love, the blues singer often emerges as a griot ready to pass on wisdom gained through personal experience. In "Bad Luck" blues, for example, Ma Rainey sings:

> Hey, people, listen while I spread my news
> Hey, people, listen while I spread my news
> I want to tell you people all about my bad luck blues. (A. Davis: 200)

Or, in "Trust No Man," she warns other women:

> I want all you women to listen to me.
> Don't trust your man no further'n
> your eyes can see. I trusted mine with my
> best friend. But that was the bad part in the end. (A. Davis: 251).

The blues also included spiritual (biblical) diction. On the one hand, the blues sometimes referred directly to biblical passages. In "Down-Hearted Blues" (1922), Bessie Smith's response to a man's mistreatment is a paraphrase of Gal 6:7 ("Do not be deceived; God is not mocked, for you reap whatever you sow"):

> 'Cause he mistreated me and he drove me from his door,
> Yes, he mistreated me and he drove me from his door
> But the Good Book says you'll reap just what you sow.
> (Gates and McKay: 27; cf. Spencer 1993: 77–81)

On the other hand, the blues sometimes indirectly alluded to biblical passages. According to Angela Y. Davis (108–11), Bessie Smith's "Back-water Blues" (like Charley Patton's "High Water Everywhere") was both a response to the flooding of the Mississippi River in 1927 and an allusion to Noah's ark (Gen 6–8). That is, like the biblical story, the blues song describes continuous rain, safety in a boat for a few, horrific devastation for many, and a boat's rest on a hill or on mountains.

The blues singers' self-conscious critique of the "Christian monopolization of black spirituality" is clear in Bessie Smith's "Preachin' the Blues." "Preachin' the Blues," while not a blues song itself, provides a discourse on the spirituality of the blues. The discourse uses terms conventionally associated with spirituality (preach, convert, save) to teach women how to "take charge of their sexuality and implicitly challenges the church's condemnation of sexuality" (A. Davis: 130–31):

> Preach them blues, sing them blues, they certainly sound good to me....
> Moan them blues, holler them blues, let me convert your soul.... I ain't
> here to try to save your soul. Just want to teach you how to save your
> jelly roll. (A. Davis: 328)

Accordingly, rather than see a distinction between the blues and religion, one should see the ways in which the blues person competed with gospel music singers and other practitioners of Christianity to continue the spirituals' holistic concern for all of life and to offer advice on the everyday struggles of postslavery black men and women. Moreover, this view of the blues and of the blues person sheds light on the significance of Harriett Williams as a blues person in *Not without Laughter*.

Although Hughes made a distinction between the sadness of the blues and that of the spirituals, all black music moved him (Wall 1995, 40, in Kellner 1979, 46). He called "spirituals and blues the 'two great Negro gifts to American music'" (in Tracy: 53). He also wrote *Tambourines to Glory*, a gospel musical featuring Sister Rosetta Thorpe (Hernton: 117). Furthermore, he spoke affectionately of jazz as the child of ordinary black people (Hughes 1995a: 306).

Yet Hughes's identification with working-class black people gave him a keener proclivity toward the blues and the blues person. The blues helped him to catch the vernacular of ordinary black people (Jemie: 31). As well, the blues imbued a philosophical and cathartic spirituality that spoke to the anguish and needs of black men and women. According to Jemie (12), the blues for Hughes was "a philosophy of endurance of the apparently unendurable ('pain swallowed in a smile')." Furthermore, the blues singer for Hughes was the everyday black people's "representative, a mirror of their lives, a priest and chief celebrant in a ritual of confession and cleansing. By admitting their failures, singer and audience admit to the simultaneous absurdity and beauty of life" (41).

Among the blues singers noted by Hughes, the blues woman was prominent. He spoke fondly of "the bellowing voice of Bessie Smith singing the Blues" (Hughes 1995a: 309). He was the first notable figure to mention the blues woman (Wall: 39). According to Wall, Hughes's work *Not without Laughter* features Harriett Williams, who "should be considered a precursor to the memorable blues women invented by Alice Walker in *The Color Purple*, Toni Cade Bambara in 'Medley,' and Sherley Anne Williams in *Someone Sweet Angel Child*." Moreover, his poems and novels reverberate with variations on the blues woman: from the venerable Sister Bradley, whose blues singing "can roll like thunder"; to the independent Alberta K. Johnson, who does not have to have a man to survive; to the proud Harriett Williams, who is equal to Jimboy, her brother-in-law, and defiant toward the "strictures of culture, state, racism, sexism, and all the controlling forces and institutions of society" (Hernton: 112).

Hughes's Harriett Williams, like other blues persons, criticizes the hypocrisy of the church and Christianity's strictures (Hunter-Lattany: 142). In a critique of the black church's internal focus, she laments:

"Darkies do like the church too much, but white folks don't care nothing about it at all. They're too busy getting theirs out of this world, not from God" (Hughes 1995b: 82). In a critique of the church's focus on morality, she tells her mother: "Aw, the church has made a lot of you old Negroes act like Salvation Army people.... Afraid to even laugh on Sundays, afraid for a girl and boy to look at one another, or for people to go to dances. Your old Jesus is white, I guess, that's why!" (55).

Yet, Harriet is deeply spiritual. In contrast to her sister, Tempy, she appreciates and affirms blackness and thus has a healthy self-respect (54; Wall: 46). She is recognized as an authority figure by the masses because she helps others to deal with the plights of existence in a defiant way. In the novel's closing dance and song routine, members of Chicago's Monogram theater audience repeatedly say "Lawd" or "True Lawd" in assent to the truth of Harriett's blues singing (Hughes 1995b: 293). Furthermore, she is community-minded: she agrees to pay for Sandy's education to ensure that he will become a leader for his race (296–98).

Thus, Hughes's Harriett Williams is not antireligious, though she strains against organized Christianity. And as scholars such as Cone, Levine, Spencer, and Davis have shown, the blues singer's critique of organized Christianity is not a critique of religion altogether. Rather, it is a critical quest for the world's truth free of institutional Christianity's other-worldly orientation and puritanical excesses. Accordingly, Harriett Williams's truth-seeing eye, voice of authority, and community-mindedness all bespeak a person of deep spirituality—a spirituality with which readers must reckon to see how her character functions in Hughes's first novel.

2. The Blues Singer As a Prodigal Son or Daughter

Spencer cites St. Clair Drake and Horace Cayton's description of some Chicagoans as "Prodigal Sons and Daughters" and agrees with their argument that "most African Americans were familiar with this theological scheme and the ritual requirements for salvation" (Spencer 1993: 64; Drake and Cayton: 616). Furthermore, the epithet was often used to describe the blues person. That is, the parable of the Prodigal Son provided the basic model for many blues singers because of their travel away from home, their experience of deprivation especially in the big cities, or their return to the church from a life of singing the blues.

Travel was indeed a part of the blues singer's life. The blues continued the spirituals' tradition of evoking the theme of travel. In slavery, the theme was evoked in the spirituals to overcome the geographical limitations of slavery on the plantations of the South. For example, one can clearly see the focus on travel in those spirituals that emphasize "home" as a place apart from the present circumstances of the enslaved. In "City Called Heaven," the enslaved African is depicted as "a poor pilgrim of sorrow" who is "tryin' to make heaven my home" (Gates and McKay: 8). In "Soon I Will Be Done," the enslaved African draws a contrast with the present "troubles of this world" with the refrain "Goin' home to live with God" (Gates and McKay: 11). Or, in "Steal Away to Jesus," the goal is to move away "home," whether home is literally with Jesus in heaven or to a rendezvous place along the Underground Railroad (Gates and McKay: 13).

In postslavery days, the blues picked up the image of travel to laud the newly found autonomy (especially in the case of the blues women, who were not defined by domesticity). For example, in "Traveling Blues," Ma Rainey avers,

> I'm dangerous and blue, can't stay here no more
> I'm dangerous and blue
> can't stay here no more
> Here comes my train,
> folks, and I've got to go. (A. Davis: 73)

Furthermore, many blues singers (Ma Rainey in "Lost Wandering Blues" and "Slow Driving Moan" and Bessie Smith in "Lookin' for My Man Blues") sang of their travel away from home as an opportunity to make it on their own away from the confines and strictures of home and church life (A. Davis: 66–90).

Deprivation was also woven into the fabric of the blues singer's career. In some cases (as with Bessie Smith), blues singers offered sanguine and sober commentary on the alienation of the new urban environments to which black men and women had traveled in search of a better life than the one they found in the rural parts of the South. Blues singers admitted that their travels in search of a better life had failed and that the northern and southern cities to which they fled had not offered them the escape they had sought in traveling there (A. Davis: 66–90).

Spencer argues that for those blues singers who stopped singing the blues and began to sing or preach in church, a "turning" or "return" moment was pivotal for them. Examples could include J. B. Lenoir, Blind Willie McTell, Flora Molton, Nehemiah "Skip James," Gary Davis, and Sara Martin (cf. 1993: 65–66).

The "turning" moment sometimes was reflected in the composition of a gospel song from the words or tune of a blues song. For Sara Martin, a former blues singer who turned to gospel music, for example, Thomas A. Dorsey composed the gospel song "I Surely Know There's Been a

Change in Me" as a "variation of the old [blues song] 'There'll Be Some Changes Made'" (Heilbut 1989: 28).

For some blues singers, moreover, the singing of the blues was but an interlude between periods of deep devotion to the church (Spencer 1993: 2–3, 63–67). For others, the "return" was simply the beginning of a different life—a life in the church. As Spencer also notes, the blues life was "a reliving of the parable of the Prodigal Son, so that blues songs are raw religious reflections of individual and ritually synchronized sojourns in moral maturity" (1990: ix).

Thus, the Prodigal Son/Daughter epithet, with its intimations of travel, deprivation, and "turning" ("return"), was a familiar appellation for the blues singer. It is not surprising, then, that the narrator of *Not without Laughter* calls Harriett a prodigal (164). To appreciate more fully Hughes's characterization of Harriett as a blues singer, moreover, readers must carefully examine the novel for its many evocations of this epithet.

3. *Not without Laughter*'s Extended Typological Appropriation of the Prodigal Son Parable

While *Not without Laughter* is not replete with biblical imagery, as we shall see, the novel certainly includes a number of direct biblical citations, biblical allusions, and extended biblical typologies carefully selected to critique certain characters, to comment on everyday life, or to indicate a phenomenon in a metaphorical manner (Brickell; Miller: 362–69).

Not every use of the Bible receives favorable notice. When the Bible is exploited in the production of class or moralizing propaganda, the characters doing so are severely critiqued. For example, neither Sister Flora Garden (125) nor Madam de Carter (124) fare well despite their use of the Bible, because both ape bourgeois ways. Nor does a Presbyterian minister and author of the book *The Doors of Life* fare well because his book— despite its citation of biblical material ("Avoid evil companions lest they be your undoing [see Psalms cxix, 115–20]; and beware of lewd women, for their footsteps lead down to hell [Proverbs vii, 25–7]")—does not speak to the lived experiences of simple folks, including those of Sandy (258).

The use of the Bible as commentary on ordinary life, however, resonates better with the perspective of the novel. Repeatedly, Aunt Hager draws on biblical images or diction to speak about the situations introduced in the novel. Her ability to see the storm coming from the signs in the western sky is reminiscent of Luke 12:54 ("When you see a cloud rising in the west, you immediately say, 'It is going to rain'; and so it happens" [NRSV]):

> Aunt Hager Williams stood in her doorway and looked out at the sun.
> The western sky was a sulphurous yellow and the sun a red ball drop-
> ping slowly behind the trees and housetops. Its setting left the rest of the
> heavens grey with clouds. "Huh! A storm's comin'," said Aunt Hager
> aloud. (Hughes 1995b: 19)

Her plea for Sandy and others to forgive white people who have refused
the entrance of black children to a Children's Day Party at a local amusement park mimics the forgiveness lines attributed to Jesus on the cross
("Father, forgive them; for they do not know what they are doing," Luke
23:34 [NRSV]; this verse is not found in the earliest manuscripts of Luke's
Gospel) or to Stephen before his death by stoning ("Lord, do not hold this
sin against them," Acts 7:60 [NRSV]): "They's po' trash owns that park
what don't know no better, hurtin' chillens' feelin's, but we'll forgive
'em" (199). Furthermore, her description of the arrest of Harriett as a case
of one who "turned from de light an' is walkin' in darkness" (207) may
well be an inverted rendering of 1 Pet 2:9 ("[God] called you out of darkness into his marvelous light" [NRSV]).

The Prodigal Daughter characterization of Harriett, however, belongs
to a third use of the Bible in the novel, namely, to indicate a phenomenon
in a metaphorical way. Obviously, one example of this metaphorical use
of the Bible appears in the title of chapter 22, namely, "Beyond the
Jordan." The title metaphorically speaks about Aunt Hager's death. The
narrator's earlier description of Harriett as a prodigal, however, is a
uniquely nuanced exploitation of a metaphor to speak of Harriett's return
from a life of wantonness. That is, Hughes's use of the Prodigal Son
metaphor is actually an extended typology fully drawing on some of the
distinctive features of the schema and readjusting the schema in an
important way to celebrate what Harriett learns as a result of her prodigality. As the remainder of this article will demonstrate, the Prodigal Son
metaphor in *Not without Laughter* includes the following features: (1) Harriett as the youngest daughter; (2) Harriett's travels away from home; and
(3) Harriett's deprivation and return.

3.1. The Prodigal As a Younger Sibling

> There was a man who had two sons. The younger of them said to his
> father, "Father give me the share of the property that will belong to me."
> So he divided his property between them. (Luke 15:11–12 NRSV)

In the folklore of Israel's ancient traditions, a prominent theme is the
contrast between an elder son and a younger son, with favoritism clearly
given to the younger one. The theme is seen in those stories in which
there are only two sons (e.g., "the stories of Cain and Abel, Ishmael and

Isaac, Esau and Jacob" [Scott: 112]). According to Scott (111), this theme of biblical literature was a part of the basic "repertoire of narrative possibilities" in the parable of the Prodigal Son (cf. Luke 15:11). As Scott notes, however, the usual favoritism toward the younger son is subverted in Luke's account, for "the father [of the parable] rejects no one; both [sons] are chosen" (125).

Hughes's *Not without Laughter* presents Harriett Williams as the youngest of Aunt Hager's three daughters, and she is clearly the favorite of the three. As Sterling A. Brown noted in his review of the novel, "Harriett, young, full of life and daring, is her [Aunt Hager's] worry" (1930: 15). Of the three daughters, Harriett is the one most frequently mentioned by her mother and the only one to receive a golden watch from her mother (Hughes 1995b: 38). Indeed, because Harriett pawns the watch to travel with a carnival, the mother has to purchase the watch a second time and later she presents it to her daughter as a gift from her deathbed. As well, Harriett was favored by her father. As Aunt Hager notes: "His [Harriett's father] last dyin' words was: 'Look out fo' ma baby Harriett.' You was his favourite chile" (56–57). Furthermore, Aunt Hager attributes the wantonness of Harriett to the latter's youth as compared to Tempy, the oldest daughter, or Anjee, the second child. As the novel opens, Harriett is only sixteen (while Tempy is thirty-five and Anjee is twenty-eight). Throughout the novel, Aunt Hager describes Harriett as one who hangs with a "wild crowd o' young folks" (38–39) or as one "runnin' wild" (54) or "runnin' round" (39) or as one who "wants to run de streets tendin' parties an' dances" (35). Harriett's next-older sister, Anjee, agrees, describing the younger sister as one who should "stop runnin' the streets so much" (46). The narrator's voice also agrees with this assessment of Harriett, for the narrator says: "Harriett was the youngest and wildest of the three children" (45).

3.2. The Travels of a Prodigal

> A few days later the younger son gathered all he had and traveled to a distant country, and there he squandered his property in dissolute living. (Luke 15:13 NRSV)

The parable of the Prodigal Son depends heavily on the travel or movement of the Prodigal. The Prodigal must travel away from home to suffer loss and to see the greater value of his father's structured environment. For Luke, moreover, the absence of the younger son sets up the dynamics for the elder son's suspicions both of the father's favoritism (which the Lukan narrator subverts) and of the younger son's sexual rendezvous with prostitutes (which the Lukan narrator does not affirm).

In *Not without Laughter*, travel is also a significant feature. Indeed, Harriett rarely stays at home. Like other women blues singers, she cannot remain constrained by the limits of her mother's house (Wall: 42). Harriett rebels against the governing strictures of her mother's home, whether that of a hypocritical form of Christianity or that of pandering to the racist whims of the whites in Stanton, Kansas. Against the hypocrisy of white men who decry the mixing of races in orphanages but not in brothels, Harriett declares: "It ain't Christian, is it?" (88). Against the passive acquiescence of Stanton's blacks, she avers: "You [Aunt Hager] and Anjee are too easy. You just take whatever white folks give you—coon to your face, and nigger behind your backs—and don't say nothing"(86).

As with the parable of the Prodigal Son, moreover, sexual innuendo is a part of Hughes's plot. In the case of Hughes's plot, however, the sexuality of Harriett is viewed as the expression of freedom in an otherwise sexually repressive environment (55). Whereas the elder brother assumes that his brother has used up his father's living with prostitutes (Luke 15:30), Hughes's novel suggests that Harriett explored sexual freedom, as was typical of the early blues woman (A. Davis: 38–41). Thus, Hughes's novel not only depicts Harriett as a younger sibling with all the recklessness that her youth entails, but also exploits the travel theme to show how Harriett's spatial freedom contributes to her blues woman's rebellion against the ideological strictures of persons confined to the limiting geography of her mother's hometown.

3.3. The Deprivation and Return of a Prodigal

> When he had spent everything, a severe famine took place throughout that country, and he began to be in need.... So he set off and went to his father. But while he was still far off, his father saw him and was filled with compassion; he ran and put his arms around him and kissed him. (Luke 15:14, 20 NRSV)

In the account of the Prodigal Son, the experience of deprivation drives the Prodigal to return home. Physical deprivation or lack leads to a moment of reflection (even if, in the estimation of some parable scholars, the reflection is not true repentance), which, in turn, leads to the return trip home (Scott: 115–16; Derrett: 103; Evans: 590–91).

To be sure, Harriett's initial geographical "return" is based on physical deprivation. An entire chapter is devoted to the "Return," and the diction of a letter from Harriett strikingly reveals the deprivation in images reminiscent of the ones found in the parable of the Prodigal Son. In the parable, the narrator states: "When he [the Prodigal] had spent everything, a severe famine took place throughout that country, and he began to be in need" (Luke 15:14). And in the novel, Harriett's letter states: "Dear Sister. I am stranded in Memphis, Tenn. And the show has gone on to New Orleans. I can't buy anything to eat because I am broke and don't know anybody in this town. Anjee, please send me my fare to come home" (146–47). As well, the novel's descriptions of her family's reception in the "Return" chapter appear to mimic the description of the reception given to the biblical prodigal. Both Sandy and Anjee kiss and hug Harriett (164) while Aunt Hager receives her with open arms and with the expression: "Done come home again! Ma baby chile come home" (164). In the parable of the Prodigal Son, the father "put his arms around him [the Prodigal] and kissed him (Luke 15:20) and exclaimed: "this son of mine was dead and is alive again; he was lost and is found!" (Luke 15:24).[3]

Yet, in *Not without Laughter*, Harriett's true "return" should not be understood simply as her physical return to Stanton, for she makes several returns to her home, and she goes back to the "far country" again in a geographical sense. What marks her genuine "return," however, is when she moves away from the "individuality" of her prodigality to adopt the "community-mindedness" of her mother. Indeed, at the end of the novel, she adopts her mother's community-minded vision for Sandy, that is, that Sandy should become a leader for his race. Harriett once sang for the church choir (56), thus giving of herself to the community. Now, as she sings the blues, her money will be used to help educate a leader among her people. No longer is she living for herself but for the growth of her family and, through it, for the growth of her race. Thus, Hughes's novel extends the Prodigal Son analogy and, in doing so, brings together the strands of an otherwise apparently disparate plot. The plot, then, is indeed about Sandy's coming of age but only in combination with another character who also comes of age—a prodigal daughter who weds the ideological expansiveness gained by her blues-singing travels to the community-mindedness of her mother's race vision.

CONCLUSION

Beyond the issue of the coming of age of Sandy and Harriett, perhaps Hughes's *Not without Laughter* is also a novel about success in

---

3 The novel's repeated references to a gold watch may be yet another allusion to the Prodigal Son parable. As noted earlier, Harriett actually pawned the watch before she and the carnival left Stanton (124), but her mother's reclamation of the watch for Harriett perhaps alludes to the father's restoration to the Prodigal Son of some important items lost by the latter through dissolute living in the far country: a robe, sandals for his feet, and a ring for his finger (Luke 15:22).

urban America. The problem of urban life faced by those who migrated from the rural areas of the South was a significant theme exploited by members of the Harlem Renaissance (and it continues to be a theme in later African American novels; Locke: 47–56: A. Smith 1995: 107–15). Hughes certainly gave the matter his attention in his later autobiographical work, *The Big Sea*. With *Not without Laughter*, Hughes depicts Harriett Williams as a symbol of urban success because her coming of age—through the basic plot of the (blues and biblical) Prodigal Daughter/Son—makes it possible for another person to come of age, her nephew Sandy.[4]

As I have shown, Hughes's exploitation of the Prodigal Son is an extended one. The plot aids Hughes in bringing together large parts of an otherwise apparently disparate story. Read against the backdrop of the Prodigal Son's account, however, *Not without Laughter* not only coheres as a whole but illustrates dramatically Hughes's salutation to the plights of many traveling prodigals—blues persons or not—who traveled to urban areas in the hope of finding success or a better life. For Hughes, notwithstanding the ideological benefits of the urban life, success was impossible until the travelers had experienced a "return," a shift away from the individuality of the urban phenomenon to the "community-mindedness" of a race vision.

It must be noted, moreover, that the characterization of Harriett Williams in the novel extends beyond the limits of the Prodigal Son's description as found in Luke's Gospel, for in the novel, Harriett, unlike Luke's Prodigal Son, actually experiences redemption and growth through her race vision. Thus, although Hughes clearly uses the Prodigal Son epithet, he refuses to allow his novel to be imprisoned within the parameters of the biblical story. Instead, his invention or creation of the novel emerges out of a commitment to the retelling of the lived experiences of African American people in general and African American blues singers in particular. In this sense, Hughes's novel is itself an extension of the same drive that created both the spirituals and one of its literary descendants, the blues, namely, the "search for the truth of the black experience" (Cone 1972: 100).

---

4 Chapter 15 ("One by One") dramatically indicates the impact of black migration.

RESPONSES

YET WITH A STEADY BEAT: THE TASK OF AFRICAN AMERICAN BIBLICAL HERMENEUTICS

Carolyn M. Jones
University of Georgia

The questions raised by the essays in *Yet with a Steady Beat* are interlocking ones about the function of metaphor in African American self and cultural understanding. These essays raise the following questions. First, what are the available models for creating an African American discourse on agency and community? What metaphors are available and viable, and how do both those who are religious people and those who are engaged in artistic representations in the black community use them? Second, the essays raise questions similar to those of African scholars such as Chinua Achebe concerning the "oppressor's tongue" (74). How do and can African Americans use the oppressor's language to attain liberation? Finally, Edward Said speaks of the problem of traveling theory, citing a conflict inherent in re-presentation. What a text means in its original location is transformed, Said argues, as that theory travels—and sometimes in destructive ways (241–42). These essays examine the implications of the "travel" of biblical myth into America and the implications of its ideological, political, and religious use for African Americans. For what are these stories, these representations? How does use of the available metaphors lead to a more just society?

Hermeneutics is about, above all, bridging. The hermeneutic space is that space between opposites—usually self/other—in which a transaction, negotiation, conversion, or meeting takes place (Bentley: 6, 8). The hope of the hermeneutic interpretative work is that a relation will be established and that an understanding can be reached. Hermeneutics, in the black experience, has, in my understanding, different concerns than traditional hermeneutics, and those understandings are explored in these essays. I understand that traditional hermeneutics is about, finally, the self, not the other with whom the self comes into negotiation. Self moves toward its horizon through the understanding of the other, which becomes, in one way or another, part of the self (Gadamer: 271–72). Such a luxury has and has not been available to African Americans, who have not been accorded, historically and politically, full selfhood until the twentieth century. As Wole Soyinka suggests in his preface to the play *Death and the King's Horseman*, the term *contact*, as in cultural contact in colonial/slave society, is, in many ways a misnomer. *Contact* in general has meant meeting and exchange, but that exchange has been on the terms of the "majority" culture and has sometimes meant destruction of the black "other" (Soyinka: i–ii). The African American colonial condition was, as Charles Long puts it, an opaque one, in which the slave not only had to "experience the truth of his negativity" but at the same time "transform [it] and create *an-other* reality" (1997: 27).

Black hermeneutics, therefore, faces a unique task. Such a hermeneutic must engage the issues suggested by what Paul Gilroy calls "the black Atlantic." That designation offers, immediately, a variety of complications, a double discontinuity. The bridge must be made between not just the antinomies of African and American, Old World and New, Europe and Africa, memory and history, and so on, but also within the self, moving through and lifting the veil of the double consciousness that is the schism, as DuBois described it, within the souls of black folks. As Vincent Harding has pointed out in *There Is a River*, the bodies of water across which black people were transported and the holding places in which they found themselves were the first hermeneutic spaces. These became not only the symbols of separation but also sites of a new creation. It was in the Middle Passage that those from different tribes, with different religions and different languages, began to form the African American (xix, 5). But, as Gilroy reminds us, the Black Atlantic was also a space of return. Frederick Douglass learned about freedom while working on slave ships with Irish sailors in a Maryland shipyard. Ida B. Wells, described her time in England like "being born again in a new condition" (Gilroy: 18). This transactional space, therefore, shapes and reshapes identity.

Any metaphor becomes, in this context of continuing formation and reformation, either a sturdy vessel, holding up under tremendous assault, or a simple raft, doing a job but not forever and not in a steady way. All metaphors are necessarily imperfect, and all, finally, are about making the Atlantic "black"—that is, facing and claiming the wound. No metaphor can heal the fracture, the fissure, the break that the slave trade tore into the body and consciousness of those it turned into products. There is always a scar, a mark. And, in many ways, that mark is what the authors of these essays are finding ways to narrate.

We should not forget that in metaphor and in myth, as James D. Hardy Jr. helps us to understand, everything is true except the figure, the story, itself. This displacement of truth to a space, the space of religion, other than the historical, the sociological, or the political, for example, opens possibilities for signification and for a different kind of precise story-telling. Art, story, and music, then, are where I, from the discipline of arts, literature, and religion, would want to locate such a possibility of narration because I think a performed identity signifies on metaphor in important ways. One's style both retains and transforms, individualizes and influences tradition. This is what I am delighted to see explored in these essays.

Gilroy argues that art was what was allowed slaves in the forms, particularly, of music and dance. As such, art becomes the backbone of black political culture and history, he says; I would add, also, of religion. Art retains memory, the needs and desires of a people, that can make a "redemptive critique" of the present and generate hope for the future (56–57). As Wilma Bailey points out in "The Sorrow Songs," art is prophetic, describing metaphorically the realities of a present situation and suggesting its future implications. Such art is, as she continues, paradoxical. It describes the dichotomy between the horrors of the present and the necessity to preserve and persevere and the black understanding of the goodness of God, which will fulfill the spiritual desire for home. Art, then, as Abraham Smith points out in his discussion of blues women, uses ideas of transcendence to construct a this-worldly critique and orientation.

As Bailey suggests and as Cheryl A. Kirk-Duggan argues in her essay "Let My People Go," African Americans, in their arts, are always in a complicated relationship with the "majority" culture's stories. That hermeneutic means that African Americans almost never "buy" all the implications of a myth like the exodus myth and may even be able to appropriate in creative ways those implications. The significance of that myth in black culture, for example, is an expression of a desire for freedom, as the essays suggest. The exodus myth, as utilized by black Americans, I think, also points to the contradictions within the majority culture that also claims that myth as its own. That is to say, it becomes what I have called a "cry from within: a reminder and a cultural conscience" (C. Jones: 381). What that story shows us is twofold. First, the hermeneutic field is a complicated one. While we may bring and claim as our own the same language to the table of negotiation, the nuances of meaning that that language carries for the "self" and the "other self" may be very differently understood. Second, however, as Kirk-Duggan puts it, "The 'I shall be who I shall be' places God in the future, in process, if you will, which means humanity can never catch up with God." Hence, Moses, who embodies the "homeless spirit" of the exodus process and who never enters the land, comes to represent a possibility and a power always available to oppressed peoples when they call. That power is also a reminder to the oppressor that there is always some other, upsetting, power available, as Kirk-Duggan illustrates in her reading of *A Raisin in the Sun*.

African Americans, therefore, have always had a unique relationship to the biblical text, that master narrative for understanding culture and self. As Charles H. Long says in "Perspectives for A Study of African-American Religion in the United States," while specific African cultural content may not have survived the Middle Passage intact, a "characteristic mode of orienting and perceiving reality"—in my terms, a style—probably did (1997: 25). The biblical text, therefore, plays a role in African American symbolic presentations and representations, but in a unique way. Long explains that such imagery was never understood as presented or accepted wholesale; instead, it was transformed as a new consciousness met it. "The biblical imagery was used because it was at hand; it was adapted to and invested with the experience of the slave" (29).

This leads to a creative use of story, of metaphor that is the basis of a culture of resistance. As Kirk-Duggan points out, "Many Black theologians see in Jesus the existential reality of the Mosaic God of Liberation." Dwight Hopkins makes this argument in "Slave Theology in 'The Invisible Institution.'" Hopkins, citing a spiritual, "Jesus Said He Wouldn't Die No Mo',"[1] argues, as Bailey does, that the slaves, working orally with biblical text preached to them, linked Jesus, on whom their hopes for freedom centered, with Moses. The point that I take from these arguments is that oral imagination is figural imagination. Figural imagination makes connections and creates links in the biblical text that a culture of writing might not make. For example, an oral culture would not concentrate on the distinctions of "Old" and "New" Testaments. Such an imagination also sees classical biblical figures as types foreshadowing a future to come. This mythical, figural view of time and story does not forget and is open-ended and inclusive. That is to say, story is not static: it involves/describes not just the past but also the present moment. As Hopkins explains,

---

1 Jesus said He wouldn't die no mo'
Said He wouldn't die no mo',
So my dear chillens don' yer fear,
Said He wouldn't die no mo'

De Lord tole Moses what ter do,
Said He wouldn't die no mo',
Lead de chillen ob Isr'el froo',
Said He wouldn't die no mo'. (20)

far from being a whimsical interpretation of the Bible, black folks' retro-projection of Jesus to Moses' days reflects an authentic and faithful reading [*sic*] of scripture. The slaves correctly followed the instructions from the prologue of John's gospel, which didactically states, "In the beginning was the Word and the Word was with God." If the Word, who is Jesus, existed in the beginning of time, then surely Jesus had the ability and the power to exhort Moses during the latter's time. (20)

Hence, for African Americans, the "conquest" is quite a different construction than it was for colonial cultures. It is conquest of the oppressive structure and its effects on the self.

These essays made me, rethinking in their context, refine my reading of the exodus story. The exodus is the leaving. As in Zora Neale Hurston's masterful rendering of a "Middle Passage" in *Moses, Man of the Mountain*, the exodus is the "crossing over," which is defined by what you are now not.[2] The exodus is a *limen*, the stripping down and cleansing that makes the potential moment: the imaginative claim on a new home and the first step out of the old one. When the actual claim is begun on the new place, which is never new, the exodus is over, and a new metaphorical system begins.[3] In *Beloved*, Baby Suggs says that the grace that you can have is the grace that you can imagine (Morrison 1988: 88). In the end, in facing the other, our imaginations fail us, and we exert self and claim power, losing the possibility of grace. It is the rare man and woman who can imagine what he or she has never experienced and, once having it, remain compassionate. Few of us can, as Alice Walker puts it, make wounds into worlds (x).

Except perhaps in one story: that of the deeply flawed Jacob, a trickster and thief. His experience of wrestling with a "man" is the metaphor of the hermeneutical space that I want to put forth in these, the final words, of my remarks. Jacob is like all of us, loyal and selfish, jealous and generous, and cocky and scared. In Gen 32, he, as Moses will do later, is

---

2 "Moses had crossed over. He was not in Egypt. He had crossed over and now he was not an Egyptian. He had crossed over. The short sword at his thigh had a jeweled hilt, but he had crossed over and so it was no longer the sign of high birth and power. He had crossed over, so he sat down on a rock near the seashore to rest himself. He had crossed over so he was not of the house of Pharaoh. He did not own a palace because he had crossed over. He did not have an Ethiopian Princess for a wife. He had crossed over. He did not have friends to sustain him. He had crossed over. He did not have enemies to strain against his strength and power. He had crossed over. He was subject to no law except the laws of tooth and talon. He had crossed over. The sun who was his friend and ancestor in Egypt was arrogant and bitter in Asia. He had crossed over. He felt as empty as a post hole for he was none of the things he had once been. He was a man sitting on a rock. He had crossed over" (Hurston: 78).

3 I would argue that the exodus ends with Moses' death.

crossing over. He, like the blues women Abraham Smith writes about, is the prodigal, son and brother, headed home, after his travels, unsure whether he will be welcome. At the Jabbok, his best and worst selves are challenged. Jacob is alone, and the "man," it seems, attacks and wrestles with him. Wrestling is, as Roland Barthes suggests, a working out of relationship over an extended period of time (1972: 23) and, I would add, in intimate contact in a designated, bounded space. It ends either with submission, one person stilled by another, or with balance, the recognition that the combatants are equal. In wrestling, force breaks form, upsetting balance, so that something new can emerge (Barthes 1974: 25, 28).[4] Strength may not be the only force that triumphs. Leverage, quickness, and the capacity to use the opponent's own strength against him may lead to victory; indeed, Jacob is weaker than his angelic opponent, but he holds the man "until the break of day." In his dark night of the soul, Jacob wrestles with many people in the figure of the angel: with his brother whom he has wronged, with God, and with himself. In this, he is transformed. Even after the man wounds him—cheating, I think, as Jacob cheats in his life—Jacob holds the man. Jacob, wounded and tired, nevertheless keeps his/the spirit: he holds on and demands a blessing. The man, keeping some of his own power, gives Jacob a new name but withholds his own. Jacob is triumphant—he gets his blessing as the founder of Israel—but he is also marked: he limps. The mark is what he takes into his new life. The mark is a sign of his identity as much as the name is: to change is painful; wounds mark the world. The sun rises upon Jacob, limping toward home.[5]

Elaine Scarry in *The Body in Pain* argues that in the Hebrew Scriptures, God usually marks with a weapon. God, she maintains, remains disembodied while human beings are embodied. The marking of the human body with a weapon, the alteration of the human body, is the way the invisible God is made visible. Marking is how God's "invisible presence is asserted" (183). Yet in the Jacob story, God is not distant but, if God is the man, intimate and present, touching Jacob directly and intimately and, as significantly, being touched and held.

The intimate presence, who may in Ashis Nandy's terms be an "intimate enemy," the wrestling, and the wound seem to me to be what the African American hermeneutical space, finally, involves. Since the first ships sailed onto the West African coast, black people have been crossing

---

4 Barthes reads the story of Jacob as one of branding, of culling out and setting apart.

5 In a talk at the University of Georgia, Jon Michael Spenser spoke of the African American love of asymmetry. I see Jacob, moving with his limp, asymmetrical, yet cocky and triumphant, as a black figure.

over and, in the vernacular, "wrestling with the man." The biblical text is part of what M. H. Abrams would call our "usable past" (194), and as such, it is what we wrestle with as well. While we cannot forget the wounds of the past, for we, like Jacob are marked and scarred, we wrestle and, like him, we rise, with a new name. Wilma Bailey, commenting on the lament, says that "The grieving [cannot] come to an end until [enslaved Africans] were free to live as whole human beings." The grief, I would suggest, remains, even as we rise. Perhaps true freedom is never forgetting the past, even as we step, like Jacob, battered yet boldly into the future. As Maya Angelou, in a poem that evokes Jacob's story, writes:

> Out of the huts of history's shame
> I rise
> Up from a past that's rooted in pain
> I rise
> I'm a black ocean, leaping and wide
> Welling and swelling, I bear in the tide.
>
> Leaving behind nights of terror and fear
> I rise.
> Into a daybreak that's wondrously clear
> I rise
> Bringing the gifts that my ancestors gave,
> I am the dream and the hope of the slave
> I rise
> I rise
> I rise. (42)

ON THE BLURRING OF BOUNDARIES

Tina Pippin
Agnes Scott College

Every semester I teach an introduction of one of the two biblical Testaments, and I always offer the same critique of the available textbooks to a class at my overwhelmingly white women's college in the South. Early each semester I quote a colleague at an across-town seminary, Randy Bailey, the editor of this volume and a yearly guest speaker in my Hebrew Bible course, on the white supremacy of biblical textbooks. As I explain my textbook choice to students (with concerns for cost a high priority), I also critique the ideological stance of most of the introductory texts. I hold up the textbook and quote Randy's charge of white supremacy. The students, even as my classroom becomes increasingly diverse, always look shocked for a variety of reasons: (1) they are not used to a professor being so blunt; (2) they have never imagined that a textbook could have such ideological ties; (3) they see such a statement as immediately excessive and aggravating; (4) they think I am making up this analysis out of my own singly weird, postmodern, feminist world; (5) they cannot imagine why a white woman from Jesse Helms's country would admit to her own complicity and accountability in racist structures and the material goods that support these structures; (6) they wonder why, if I feel this way, that I would even use a textbook. One reason I make this statement is partly pragmatic. I want to wake them up—both to the ideological complexities of the Bible (and bibles) and to our shared context at a church-related liberal arts college in the South that continues the legacy of the neo-plantation mentality and the racial, classist, gendered nature of the hierarchy of work and power on the campus. And I quote Randy to remind myself of my own role and use of my white privilege in the continuation of such structures. With this privilege and professorial authority I could easily shut my door to the ever-cyclical racial crises on campus, shut out the marginal voices in my Bible classroom, and there would be minimal, if any, protest.

As a biblical scholar and an ethicist in this context, I am constantly reminded of the centrality of the Bible in the lives of the majority of my students–from the fundamentalist Christians to the former believers, to the Muslims who follow the Gen 2–3 reading of creation rather than the more egalitarian Koranic version, to the second-generation Hindu students—all of whom are in some way under the power of a biblical culture in the United States. "In God We Trust"—which "God" and which "we" and what "trust"? Ideally, I want my students to learn to question and resist the dominant interpretations and to be challenged by the marginal voices, such as the ones represented in this volume.

The dominant, normative voice in these introductory textbooks remains the historical-critical method as performed by predominantly Anglo-European males. Even though I continue to supplement these dominant voices with various critical voices from African American biblical hermeneuts, feminists, womanists, postcolonials, and popular culture, I spend way too much time on "the basics," with all other material representing the marginal voices. Biblical studies is at a crossroads between the past and ever-present hegemonic discourses and the more recently resisting scholarship of the oppressed, the colonized, and the disenfranchised. The boundaries of "the basics" are more fluid in recent years; it is becoming harder to ignore the growing choruses. But as I repeatedly heard as a child, "You give them [insert racial or religious minority or foreign country here] an inch, and they take a mile." Such a racist, colonizing proverb works to reinstate white supremist ideologies. The few introductory textbooks that do let in other voices tend to control the (white) space in various ways that nonetheless continue to privilege white, male voices.

The articles in this volume continue the discourse begun in *Stony the Road We Trod* by adding more voices outside and beyond biblical studies and the church. This volume represents the continued move in African American biblical hermeneutics from the search to recover African faces in the Bible to uncovering the ideologies of biblical texts. There is the naming and claiming of race and community. The issue of biblical authority and the canon is raised (Liburd; Williams) in ways that call for a continued hermeneutical challenging of (biblically mandated) slavery, as well as the concerns of the roles of women and homosexuals in the African American church. Demetrius Williams finds a liberative note in Gal 3:28; while acknowledging that this passage is also problematic, "it does ... provide a paradigm that can include in its orbit a vision of equality regardless of race, class, and sex/gender." Thus, ancient black Africans are not the only ones invisible in the history of biblical interpretation, and the authors of this volume come face to face with the problematic texts to excavate the ancient possibilities and create a vision for the present-day "invisible" and disempowered ones.

So the biblical canon is open for these authors, and in this opening there is much to celebrate: inclusivity of gender/sexualities, of secular or "pagan" rituals (e.g., Kwanzaa; see Braxton), of historical voices from slavery and racism in the United States, of racial identity and heritage. In an earlier draft of his essay, Braxton summarized these strategies in his reading of 1 Cor 7:17–24 as starting "with a view to forging analogies between the ancient text and contemporary (African American) life." Sometimes this approach involves revisiting the slave narratives and spirituals of the past, and sometimes more contemporary cultural expressions are reclaimed.

These various past and more recent conversation partners engage the reader in the present-tense realities of racism as a lived experience by African Americans. For example, as Cheryl Kirk-Duggan relates, "let my people go" is a thread that goes from Moses through slaveries (Egyptian and colonialist eras) to twentieth-century African American plays such as Lorraine Hansberry's *A Raisin in the Sun.* But Kirk-Duggan is aware of what she calls "the two-edged nature of the texts" such as the exodus and the often-confusing swirl of liberation and oppression in the interpretive process. She acknowledges that "To extol liberation is one thing, but to embody that liberation in the guise of a patriarchal, warfare-focused God is problematic," for the Egyptians and especially the Canaanites are the losers in God's liberation scheme. This open canon also involves what Abraham Smith terms "the use of the Bible as commentary on ordinary life." The biblical gaps and silences are named and measured against life, family, and the larger African American community. Thus, voices from history, fiction, and song create ever new ways of rediscovering the biblical text and working through/with the problems the Bible brings in reclaiming community.

Along these lines, Harold Bennett reveals that the Deuteronomic passages on the widow, stranger, and orphan relegate these outsiders to a marginal position in society. Bennett calls for a reading "from the perspective of the underdog" as a critique of community service programs of churches. He states, "The Black church, in particular, should ensure that it affirms these persons, while addressing the causes of their predicament." His main interest, shared by the authors in this volume, is using biblical criticism and critique of the Bible to move toward systemic, transformative social change. Some key questions include: In taking the Bible seriously, what is discovered about the situation and experience of the poor, of women, of children, of survivors of abuse, of refugees, of LGBTQ (lesbian-gay-bisexual-transgendered-queer) peoples? And when the Bible is silent or speaks negatively about a marginalized group, how does the biblical scholar, and the church, work toward a humanizing solution? This volume raises many important questions around "the ethics of reading" and shows that a genuine respect of the Bible necessitates a critical engagement/ confrontation/challenging/reworking of

the texts toward human rights and not a wholehearted approval of biblical authority. In other words, a human-rights framework guides the
reading and sets high standards for what texts are authoritative. The
question becomes what texts speak the truths from the African American
experience, and what are the inherent complexities that come with such
truth-claims, as the exodus example shows.

Thus, the critical use of the Bible is possible in a multidisciplinary
dialogue. Perhaps what is needed is a sort of Truth and Reconciliation
Commission for biblical scholars. Kirk-Duggan reveals that "Black theology, however, has often been located in predominately White academia,
dissociated from lived Black religion." From my social location I am primarily interested in the first part of this statement, for this volume
appears in a historically predominantly white book series in a currently
predominantly white (SBL) structure. What I mean by "white" has been
explained best by Ruth Frankenberg as "a location of structural advantage, of race privilege ... a 'standpoint,' a place from which white people
look at ourselves, at others, and at society ... a set of cultural practices
that are usually unmarked and unnamed" (1). This definition is carried
further in the collection of essays in the book, *White Reign: Deploying
Whiteness in America.* Educational theorist Peter McLaren defines whiteness as

> a sociohistorical form of consciousness, given birth at the nexus of capi-
> talism, colonial rule, and the emergent relationships among dominant
> and subordinate groups.... Whiteness is also a refusal to acknowledge
> how white people are implicated in certain social relations of privilege
> and relations of domination and subordination. Whiteness, then, can be
> considered as a form of social amnesia associated with certain modes of
> subjectivity within particular social sites considered to be normative. (66)

Whites engage in "thinking through race" as a mark of difference
(Frankenberg). So what would an antiracist academic society look like?
Or as Becky Thompson asks in her study of antiracist activists, "Why do
I believe we need to think about antiracism not only as a specific set of
acts, principles, and alliances but also as a way of life? Because
antiracism does not stand up to the test of time unless it is fully integrated into people's lives" (362). The call from the authors in this
volume is to call attention to the need for constant conversations about
the Bible and race and on to the interstructured nature of oppression.
These scholars are listening to the voices of the past and passing on the
multiple messages of domination and freedom, exclusion and inclusion.
And they are asking what difference their scholarship makes—for race,
gender, and sexual relations and for the church's work and presence in
the world.

More links could be made in this volume between African American biblical her-meneutics and the interfaith and global conversations. In their discussion of their concept of empire, or how the new world order continues to be shaped around postmodern lines of globalization, Michael Hardt and Antonio Negri discern that racism and racist systems of oppression are no longer built around binary and hierarchical lines. Racism and white supremacy have taken more fluid forms of organization. Hardt and Negri are interested in examining "how imperial theory can adopt what is traditionally thought to be an anti-racist position and still maintain a strong principle of social separation" (193). In other words, they find the theoretical positions of "imperial racist theory and modern anti-racist theory" (192) to be almost identical in their move from a biological to a cultural determinism. "White supremacy functions rather through first engaging alterity and then subordinating differences according to degrees of deviance from whiteness" (194; see also Becky Thompson, who argues there is no such thing as an antiracist culture). White supremacy remains intact because it can morph across the traditional boundaries. Colin Powell can be secretary of state and Clarence Thomas a Supreme Court justice; the college where I teach can increase enrollment of African American students to just below 20 percent but not change the institutional structures that maintain what Étienne Balibar calls "differential inclusion" (Hardt and Negri: 194), which supports a white leadership and ideology. Furthermore in the postmodern empire, "Imperial racism, or differential racism, integrates others with its order and then orchestrates those differences in a system of control" (195). The system of control includes endless dialogues on race and diversity issues (mostly on the level of the interpersonal and not the systemic) in order to quell the frequent, cyclic uprisings by students (African American and white) for institutional transformation. This same critique could be applied to (almost?) any academic society in the West, including our own Society of Biblical Literature. There is that "differential inclusion" at work with the maintenance of white supremacy and power in ever more subtle and shifting ways. How can I, claiming to do antiracist work, not get caught in the trap? What is an antiracist position in such fluid global—and local—relationships?

Perhaps by choosing to use a textbook in my introductory Bible courses I am buying into the dominant paradigm more than I want to imagine. The academic discipline of biblical studies alone serves to alienate many of my students. Still, many want to learn the discourse as part of being educated and do not want to deal with any further complications or textbook critique on the basis of race, class, gender, and so forth. This past year I began an experiential learning track in my Bible courses (similar to a program at Belmont University); about one-third of the students in each class choose to work thirty hours in a placement at Decatur Cooperative Ministries, located right across the tracks from the college. DCM provides a range of services, from training on budgets to a temporary shelter for homeless women and children (aptly named Hagar's House). Students read a book about homelessness in Atlanta by two Columbia Theological Seminary professors, *The Word on the Street: Performing the Scriptures in the Urban Context,* who relate their experiences with seminary classes working with systemic issues of economic justice at a Christian base community, The Open Door. In examining the roots of homelessness, solutions of empowerment, and the faces of the homeless, students engage the biblical texts in the context of interacting with women and children who are displaced from their homes. Since the Bible is not a sacred text for some of the students (some are Hindu, Muslim, or Pagan, for example), there is an interesting range of reflections and critiques on the texts and the various ways this church-supported organization seeks to live out what they see as a biblical mandate of solidarity with the poor. Knowledge of, for example, the Four Source Hypothesis or the eighth-century prophets is background for larger and more immediate hermeneutical concerns. Perhaps the most I can hope is that this experience helps to disrupt the dominant paradigms of biblical studies.

So too the authors in this volume combine their concerns for the intellectual discernment of texts with political realities. They help me "see race" and the roots and effects of racial exclusion more clearly. At a "Race Matters Conference" at Princeton University in the late 1990s, some of the best thinkers gathered to discuss "that race not only mattered but is central to a profound betrayal of democracy taking place throughout contemporary American culture" (Lubiano: viii). Toni Morrison talks in the lead article about "the ways the racial house has troubled my work." She relates that the main questions involve: "How to be both free and situated; how to convert a racist house into a race-specific yet nonracist home. How to enunciate race while depriving it of its lethal cling?" (1998: 5). For scholars (like me) she gives a warning, that we gain awareness of our "own participation in the maintenance of the race house" (12).

The authors in this volume accomplish what Morrison describes as "clearing intellectual and moral space where racial constructs are being forced to reveal their struts and bolts, their technology and their carapace, so that political action, legal and social thought, and cultural production can be generated sans racist cant, explicit or in disguise" (1998: 11). Biblical exegesis and hermeneutics continues to be a political act, although this factor is often unacknowledged. Academics is certainly not a democratic space, but in what ways does the normative nature of biblical studies textbooks betray the real discourses in the discipline? In what ways do they maintain the race house?

Vincent Wimbush offers some useful suggestions. What is needed to break the silence is a reorientation of the discipline of biblical studies. Wimbush states:

> Informed by African American experience, the academic study of the Bible would then need to reconsider its primary agenda as the study of history and of texts.... It should always raise the question whether one can be or should be said to be a scholar of the Bible without taking seriously the problematics, including the determinants of historical-cultural receptions, of the Bible. (2000a: 14)

Wimbush questions the very assumptions of mainstream biblical studies, the taken-for-granted starting points. Maintaining the race house means holding on to the old, and some of the new, assumptions about the Bible. It demands an examination of all our presuppositions and an openness to the possibilities of transformation.

In the end it comes down to how I am "implicated in certain social relations of privilege and relations of domination and subordination" (McLaren: 66). What would my classroom look like if I was ever able to fully integrate my antiracist work? From my social location in the city of Atlanta in a neighborhood experiencing ever-encroaching white gentrification, with the corner at the end of my block consisting mostly of Korean American store owners and outside drugs and prostitution, with almost completely re-segregated (approximately 98 percent African American) public schools—I can almost be in a time warp of race relations. The boundaries of race are constantly being redrawn, but too often along the old lines. The articles in this volume serve as another, needed wake-up call to a world where these old boundaries are in dispute.

The main reason I choose to respond from my own social location and privilege comes from my need to investigate the nature of center and margins in my field. I believe, with bell hooks, that all the spaces we inhabit are political spaces and that our academic languages are highly politicized ways of keeping or challenging privilege or power. The academic languages in the essays in this volume reflect hooks's notion of language as "a place of struggle" to remember and create spaces of resistance (1990: 145). The African American academic is at least bilingual, able to speak to the dominant community in its language but also to speak another, resisting, home language. hooks spells out the nature of this resistance: "We are transformed, individually, collectively, as we make radical creative space which affirms and sustains our subjectivity, which gives us a new location from which to articulate our sense of the world" (153). The academic discourse in this volume at times speaks too much to the center, to the dominant group. There is appropriation of and fluency in the dominant discourses of biblical studies. Also what this volume does is the necessary work of reclaiming "home" and those "spaces of resistance" within the academy. There are hints at the nature of the continued struggle. The disruption and transformation of power relations—and of textbooks—will take a more "radical creative space."

African American Biblical Hermeneutics: Major Themes and Wider Implications

Norman K. Gottwald

The essays in this volume abundantly demonstrate the editor's observation that African American biblical studies have increasingly branched out to embrace a wide range of critical methodologies while keeping a decided focus on how the Bible functions in black experience and culture. Rather than respond to the essays one by one, I will focus on certain themes that recur in several of the contributions and on some implications of these themes for my own context.

Thematic Issues

The Role of the Bible in African American Culture and Literature

The prominence of the Bible in black preaching is accentuated by Kirk-Duggan and Liburd. The former shows that, while the exodus motif has resounded frequently in black sermons, it has been employed with strikingly different emphases. The latter argues that the analogical freedom with which New Testament writers "re-actualize" Old Testament texts is appropriately paralleled by a similar practice in black preaching. The unease that both these writers express about much Bible-based black preaching will be commented on below. Page's highly intriguing study of Prince Hall's masonic "charges" illuminates a form of quasi-preaching in a para-church context, causing one to wonder about other venues that may have attracted a "spillover" of black preaching. Bailey's extensive inquiry into the "sorrow songs" in relation to biblical laments greatly enriches our understanding of the complex cultural matrix in which they developed, as well as raising the issue of how much these folk songs may have been censored in the process of transmission. Of further note, she indicates that the Christian content of the songs is mixed with African religion and that a fair number of the songs lack any religious idiom.

Smith's claim that the Langston Hughes novel is structured on the Prodigal Son/Daughter pattern seems more effectively demonstrated than Kirk-Duggan's belief that Lorraine Hansberry's play follows an exodus script dependent on the Bible.

The Bible As a Highly Problematic Resource for Liberating Faith and Practice

The most striking feature of these essays is the near unanimity with which they caution against assuming that the Bible is uniformly and reliably supportive of liberation. In its inception, black theology appeared to place confidence in an unquestioned biblical foundation. Beginning, however, with the South African Itumeleng Mosala, a hermeneutic of suspicion toward the biblical text has steadily grown in black theology, and this trend, augmented by womanist theology, ideological criticism, and culture criticism, appears full-blown in the present essays. It is not that the Bible is abandoned as a basic resource, but it certainly is sharply interrogated and evaluated in terms of criteria for liberation formulated out of black experience. Kirk-Duggan, and Williams as well, insist that the exodus-conquest story simply cannot be invoked without awareness of the fate of the Egyptians and Canaanites. Bennett argues that the Deuteronomic provisions for widows, strangers, and orphans were of dubious practical help beyond the illusion of social compassion that they fostered. Williams further contends that while their firsthand experience of enslavement allowed African Americans to transcend the Bible's permissiveness toward slavery, blacks have continued to be hobbled by the Bible's subordination of women and antipathy to homosexuality. This revolt against naïve confidence in a spontaneously liberating Bible goes well beyond the witty lyric from *Porgy and Bess,* "the things that you're liable to read in the Bible, it ain't necessarily so." The more serious insight is that the reactionary moral and social views you are "liable" to derive from large parts of the Bible are indeed "necessarily so," that is, well entrenched in much biblical discourse and decidedly harmful to the welfare of African Americans.

The Urgency of Expanding Black Theology beyond Race to Include Gender, Class, and Other Forms of Oppressed Social and Cultural Identity

Williams and Liburd are particularly blunt in insisting that black biblical interpretation, theology, and preaching must enlarge their repertory of social oppressions that demand to be as vehemently opposed as racism. These authors have sexism and homophobia immediately in mind, in part because black women and black homosexuals are doubly oppressed but also because the credibility of black liberation is undermined if African Americans do not oppose oppression in all its forms both within and beyond the black community. Relevant to this issue is Braxton's astute insight that Paul's nonchalance toward both circumcision and uncircumcision as Christian identity markers may have had the ironic consequence, unintended by Paul, of freeing some Christians to be participants in synagogue and gymnasium without compromising their Christian identity. Williams's exploration of Gal 3:28 as a possible model for African American liberation opens up similar options for multiple identities in the black experience (as woman, as homosexual, even as mason [in the manner of Prince Hall], etc.). Each of these extraracial identities can be seen both to enrich black community and to build solidarity with nonblacks of similar identity. Much of this nuanced inquiry focuses on the thorny issue of how the spectrum of multiple identities and multiple forms of oppression can be comprehended within black experience without "sacrificing" the racial identity in which all black extraracial subidentities are necessarily enmeshed. In my fifteen years of teaching in a seminary with a majority of African American students, I have witnessed the emergence of a womanist movement and even a tentative grappling with black homosexuality. On the one hand, the frequent gut reaction was that focus on the legitimacy of these "alien" identities would divide and weaken the black community in its struggle for liberation. On the other hand, more seasoned reflection contended that black liberation from external forces could only be achieved to the degree that the black community acknowledged and struggled against its internal oppressions.

IMPLICATIONS FOR MY CONTEXT

Novel Perspectives on the Bible

The first value I see in these contributions is their reminder that there is always something "new" to be seen in biblical texts, either as novelties in the text itself or as novelties in the inferences drawn by interpreters in varied life situations. Bennett's exposure of the basic ineffectuality of the supposedly generous Deuteronomic "poor laws" invokes socioeconomic dynamics and ideological considerations to validate his claim. This unmasking of the poor laws fits well within a body of studies that has shown the social legislation of Deuteronomy to have been a part of the religious and political centralization program of Josiah. To gain support, this program offered some limited benefits in exchange for greater political control over the populace. Similarly, a new reading of Paul's insistence on the irrelevance of circumcision/

uncircumcision by Braxton suggests that, in clearing away particular social or religious identities as a precondition of membership in the church, Paul unintentionally validated those extra-Christian identities as valid in the eyes of some Corinthian Christians. This throws further light on the controversies in Corinth.

In a related study of Gal 3:28, Williams concurs with a majority of interpreters that Paul did not intend to abolish social roles and social hierarchy, but going beyond authorial intention he sees the text as an inclusive model for the multiple struggles of African American, embracing as it does race, class, and gender.

The Danger of Uncritical Reliance on a Liberating Bible

As noted above, common to all the biblical exegeses and expositions in this volume is a sustained "hermeneutic of suspicion," both as to how the text functioned in its social world and how it speaks, both negatively and positively, to the current social world(s) of African Americans. For quite some years it seemed that the South African Mosala stood virtually alone among black scholars in his articulate insistence on de-ideologizing the Bible. Now, however, it is clear that the stance of many black scholars has shifted dramatically in Mosala's direction. Given the high place of honor accorded the Bible in the black church, it is salutary to see such a bold tackling of the insufficiencies and harmful effects of the Bible when it is taken uncritically. Unquestionably the struggle against idolizing/ idealizing the Bible takes specific forms in the black church. It is, however, in one sense but a variant of the same struggle within white churches. The two struggles are linked by the historically negative input of white fundamentalism/conservatism to the formulations of biblical literalism, even inerrancy, in some black church circles, as also by white political conservatism fueled by a harsh biblical literalism that continues to impede the struggle for black liberation. Moreover, in my judgment, this kind of "Bible worship" is a grave impediment to the social and political relevance of the church in wide sectors of "the two-thirds world." It is heartening to see ethnic minority biblical scholars in the first world tackling this impediment on their home ground. It gives courage and inspiration to those of us fighting the battle in white churches to see black colleagues doing the same in their churches.

The Difficulty in Sustaining Communication between Differing Social Contexts

These essays also lead me to a concern over the context of my own interpretation. My widest context is clearly a cluster of practices in academia, the white church, and social-change movements in the United States and abroad. My actual performance in retirement from academia consists of teaching occasional courses at seminaries and universities, research and writing, and from time to time providing biblical resources for social-change organizations within and beyond the church. A measurable restriction in my operative context has thus resulted from "retirement" (which I prefer to think of as a "recycling"). Although I continue to do the things I have always done, only now on a reduced scale, my experience of and communication with minority communities has slackened. While teaching at New York Theological Seminary, I was in active participation and dialogue with developments in black and Latino biblical studies and theology. Nowadays, I depend on more limited professional and ecclesial contacts with minority students and scholars and a reading of their contributions such as appear in this volume. The links to black and Latino experience are no longer a daily reality, an intrinsic part of my work, but must be consciously sought out amid all the appeals for my attention and support. While this may appear to be a dilemma peculiar to retired folks, I cannot help but feel that many white biblical scholars, who have never had a New York Theological Seminary type of immersion in black and Latino culture and religion, may be oblivious to the social and religious matrix that has generated black biblical studies. This results in an asymmetrical relationship in which black scholars know white culture(s) experientially in a way that white scholars by and large do not know black culture(s) experientially. This is bound to have deleterious effects on the reception of black biblical scholarship by mainstream white scholarship. This is less a personal indictment than it is a description of the racial divisions that are replicated in supposedly neutral academia, as they are replicated throughout society. I do not see any certain way out of this haunting dilemma, but that this collection of essays has posed the dilemma afresh for me is one of the best reasons for keeping in as close touch with black biblical scholarship as I possibly can.

BIBLIOGRAPHY

Abrams, M. H. 1979. Abram's Reply. Pages 175–94 in *Critical Understanding: The Powers and Limits of Pluralism*. Edited by Wayne C. Booth. Chicago: University of Chicago Press.

Achebe, Chinua. 1988. *Hopes and Impediments: Selected Essays*. New York: Doubleday.

Allen, William Francis, Charles Pickard Ware, and Lucy McKim Garrison, eds. 1971. *Slave Songs of the United States*. 1867. Reprint, Freeport, N.Y.: Books for Libraries Press.

Anderson, A. A. 1985. *Psalms 73–150*. NCB. 1981. Reprint. Grand Rapids: Eerdmans.

Andrews, William L. 1986. *Sisters of the Spirit: Three Black Women's Autobiographies of the Nineteenth Century*. Bloomington: Indiana University Press.

Angelou, Maya. 1978. *And Still I Rise*. New York: Random House.

Bailey, Lloyd R. 1989. *Noah: The Person and the Story in History and Tradition*. Studies on Personalities of the Old Testament. Columbia: University of South Carolina Press.

Bailey, Randall C. 1991. Beyond Identification: The Use of Africans in Old Testament Poetry and Narratives. Pages 165–84 in *Stony the Road We Trod: African American Biblical Interpretation*. Edited by Cain H. Felder. Minneapolis: Fortress.

———. 1994. "And They Shall Know That I Am YHWH!": The P Recasting of the Plague Narratives in Exodus 7–11. *Journal of the Interdenominational Theological Center* 22:1–17.

———. 1995. "Is That Any Name for a Nice Hebrew Boy?" Exodus 2:1–10: The De-Africanization of an Israelite Hero. Pages 25–36 in *The Recovery of Black Presence*. Edited by Randall C. Bailey and Jacqueline Grant. Nashville: Abingdon.

———. 1998. The Danger of Ignoring One's Own Cultural Bias in Interpreting the Text. Pages 66–90 in *The Postcolonial Bible*. Edited by R. S. Sugirtharajah. Sheffield: Sheffield Academic Press.

———. 2000. Academic Biblical Interpretation among African Americans in the United States. Pages 696–711 in *African Americans and the Bible: Sacred Texts and Social Textures*. Edited by Vincent L. Wimbush. New York: Continuum.

———., ed. 1994. *Journal of the Interdenominational Theological Center* 22.

Baker-Fletcher, Karen. 1993. A Womanist Ontology of Freedom and Equality. *JRT* 49/2:60–71.

Bannerji, Himani. 1995. *Thinking Through: Essays on Feminism, Marxism, and Anti-Racism*. Toronto: Women's Press.

Bartchy, S. Scott. 1973. ΜΑΛΛΩΝ ΧΡΗΣΑΙ: *First-Century Slavery and the Interpretation of First Corinthians 7:21.* SBLDS 11. Missoula, Mont.: Scholars Press.

Barth, Fredrik. 1981. *Process and Form in Social Life: Selected Essays of Fredrik Barth,* vol. 1. London: Routledge & Kegan Paul.

Barthes, Roland. 1972. *Mythologies.* Translated by Annette Lavers. New York: Hill & Wang.

―――. 1974. The Struggle with the Angel: Textual Analysis of Genesis 32:22–33. Pages 21–33 in *Structural Analysis and Biblical Exegesis: Interpretational Essays.* Edited by François Bovon. Translated by Alfred M. Johnson Jr. Pittsburgh: Pickwick.

Barton, John. 1988. *Ethics and the Old Testament.* Harrisburg, Pa.: Trinity Press International.

Baur, Ferdinand Christian. 1878. *The Church History of the First Three Centuries.* London: William & Norgate.

Bell, Charles. 1970. *Fifty Years in Chains.* 1837. Reprint, New York: Dover.

Bennett, Harold V. 1999. Social Injustice and Biblical Law: The Case of Widows, Strangers, and Orphans in the Deuteronomic Code. Ph.D. diss. Vanderbilt University.

Bentley, Jerry H. 1993. *Old World Encounters: Cross-Cultural Contacts and Exchanges in Pre-Modern Times.* New York: Oxford University Press.

Berger, Peter. 1992. *A Far Glory: The Quest for Faith in an Age of Credulity.* New York: Free Press.

Berger, Peter L., and Thomas Luckmann. 1966. *The Social Construction of Reality.* Garden City, N.Y.: Doubleday.

Betz, Hans Dieter. 1979. *Galatians: A Commentary on Paul's Letter to the Churches in Galatia.* Philadelphia: Fortress.

Bilde, Per, Troels Engberg-Pedersen, Lise Hannestad, and Jan Zahle, eds. 1992. *Ethnicity in Hellenistic Egypt.* Aarhus: Aarhus University Press.

Bloch, Renée. 1978. Midrash. Pages 29–50 in *Approaches to Ancient Judaism: Theory and Practice.* Edited by William S. Green. BJS 1. Missoula, Mont.: Scholars Press.

Bone, Robert. 1965. *The Negro Novel in America.* New Haven: Yale University Press.

Bousset, Wilhelm. 1970. *Kyrios Christos: A History of the Belief in Christ from the Beginning of Christianity to Irenaeus.* Translated by John E. Steely. Nashville: Abingdon.

Boyarin, Daniel. 1994. *A Radical Jew: Paul and the Politics of Identity.* Berkeley and Los Angeles: University of California Press.

Brickell, Herschel. 1930. Review of *Not without Laughter. Saturday Review:* September 6, 1930.

Brown, Laurence, Bernard C. Farr, and R. Joseph Hoffman. 1997. *Modern Spiritualities: An Inquiry.* Amherst, N.Y.: Prometheus.

Brown, Robert McAfee. 1978. *Theology in a New Key: Responding to Liberation Themes.* Philadelphia: Westminster.

Brown, Sterling A. 1930. Review of *Not without Laughter. Opportunity:* September, 1930.

―――. 1937. *Negro Poetry and Drama.* Washington, D.C.: The Associates of Negro Folk Education.

Brueggemann, Walter. 1994. Exodus. *NIB* 1:677–981.

Budde, Karl D., Alfred Bertholet, and D. G. Wildeboer. 1898. *Die Fünf Megillot.* Freiburg: Mohr Siebeck.

Bultmann, Rudolf. 1956. *Primitive Christianity: In Its Contemporary Setting.* Translated by R. H. Fuller. New York: World Publishing Company.

———. 1958. *Jesus Christ and Mythology.* New York: Charles Scribner's Sons.

———. 1960. *Existence and Faith: Shorter Writings of Rudolf Bultmann.* Translated by Schubert Ogden. New York: World Publishing Company.

Callahan, Allen D. 1998. "Brother Saul": An Ambivalent Witness to Freedom. *Semeia* 83/84:235–50.

Cannon, Katie G. 1988. *Black Womanist Ethics.* AAR Academy Series 60. Atlanta: Scholars Press.

Cannon, Katie G., and Elisabeth Schüssler Fiorenza, eds. 1989. *Interpretation for Liberation. Semeia* 47.

Carson, Sharon. 1994. Dismantling the House of the Lord: Theology As Political Philosophy in *Incidents in the Life of a Slave Girl. JRT* 51:53–66.

Carter, Steven R. 1991. *Hansberry's Drama: Commitment amid Complexity.* Urbana: University of Illinois Press.

Chalcraft, David J. 1997. *Social Scientific Old Testament Criticism.* Sheffield: Sheffield Academic Press.

Chaney, Marvin. 1986. Systemic Study of the Israelite Monarchy. *Semeia* 37:53–76.

Christ, Carol P. 1984. Feminist Liberation Theology and Yahweh As Holy Warrior: An Analysis of Symbol. Pages 202–12 in *Women's Spirit Bonding.* Edited by Janer Kalven and Mary Buckley. New York: Pilgrim.

Cleage, Albert B., Jr. 1968. *The Black Messiah.* New York: Sheed & Ward.

Cohen, Shaye. 1993. "Those Who Say They Are Jews and Are Not": How Do You Know a Jew in Antiquity When You See One? Pages 1–45 in *Diasporas in Antiquity.* Edited by Shaye D. Cohen and Ernest S. Frerichs. Atlanta: Scholars Press.

Coil, Henry W. 1954. *A Comprehensive View of Freemasonry.* New York: Macoy.

Collins, John J. 1985. A Symbol of Otherness: Circumcision and Salvation in the First Century. Pages 163–86 in *"To See Ourselves As Others See Us": Christians, Jews, "Others" in Late Antiquity.* Chico, Calif.: Scholars Press.

Cone, James H. 1969. *Black Theology and Black Power.* New York: Seabury.

———. 1972. *The Spirituals and the Blues: An Interpretation.* Maryknoll, N.Y.: Orbis.

———. 1975. *God of the Oppressed.* New York: Seabury.

———. 1976. What Does It Mean to Be Saved? Pages 20–24 in *Preaching the Gospel.* Edited by Henry J. Young. Philadelphia: Fortress.

———. 1984. *For My People: Black Theology and the Black Church.* Maryknoll, N.Y.: Orbis.

———. 1986. *Black Theology of Liberation.* 2d ed. Maryknoll, N.Y.: Orbis.

———. 1990a. *A Black Theology of Liberation: Twentieth Anniversary Edition.* Maryknoll, N.Y.: Orbis.

———. 1990b. *For My People: Black Theology and the Black Church.* Maryknoll, N.Y.: Orbis.

Copher, Charles B. 1993. *Black Biblical Studies: An Anthology of Charles B. Copher.* Chicago: Black Light Fellowship.

Craigie, Peter C. 1976. *The Book of Deuteronomy*. NICOT. Grand Rapids: Eerdmans.

Craven, Toni. 1992. *The Book of Psalms*. Collegeville, Minn.: Liturgical Press.

Crawford, George W. 1971. *Prince Hall and His Followers*. New York: AMS.

Crenshaw, Kimberlé, et al. 1995. *Critical Race Theory*. New York: New Press.

Crüsemann, Frank. 1996. *The Torah: Theology and Social History of Old Testament Law*. Translated by Allan W. Mahnke. Minneapolis: Fortress.

Davis, Angela Y. 1998. *Blues Legacies and Black Feminism: Gertrude "Ma" Rainey, Bessie Smith, and Billie Holiday*. New York: Pantheon.

Davis, Gerald L. 1985. *I Got the Word in Me and I Can Sing It, You Know: A Study of the Performed African-American Sermon*. Philadelphia: University of Pennsylvania Press.

Delgado, Richard, ed. 2000. *Critical Race Theory: The Cutting Edge*. 2d ed. Philadelphia: Temple University Press.

Derrett, J. D. M. 1970. *Law in the New Testament*. London: Darton, Longman & Todd.

Dett, R. Nathaniel. 1927. *Religious Folk Songs of the Negro*. Hampton, Va.: Hampton Institute Press.

Dickinson, Donald C. 1967. *A Bio-Bibliography of Langston Hughes*. Hamden, Conn.: Shoe String.

Drake, St. Clair, and Horace R. Cayton. 1945. *Black Metropolis: A Study of Negro Life in a Northern City*. New York: Harcourt, Brace.

DuBois, W. E. B. 1907. *The Souls of Black Folk*. Chicago: A. C. McClurg.

———. 1969. *The Souls of Black Folk*. 1907. Reprint, New York. New American Library.

Duling, Dennis C. 1993. Matthew. Pages 1857–1914 in *The HarperCollins Study Bible: New Revised Standard Version*. Edited by Wayne A. Meeks. New York: HarperCollins.

Dunn, James D. G. 1993. *The Epistle to the Galatians*. Peabody, Mass.: Hendrickson.

Elliott, John H. 1993. *What Is Social-Scientific Criticism?* Minneapolis: Fortress.

Epsztein, Léon. 1986. *Social Justice in the Ancient Near East and the People of the Bible*. Translated by John Bowden. London: SCM.

Evans, C. F. 1990. *Saint Luke*. Trinity Press International New Testament Commentaries. London: SCM.

Even-Shoshan, Abraham. 1989. *A New Concordance of the Old Testament*. Jerusalem: Kiryat Sefer and Baker Book House.

Exum, J. Cheryl. 1994. Second Thoughts about Secondary Characters: Women in Exodus 1.8– 2.10. Pages 75–87 in *A Feminist Companion to Exodus–Deuteronomy*. Edited by Athalya Brenner. FCB. Sheffield: Sheffield Academic Press.

Felder, Cain H. 1989a. The Bible, Re-Contextualization and the Black Religious Experience. Pages 155–71 in *African American Religious Studies: An Interdisciplinary Anthology*. Edited by Gayraud S. Wilmore. Durham, N.C.: Duke University Press.

———. 1989b. *Troubling Biblical Waters: Race, Class, and Family*. Maryknoll, N.Y.: Orbis.

———, ed. 1991. *Stony the Road We Trod: African American Biblical Interpretation*. Minneapolis: Fortress.

Feldman, Louis H. 1996. Diaspora Synagogues: New Light from Inscriptions and Papyri. Pages 48–66 in *Sacred Realm: The Emergence of the Synagogue in the Ancient World*. Edited by Steven Fine. Oxford: Oxford University Press.

Ferris, Paul Wayne, Jr. 1992. *The Genre of Communal Lament in the Bible and the Ancient Near East*. SBLDS. Atlanta: Scholars Press.

Fisher, Miles Mark. 1949. *The Evolution of the Slave Songs of the United States: A Dissertation*. Chicago: University of Chicago Press.

Frankenberg, Ruth. 1993. *The Social Construction of Whiteness: White Women, Race Matters*. Minneapolis: University of Minnesota Press.

Franklin, John H., and Alfred A. Moss Jr. 2000. *From Slavery to Freedom: A History of African Americans*. Boston: McGraw- Hill.

Gadamer, Hans-Georg. 1986. *Truth and Method*. New York: Crossroads.

Gager, John G. 1998. Jews, Gentiles, and Synagogues in the Book of Acts. *HTR* 79:91–99.

Garon, Paul. 1979. *Blues and the Poetic Spirit*. New York: Da Capo.

Gates, Henry Louis, Jr., and K. Anthony Appiah, eds. 1993. *Langston Hughes: Critical Perspectives Past and Present*. New York: Amistad.

Gates, Henry Louis, Jr., and Nellie Y. McKay, eds. 1997. *The Norton Anthology of African American Literature*. New York: Norton.

Geertz, Clifford. 1973a. *The Interpretation of Cultures*. New York: Basic Books.

———. 1973b. Thick Description: Toward an Interpretive Theory of Culture. Pages 3–30 in *The Interpretation of Cultures*. New York: Basic Books.

———. 2000. *Local Knowledge: Further Essays in Interpretive Anthropology*. New York: Basic Books.

Geffré, Claude. 1987. *The Risk of Interpretation: On Being Faithful to the Christian Tradition in a Non-Christian Age*. Translated by David Smith. New York: Paulist.

General Conference of Seventh-day Adventists. 1995. *Seventh-day Adventist Church Manual*. 15th ed. Hagerstown, Md.: Review & Herald Publishing Association.

Gibboney, Ted. 2000. Conversation, Oct. 31, 2000.

Gilkes, Cheryl Townsend. 1987. "Some Mother's Son and Some Father's Daughter": Gender and Biblical Language in Afro-Christian Worship Tradition. Pages 73–99 in *Shaping New Visions: Gender and Values in American Culture*. Edited by Clarissa Atkinson et al. Ann Arbor, Mich.: UMI Research Press.

———. 2000. The Virtues of Brotherhood and Sisterhood: African American Fraternal Organizations and Their Bibles. Pages 389–403 in *African Americans and the Bible: Sacred Texts and Social Textures*. Edited by Vincent L. Wimbush. New York: Continuum.

Gilroy, Paul. 1998. *The Black Atlantic: Modernity and Double Consciousness*. Cambridge, Mass.: Harvard University Press.

Gottwald, Norman G. 1985. *The Hebrew Bible: A Socio-Literary Introduction*. Philadelphia: Fortress.

Goudriaan, Koen. 1992. Ethnical Strategies in Graeco-Roman Egypt. Pages 74–99 in *Ethnicity in Hellenistic Egypt*. Edited by Per Bilde, Troels Engberg-Pedersen, Lise Hannestad, and Jan Zahle. Aarhus: Aarhus University Press.

Gowan, Donald. 1994. *Theology in Exodus: Biblical Theology in the Form of Commentary*. Louisville: Westminster John Knox.

Grant, Jacquelyn. 1989a. *White Women's Christ and Black Women's Jesus: Feminist Christology and Womanist Response*. AAR Academy Series 64. Atlanta: Scholars Press.

———. 1989b. Womanist Theology: Black Women's Experience As a Source for Doing Theology, with Special Reference to Christology. Pages 208–27 in *African American Religious Studies: An Interdisciplinary Anthology.* Edited by Gayraud S. Wilmore. Durham, N.C.: Duke University Press.

———. 1995. Womanist Jesus and Mutual Struggle for Liberation. Pages 129–42 in *The Recovery of Black Presence.* Edited by Randall C. Bailey and Jacqueline Grant. Nashville: Abingdon.

Greene, Lorenzo J. 1961. Prince Hall: Massachusetts Leader in Crisis. *Freedomways* 1:238–58.

Grimshaw, William H. 1969. *Official History of Freemasonry among the Colored People in North America.* New York: Negro Universities Press.

Gunkel, Hermann. 1995. *Introduction to the Psalms: The Genres of the Religious Lyric of Israel.* Translated by James D. Nogalski. Macon, Ga.: Mercer University Press.

Haas, Peter J. 1989. "Die He Shall Surely Die." The Structure of Homicide in Biblical Law. *Semeia* 45:67–87.

Haik-Ventoura, Suzanne. 1991. *The Music of the Bible Revealed.* Translated by Dennis Weber. Edited by John Wheeler. Berkeley, Calif.: Bibal Press. [Orig. *La musique de la Bible révélée,* 1976]

Hall, Prince. 1792. *A Charge Delivered to the Brethren of the African Lodge on the 25th of June 1792. At the Hall of Brother William Smith, in Charlestown.* Early American Imprints. Worcester, Mass.: American Antiquarian Society.

———. 1797. *A Charge Delivered to the African Lodge, June 14, 1797, at Menotomy.* Early American Imprints. Worcester, Mass.: American Antiquarian Society.

Hansberry, Lorraine. n.d.. *A Raisin in the Sun: A Drama in Three Acts.* New York: Random House.

Harding, Vincent. 1983. *There Is a River: The Black Struggle for Freedom in America.* New York: Harcourt Brace.

Hardt, Michael, and Antonio Negri. 2000. *Empire.* Cambridge, Mass.: Harvard University Press.

Hardy, James D., Jr. n.d. Daughters of Zeus and Memory. Unpublished manuscript.

Harnack, Adolf. 1986. *What Is Christianity.* Fortress Texts in Modern Christianity. Translated by Thomas B. Saunders. 1957. Reprint, Philadelphia: Fortress.

Heaton, Ronald E. 1974. *Masonic Membership of the Founding Fathers.* Silver Spring, Md.: Masonic Service Association.

Heilbut, Anthony. 1989. *The Gospel Sound: Good News and Bad Times.* New York: Limelight.

Hernton, Calvin C. 1987. *The Sexual Mountain and Black Women Writers: Adventures in Sex, Literature, and Real Life.* New York: Doubleday.

Herodotus. 1999. *The Histories.* Translated by Aubrey de Sélincourt. New York: Penguin.

Higginbotham, Evelyn Brooks. 1993. *Righteous Discontent: The Women's Movement in the Black Baptist Church, 1880–1920.* Cambridge, Mass.: Harvard University Press.

Higginson, Thomas Wentworth. 1867. *Negro Spirituals.* Boston: University of Virginia.

Hine, Darlene, Elsa Brown, and Rosalyn Terborg-Penn, eds. 1993. *Black Women in America: An Historical Encyclopedia.* Bloomington: Indiana University Press.

Hood, Robert E. 1990. *Must God Remain Greek? Afro Cultures and God-Talk*. Minneapolis: Fortress.

hooks, bell. 1989. "Raisin" in a New Light. *Christianity and Crisis* 49:21–23.

———. 1990. *Yearning: Race, Gender, and Cultural Politics*. Boston: South End Press.

Hoover, Theressa. 1979. Black Women and the Churches: Triple Jeopardy. Pages 377–88 in *Black Theology: A Documentary History, 1966–1979*. Edited by Gayraud Wilmore and James Cone. New York: Orbis.

Hopkins, Dwight. 1991. Slave Theology in the "Invisible Institution." Pages 1–45 in *Cut Loose Your Stammering Tongue: Black Theology in the Slave Narratives*. Edited by Dwight N. Hopkins and George Cummings. Maryknoll, N.Y.: Orbis.

Horsley, Richard A. 1996. 1 Corinthians: A Case Study of Paul's Assembly. Pages 242–52 in *Paul and Empire: Religion and Power in Roman Imperial Society*. Edited by Richard A. Horsley. Harrisburg, Pa.: Trinity Press International.

———. 1998. Paul and Slavery: A Critical Alternative to Recent Readings. *Semeia* 83/84:153–200.

Hughes, Langston. 1969. *The Panther and the Lash: Poems of Our Times*. New York: Knopf.

———. 1995a. The Negro Artist and the Racial Mountain. Pages 305–9 in *Voices from the Harlem Renaissance*. Edited by Nathan Irvin Huggins. New York: Oxford University Press.

———.1995b. *Not without Laughter*. Introduction by Maya Angelou. New York: Scribner's.

Hunter-Lattany, Kristin. 1995. The Girl with the Red Dress On. Pages 141–48 in *Langston Hughes: The Man, His Art and His Continuing Influence*. Edited by C. James Trotman. New York: Garland.

Hurston, Zora Neale. 1939. *Moses, Man of the Mountain*. New York: Harper Collins.

Jackson, George Pullen. 1964. *White Spirituals of the Southern Uplands*. 1933. Reprint, Hatboro, Pa.: Folklore Associates.

———. 1975. *White and Negro Spirituals: Their Life Span and Kinship*. 1943. Reprint, New York: DaCapo.

Jemie, Onwuchekwa. 1976. *Langston Hughes: An Introduction to the Poetry*. New York: Columbia University Press.

Johnson, James Weldon. 1963. Lift Ev'ry Voice and Sing. In *Saint Peter Relates an Incident*. 1917. Reprint, New York: Viking Penguin.

———. 1985. *The Book of American Negro Spirituals*. 1925. Reprint, New York: De Carpo Press.

Johnson, Luke T. 1996. *The Writings of the New Testament: An Introduction*. Rev. ed. Minneapolis: Fortress.

Johnson, Melvin M. 1983. *The Beginnings of Freemasonry in America*. Bloomington, Ill.: Masonic Book Club.

Jones, Amos, Jr. 1984. *Paul's Message of Freedom: What Does It Mean to the Black Church?* Valley Forge, Pa.: Judson.

Jones, Arthur C. 1993. *Wade in the Water: The Wisdom of the Spirituals*. Maryknoll, N.Y.: Orbis.

Jones, Carolyn M. 1994. Moses: Identity and Community in Exodus. Pages 367–84 in *In Good Company: Essays in Honor of Robert Detweiler.* Edited by David Jasper and Mark Ledbetter. Atlanta: Scholars Press.

Jones, Dwight Clinton. 1979. The Lord Is on Our Side. Pages 57–63 in vol. 2 of *Outstanding Black Sermons.* Valley Forge, Pa.: Judson.

Jones, William. 1988. *Is God a White Racist? A Preamble to Black Theology.* 2d ed. Boston: Beacon.

Kaplan, Sidney, and Emma Nogrady Kaplan. 1989. *The Black Presence in the Era of the American Revolution.* Amherst: University of Massachusetts Press.

Katz, Bernard, ed. 1969. *The Social Implications of Early Negro Music in the United States.* New York: Arno Press and the New York Times.

Kellner, Bruce. 1979. *Keep a Inchin' Along: Selected Writings of Carl Van Vechten about Black Art and Letters.* Westport, Conn.: Greenwood.

Kemble, Frances Anne. 1984. *Journal of a Residence on a Georgian Plantation in 1838–1839.* Athens: University of Georgia Press.

Kent, George E. 1989. Hughes and the Afro-American Folk and Cultural Tradition. Pages 17–36 in *Langston Hughes.* Edited by Harold Bloom. New York: Chelsea House.

Kerkeslager, Allen. 1997. Maintaining Jewish Identity in the Greek Gymnasium: A "Jewish Load" in CPJ 3.519. *JSJ* 28:12–33.

Kincheloe, Joe L., Shirley R. Steinberg, Nelson M. Rodriguez, and Ronald E. Chennault, eds. 2000. *White Reign: Deploying Whiteness in America.* New York: St. Martin's Griffin.

King, Martin Luther, Jr. 1963. *Strength to Love.* New York: Harper & Row.

Kirk-Duggan, Cheryl A. 1997. *Exorcising Evil: A Womanist Perspective on the Spirituals.* Maryknoll, N.Y.: Orbis.

Knight, Douglas A. 1994. Introduction: Ethics, Ancient Israel, and the Hebrew Bible. *Semeia* 66:1–8.

Kraabel, A. T. 1981. The Disappearance of the "God-Fearers." *Numen* 28:113–26.

Kruse, Colin G. 1996. *Paul, the Law, and Justification.* Peabody, Mass.: Hendrickson.

Kugel, James L. 1981. On the Bible and Literary Criticism. *Prooftexts* 1:217–36.

Kugel, James L., and Rowan A. Green. 1986. *Early Biblical Interpretation.* LEC. Philadelphia: Westminster.

Lategan, Bernard C. 1992. Hermeneutics. *ABD* 3:149–54.

Lategan, Bernard C., and Willem S. Vorster. 1985. *Text and Reality: Aspects of Reference in Biblical Texts.* Philadelphia: Fortress; Atlanta: Scholars Press.

Lawton, David. 1990. *Faith, Text and History: The Bible in English.* Studies in Religion and Culture. Charlottesville: University Press of Virginia.

Leazer, Gary. 1995. *Fundamentalism and Freemasonry: The Southern Baptist Investigation of the Fraternal Order.* New York: M. Evans.

LeCompte, Margaret D., and Jean J. Schensul. 1999. *Designing and Conducting Ethnographic Research.* Ethnographer's Toolkit. Walnut Creek: AltaMira.

Lerner, Gerda. 1973. *Black Women in White America: A Documentary History.* New York: Vintage.

Lerner, Michael. 1991. Breaking the Chains of Necessity: An Approach to Jewish Liberation Theology. Pages 55–64 in *Judaism, Christianity, and Liberation: An Agenda for Dialogue.* Edited by Otto Maduro. Maryknoll, N.Y.: Orbis.

Levine, Etan. 1981. *The Aramaic Version of Lamentations*. New York: Herman Press.

Levine, Lawrence W. 1997. Slave Songs and Slave Consciousness: An Exploration in Neglected Sources. Pages 59–87 in *African American Religion: Interpretative Essays in History and Culture*. Edited by Timothy Fulop and Albert Raboteau. New York: Routledge.

Levingston, Judd. 1991. Introduction: Liberation Theology and Judaism. Pages 1–19 in *Judaism, Christianity, and Liberation: An Agenda for Dialogue*. Edited by Otto Maduro. Maryknoll, N.Y.: Orbis.

Levinson, Bernard. 1997. *Deuteronomy and the Hermeneutics of Legal Innovation*. New York and Oxford: Oxford University Press.

Locke, Alain. 1995. The New Negro. Pages 47–56 in *Voices from the Harlem Renaissance*. Edited by Nathan Irvin Huggins. New York: Oxford University Press.

Long, Charles H. 1986. *Significations: Signs, Symbols, and Images in the Interpretation of Religion*. Philadelphia: Fortress.

———. 1997. Perspectives for a Study of African-American Religion in the United States. Pages 21–36 in *African-American Religion: Interpretative Essays in History and Culture*. Edited by Albert J. Raboteau and Timothy E. Fulop. New York: Routledge.

Lovell, John, Jr. 1972. *Black Song: The Forge and the Flame*. New York: MacMillan.

Lubiano, Wahneema. 1998. Introduction. Pp. vii–ix in *The House That Race Built*. Edited by Wahneema Lubiano. New York: Vintage Books.

MacDonald, Dennis R. 1987. *There Is No Male and Female: The Fate of a Dominical Saying in Paul and Gnosticism*. Philadelphia: Fortress.

Mackey, Albert G. 1927. *An Encyclopedia of Freemasonry and Its Kindred Sciences*. Chicago: Masonic History Company.

———. 1955. *The Symbolism of Freemasonry*. Chicago: Powner.

Malchow, Bruce. 1996. *Social Justice in the Hebrew Bible*. Collegeville, Minn.: Liturgical Press.

Marcus, Jacob R. 1970. How Jews Treated Their Slaves. In *The Colonial American Jew: 1492–1776*. Vols. 2–3. Detroit: Hebrew Union College-Jewish Institute of Religion.

Martin, Clarice J. 1989. A Chamberlain's Journey and the Challenge of Interpretation for Liberation. *Semeia* 47:105–35.

———. 1991. The *Haustafeln* (Household Codes) in African American Biblical Interpretation: "Free Slaves" and "Subordinate Women." Pages 206–31 in *Stony the Road We Trod: African American Biblical Interpretation*. Edited by Cain H. Felder. Minneapolis: Fortress.

———. 1998. "Somebody Done Hoodoo'd the Hoodoo Man": Language, Power, Resistance, and the Effective History of Pauline Texts in American Slavery. *Semeia* 83/84:203–33.

Matera, Frank J. 1992. *Galatians*. Collegeville, Minn.: Liturgical Press.

Mayes, A. D. H. 1991. *Deuteronomy*. Grand Rapids: Eerdmans.

Mayle, Bessie. 1932. The History and Interpretation of the Pre-Reformation Carol and the Negro Spiritual. Unpublished thesis, Boston University.

McClester, Cedric. 1990. *Kwanzaa: Everything You Always Wanted To Know But Didn't Know Where To Ask*. New York: Gumbs & Thomas.

McGrath, Alister E. 1999. *Christian Spirituality: An Introduction.* Oxford: Blackwell.

McKnight, Edgar V. 1988. *Post-Modern Use of the Bible: The Emergence of Reader-Oriented Criticism.* Nashville: Abingdon.

McLaren, Peter. 2000. Whiteness Is...: The Struggle for Postcolonial Hybridity. Pages 63–75 in *White Reign: Deploying Whiteness in America.* Edited by Joe L. Kincheloe, Shirley R. Steinberg, Nelson M. Rodriguez, and Ronald E. Chennault Kincheloe. New York: St. Martin's Griffin.

McNutt, Paula. 1999. *Reconstructing the Society of Ancient Israel.* Louisville: Westminster John Knox.

Meeks, Wayne. 1974. The Image of the Androgyne: Some Uses of a Symbol in Earliest Christianity. *HR* 13:165–208.

Mickve Israel website. 2001. www.savannahcommunity.com/servlet/so_ProcServ/GID=01006011570942678577930486.

Miller, R. Baxter. 1976. "Done Made Us Leave Our Home": Langston Hughes' *Not without Laughter*—Unifying Image and Three Dimensions. *Phylon* 37:362–69.

Mitchell, Henry H. 1991. *Black Preaching: The Recovery of a Powerful Art.* Nashville: Abingdon.

Monroe, Irene. 2001. The Struggle of Human Acceptance. *The African American Pulpit* 4/3:65–69.

Morgan, Robert, with John Barton. 1988. *Biblical Interpretation.* Oxford: Oxford University Press.

Morrison, Toni. 1988. *Beloved.* New York: Penguin Plume.

———. 1998. Home. Pages 3–12 in *The House That Race Built.* Edited by Wahneema Lubiano. New York: Vintage Books.

Mosala, Itumeleng. 1989. *Biblical Hermeneutics and Black Theology in South Africa.* Grand Rapids: Eerdmans.

Moule, C. F. D. 1987. Jesus, Judaism, and Paul. Pages 43–52 in *Tradition and Interpretation in the New Testament: Essays in Honor of E. Earle Ellis for His Sixtieth Birthday.* Edited by Gerald F. Hawthorne with Otto Betz. Grand Rapids: Eerdmans.

Mowinckel, Sigmund. 1962. *The Psalms in Israel's Worship.* 2 vols. Oxford: Basil Blackwell.

Mueller-Vollmer, Kurt, ed. 1985. *The Hermeneutics Reader.* New York: Continuum.

Muraskin, William A. 1975. *Middle-Class Blacks in a White Society.* Berkeley and Los Angeles: University of California Press.

Nandy, Ashis. 1988. *The Intimate Enemy: Loss and Recovery of Self under Colonialism.* Delhi: Oxford University Press.

Newbold, Robert T., ed. 1977. *Black Preaching: Select Sermons in the Presbyterian Tradition.* Philadelphia: Geneva.

Newton, Joseph F. 1951. *The Builders: A Story and Study of Freemasonry.* New York: Macoy.

The North Star. 1848. April 28.

Oliver, Paul. 1990. *Blues Fell This Morning: Meaning in the Blues.* 2d ed. Cambridge: Cambridge University Press.

Paris, Peter. 1985. *The Social Teachings of the Black Churches.* Philadelphia: Fortress.

———. 1995. *The Spirituality of African Peoples.* Minneapolis: Fortress.

Perkins, Lynn F. 1971. *The Meaning of Masonry.* Lakemont, Ga.: CSA.

Piatigorsky, Alexander. 1999. *Freemasonry: The Study of a Phenomenon.* London: Harvill.

Pinn, Anthony B. 1995 . *Why Lord? Suffering and Evil in Black Theology.* New York: Continuum.

―――. 1998. *Varieties of African American Religious Experience.* Minneapolis: Fortress.

Pixley, George. 1987. *On Exodus: A Liberation Perspective.* Translated by Robert Barr. Maryknoll, N.Y.: Orbis.

Raboteau, Albert J. 1978. *Slave Religion: The "Invisible Institution" in the Antebellum South.* New York: Oxford University Press.

Ragland, Alan. 1995. From Heaven to Hell: What Went Wrong in Egypt. Pages 35–44 in *Living in Hell: The Dilemma of African-American Survival.* Edited by Mose Pleasure Jr. and Fred C. Lofton. Grand Rapids: Zondervan.

Rajak, Tessa. 1985. Jews and Christians As Groups in a Pagan World. Pages 245–62 in *"To See Ourselves As Others See Us": Christians, Jews, "Others" in Late Antiquity.* Chico, Calif.: Scholars Press.

Reid, Stephen B. 1990. *Experience and Tradition: A Primer in Black Biblical Hermeneutics.* Nashville: Abingdon.

Reumann, John. 1991. Introduction: Whither Biblical Theology? Pages 1–31 in *The Promise and Practice of Biblical Theology.* Edited by John Reumann. Minneapolis: Fortress.

Roberts, J. Deotis. 1976. What Does It Mean to Be Saved? Pages 64–67 in *Preaching the Gospel.* Edited by Henry J. Young. Philadelphia: Fortress.

―――. 1983. *Black Theology Today: Liberation and Contextualization.* Toronto Studies in Theology. New York: Edwin Mellen.

Robbins, Vernon. 1996. *The Tapestry of Early Christian Discourse: Rhetoric, Society and Ideology.* New York: Routledge.

Rooks, C. Shelby. 1972. Toward the Promised Land: An Analysis of the Religious Experience of Black America. *The Black Church* 2/1:1–48.

Ruth, Lester. 2000. *A Little Heaven Below: Worship in the Early Methodist Quarterly Meetings.* Nashville: Abingdon.

Said, Edward W. 1983. Traveling Theory. Pages 226–47 in *The World, the Text, and the Critic.* Cambridge, Mass.: Harvard University Press.

Saunders, Stanley P., and Charles L. Campbell. 2000. *The Word on the Street: Performing the Scriptures in the Urban Context.* Grand Rapids: Eerdmans.

Scarry, Elaine. 1985. *The Body in Pain: The Making and Unmaking of the World.* New York: Oxford University Press.

Schäfer, Peter. 1997. *Judeophobia.* Cambridge, Mass.: Harvard University Press.

Schleiermacher, Friedrich. 1958. *On Religion: Speeches to Its Cultured Despisers.* Translated by John Oman. New York: Harper & Row.

―――. 1971. *Hermeneutics: The Handwritten Manuscripts.* Edited by Heinz Kimmerle. Translated by J. Duke and J. Forstman. AAR Texts and Translations 1. Atlanta: Scholars Press.

Schorsch, Jonathan. 2001. Jews and Blacks in the Early Colonial World, 1450–1800. Dissertation, UCLA. Fellowship Announcement: www.humnet.ucla.edu/cjs/amado_recipients.html#Jonathan_Schorsch.

Schüssler Fiorenza, Elisabeth. 1983. *In Memory of Her: A Feminist Theological Recon-struction of Christian Origins.* New York: Crossroad.

———. 1987. Rhetorical Situation and Historical Reconstruction in 1 Corinthians. *NTS* 33:386–403.

Schwartz, Hans. 1995. *Evil: A Historical and Theological Perspective.* Translated by Mark W. Worthing. Minneapolis: Fortress.

Scott, Bernard Brandon. 1989. *Hear Then the Parable: A Commentary on the Parables of Jesus.* Minneapolis: Fortress.

Scroggs, Robin. 1972. Paul and the Eschatological Woman. *JAAR* 40:283–303.

Segal, Alan F. 1986. *Rebecca's Children: Judaism and Christianity in the Roman World.* Cambridge, Mass.: Harvard University Press.

Setel, Drorah. 1992. Exodus. Pages 26–35 in *The Women's Bible Commentary.* Edited by Carol A. Newsom and Sharon H. Ringe. Louisville: Westminster John Knox.

Sherman, John M. 1962. More about Prince Hall: Notes and Documents. *Philalethes* 15:42, 45.

Smith, Abraham. 1995. Toni Morrison's *Song of Solomon:* The Blues and the Bible. Pages 107–15 in *The Recovery of Black Presence: An Interdisciplinary Exploration.* Edited by Randall C. Bailey and Jacquelyn Grant. Nashville: Abingdon.

———. 1998. Putting "Paul" Back Together Again: William Wells Brown's *Clotel* and Black Abolitionist Approaches to Paul. *Semeia* 83/84:251–62.

———. 2000. Aaron Douglas, the Harlem Renaissance, and Biblical Art: Toward a Radical Politics of Identity. Pp 682–95 in *African Americans and the Bible: An Interdisciplinary Project.* Edited by Vincent Wimbush. New York: Continuum.

Smith, Jonathan. 1986. Fences and Neighbors: Some Contours of Early Judaism. Pages 1–18 in *Imagining Religion: From Babylon to Jonestown.* Chicago: University of Chicago Press.

Smith, Theophus H. 1994. *Conjuring Culture: Biblical Formations of Black America.* New York: Oxford University Press.

Soggin, J. Alberto. 1982. *Introduction to the Old Testament: From Its Origins to the Closing of the Alexandrian Canon.* Rev. ed. Philadelphia: Westminster.

Southern, Eileen. 1971. *The Music of Black Americans: A History.* New York: Norton.

Soyinka, Wole. 1984. *Death and the King's Horseman.* New York: Hill & Wang.

Spencer, Jon Michael. 1990. *Protest and Praise: Sacred Music of Black Religion.* Minneapolis: Fortress.

———. 1993. *Blues and Evil.* Knoxville: University of Tennessee Press.

Stemper, William H., Jr. 1987. Freemasons. *ER* 5:416–19.

Stendahl, Krister. 1966. *The Bible and the Role of Women: A Case Study in Hermeneutics.* Philadelphia: Fortress.

Stewart, Warren. 1984. *God's Word in Black Preaching.* Valley Forge, Pa.: Judson.

Stowers, Stanley K. 1998. Paul and Slavery: A Response. *Semeia* 83/84:295–311.

Stuhlmacher, Peter. 1977. *Historical Criticism and Theological Interpretation of Scripture: Toward a Hermeneutics of Consent.* Translated by Roy A. Harrisville. London: SPCK.

Sugitharajah, R. S., ed. 1991. *Voices from the Margin: Interpreting the Bible in the Third World.* Maryknoll, N.Y.: Orbis.

Sweet Honey in the Rock. 1988. *Breaths.* CD FF 70105. Flying Fish Records.

———. 1993. *Still on the Journey: The Twentieth Anniversary Album.* CD 9 42536-2. Earthbeat! Records.

———. 1997. *Selections 1976–88.* CD FF 667–668. Flying Fish Records.

Tcherikover, Victor A., Alexander Fuks, Menahem Stern, and David M. Lewis. 1964. *Corpus Papyrorum Judaicarum.* Vol. 3. Cambridge, Mass.: Harvard University Press.

Thiselton, Anthony. 1998. Biblical Studies and Theoretical Hermeneutics. Pages 95–113 in *The Cambridge Companion to Biblical Interpretation.* Edited by John Barton. Cambridge Companions to Religion. Cambridge: Cambridge University Press.

Thompson, Becky. 2001. *A Promise and a Way of Life: White Antiracist Activism.* Minneapolis: University of Minnesota Press.

Thrower, Sarah Selina. 1953. The Spiritual of the Gullah Negro in South Carolina. Unpublished thesis, College of Music of Cincinnati.

Thurman, Howard. 1954. *The Creative Encounter.* New York: Harper & Row.

———. 1981. *Jesus and the Disinherited.* Richmond, Ind.: Friends United Press.

Townes, Emilie M. 1993a. Living in the New Jerusalem: The Rhetoric and Movement of Liberation in the House of Evil. Pages 78–91 in *A Troubling in My Soul: Womanist Perspectives on Evil and Suffering.* Edited by Emilie M. Townes. Maryknoll, N.Y.: Orbis.

———. 1993b. *Womanist Justice, Womanist Hope.* AAR Academy Series 79. Atlanta: Scholars Press.

Tracy, Steven C. 1995. Langston Hughes: Poetry, Blues and Gospel—Somewhere to Stand. Pages 51–61 in *Langston Hughes: The Man, His Art and His Continuing Influence.* Edited by C. James Trotman. New York: Garland.

Troeltsch, Ernst. 1992. *The Social Teaching of the Christian Churches.* 2 vols. Transated by Olive Wyon. Library of Theological Ethics. 1931. Reprint, Louisville: Westminster John Knox.

Upton, William H. 1895. Prince Hall's Letter Book. Pages 54–58 in *Ars Quattuor Coronatorum: Being the Transactions of the Lodge Quattuor Coronati, # 2076.* Margate, Eng.: Keble's Gazette.

Vago, Steven. 1997. *Law and Society.* Upper Saddle River, N.J.: Prentice Hall.

Van Gorden, John H. 1980. *Biblical Characters in Freemasonry.* Lexington, Mass.: Masonic Book Club.

———. 1985. *Modern Historical Characters in Freemasonry.* Bloomington, Ill.: Masonic Book Club.

———.1986. *Ancient and Early Medieval Characters in Freemasonry.* Lexington, Mass.: Masonic Book Club.

Vaughn, William P. 1983. *The Antimasonic Party in the United States 1826–1843.* Lexington: University Press of Kentucky.

Walker, Alice. 1983. *In Search of Our Mothers' Gardens.* San Diego: Harcourt Brace Jovanovich.

Wall, Cheryl A. 1995. Whose Sweet Angel Child? Blues Women, Langston Hughes, and Writing during the Harlem Renaissance. Pp 37–50 in *Langston Hughes: The Man, His Art and His Continuing Influence.* Edited by C. James Trotman. New York: Garland.

Warrior, Robert Allen. 1991. A Native American Perspective: Canaanites, Cowboys, and Indians. Pages 287–95 in *Voices from the Margin: Interpreting the Bible in the Third World*. Edited by R. S. Sugirtharajah. Maryknoll, N.Y.: Orbis.

Washington, Booker T. 1901. *Up from Slavery: An Autobiography*. New York: Doubleday, Page & Co.

Weems, Renita J. 1991. Reading Her Way through the Struggle: African American Women and the Bible. Pages 57–77 in *Stony the Road We Trod: African American Biblical Interpretation*. Edited by Cain Hope Felder. Minneapolis: Fortress.

———. 1992. The Hebrew Women Are Not Like the Egyptian Women: The Ideology of Race, Gender, and Sexual Reproduction in Exodus 1. *Semeia* 59:25–34.

———. 1995. *Battered Love: Marriage, Sex, and Violence in Hebrew Prophets*. Minneapolis: Fortress.

Weil, Daniel Meir. 1995. *The Masoretic Chant of the Bible*. Jerusalem: Rubin Mass.

Wesleyan Methodist, A. 1819. *Methodist Error; or, Friendly Advice to Those Methodists, Who Indulge in Extravagant Emotions and Bodily Exercises*. Trenton: S. & E. Fenton.

West, Cornel. 1982. *Prophesy Deliverance: An Afro-American Revolutionary Christianity*. Philadelphia: Westminster.

Whalen, William J. 1966. *Handbook of Secret Organizations*. Milwaukee: Bruce.

———. 1998. *Christianity and American Freemasonry*. San Francisco: Ignatius.

Wheeler, Edward. 1995. Going beyond News from the Brickyard. Pages 45–52 in *Living in Hell: The Dilemma of African-American Survival*. Edited by Mose Pleasure Jr. and Fred C. Lofton. Grand Rapids: Zondervan.

White, James, F. 1991. *John Wesley's Prayerbook: The Sunday Service of the Methodists in North America with Introduction, Notes and Commentary by James F. White*. Akron, Ohio: OSL Publications. This book contains a facsimile edition of Wesley's 1784 text.

Williams, Delores S. 1993. *Sisters in the Wilderness: The Challenge of Womanist God-Talk*. Maryknoll, N.Y.: Orbis.

Williams, Loretta J. 1980. *Black Freemasonry and Middle-Class Realities*. Columbia: University of Missouri Press.

Wilmore, Gayraud S. 1977. Blackness As Sign and Assignment. Pages 165–73 in *Black Preaching: Select Sermons in the Presbyterian Tradition*. Edited by Robert T. Newbold. Philadelphia: Geneva.

———. 1983. *Black Religion and Black Radicalism: An Interpretation of the Religious History of Afro-American People*. 2d ed. Maryknoll, N.Y.: Orbis.

Wimbush, Vincent L. 1989. Historical/Cultural Criticism As Liberation: A Proposal for an African American Biblical Hermeneutic. *Semeia* 47:43–55.

———. 1991. The Bible and African Americans: An Outline of an Interpretive History. Pages 81–97 in *Stony the Road We Trod: African American Biblical Interpretation*. Edited by Cain H. Felder. Minneapolis: Fortress.

———. 2000a. Introduction: Reading Darkness, Reading Scriptures. Pages 1–43 in *African Americans and the Bible: Sacred Texts and Social Textures*. Edited by Vincent L. Wimbush. New York: Continuum.

———, ed. 2000b. *African Americans and the Bible: Sacred Texts and Social Textures*. New York: Continuum.

Wire, Antoinette Clark. 1990. *The Corinthian Women Prophets: A Reconstruction through Paul's Rhetoric.* Philadelphia: Fortress.

Wood, Francis E. 1993. "Take My Yoke upon You": The Role of the Church in the Oppression of African-American Women. Pages 37–47 in *A Troubling in My Soul: Womanist Perspectives on Evil and Suffering.* Edited by Emilie M. Townes. Maryknoll, N.Y.: Orbis.

Work, John W. 1940. *American Negro Songs and Spirituals.* New York: Crown.

Young, Henry J., ed. 1976. *Preaching the Gospel.* Philadelphia: Fortress.

Young, Josiah. 1987. Exodus As a Paradigm for the Black Theology. Pages 93–99 in *Exodus, A Lasting Paradigm.* Concilium—Religion in the Eighties. Edited by Bas van Iersel and Anton Weiler. Edinburgh: T&T Clark.

CONTRIBUTORS

Randall C. Bailey is the Andrew W. Mellon Professor of Hebrew Bible at the Interdenominational Theological Center in Atlanta, Georgia. He is an ideological critic and the author of *David in Love and War: The Pursuit of Power in 2 Samuel 10–12* (Sheffield, 1990), co-editor with Jacquelyn Grant of *The Recovery of Black Presence: An Interdisciplinary Exploration* (Abingdon, 1995), and co-editor with Tina Pippin of the Semeia volume, *Race, Class and the Politics of Bible Translation* (1996). He may be reached at rcbailey@itc.edu.

Wilma Ann Bailey is Associate Professor of Hebrew and Aramaic Scripture at Christian Theological Seminary, Indianapolis, Indiana.

Harold V. Bennett is an Assistant Professor of Religious Studies at Morehouse College in Atlanta, Georgia. He employs social-scientific approaches to reading the Hebrew Bible. He is the author of *Injustice Made Legal: Deuteronomic Law and the Plight of Widows, Strangers, and Orphans in Ancient Israel* (Eerdmans, 2002). He may be reached at hbennett@morehouse.edu.

Brad Ronnell Braxton is the Jessie Ball duPont Assistant Professor of Homiletics and Biblical Studies at Wake Forest University Divinity School in Winston-Salem, North Carolina. He is an ideological critic and is the author of *The Tyranny of Resolution: I Corinthians 7:17–24* (Society of Biblical Literature, 2000) and *No Longer Slaves: Galatians and African American Experience* (Liturgical Press, 2002). He may be reached at braxtob@wfu.edu.

Norman K. Gottwald is Adjunct Professor of Old Testament at Pacific School of Religion, Berkeley, California, and Emeritus Professor of Biblical Studies at New York Theological Seminary. He is a social-scientific critic of the Hebrew Bible and former President of the Society of Biblical Literature. He is the author of *The Tribes of Yahweh* (Orbis, 1979; reprint, Sheffield Academic Press, 1999), The *Hebrew Bible: A Socio-Literary Introduction* (Fortress, 1985), and *The Politics of Ancient Israel* (Westminster John Knox, 2001). He may be reached at tzaddi@mindspring.com.

Carolyn M. Jones is Associate Professor of Religion at the University of Georgia. She may be reached at medine@arches.uga.edu.

Cheryl A. Kirk-Duggan is Director of the Center for Women and Religion and is an in Residence and Core Doctoral Faculty at the Graduate Theological

Union in Berkeley, California. She is a Womanist biblical scholar, theologian, and ethicist and is the author of *Misbegotten Anguish: A Theology and Ethics of Violence* (Chalice, 2001), *The Undivided Soul: Helping A Congregation Connect Body and Spirit* (Abingdon, 2001), and *Refiner's Fire: A Religious Engagement with Violence* (Fortress, 2000). She may be reached at kirkdugg@gtu.edu.

Ronald N. Liburd is Assistant Professor of Religion at Florida A & M University in Tallahassee, Florida. His area of research interest is New Testament and Christian origins, and he has special interest in interpretive models and theories that place marginalized people at the center of religious conversation. He has published an article entitled "'Like . . . a House upon the Sand': African American Biblical Hermeneutics in Perspective" (*JITC* Fall 1994). He may be reached at ronald.liburd@famu.edu.

Hugh R. Page Jr. is the Walter Associate Professor of Theology, Associate Dean for Undergraduate Studies in the College of Arts and Letters, and Director of the African and African-American Studies Program at the University of Notre Dame in South Bend, Indiana. He is a Semitic philologist and ethnological critic. He is the author of *The Myth of Cosmic Rebellion: A Study of Its Reflexes in Ugaritic and Biblical Literature* (Brill, 1996) and editor of *Exploring New Paradigms in Biblical and Cognate Studies* (Mellen Biblical Press, 1996). He may be reached at poet@hrpj.com.

Tina Pippin is Professor in the Department of Religious Studies at Agnes Scott College in Decatur, Georgia. She is a postmodern, feminist critic and activist educator and the author of *Apocalyptic Bodies: The Biblical End of the World in Text and Image* (Routledge 1999) and a co-editor (with Ronald Schleifer and David Jobling) of *The Postmodern Bible Reader*. She may be reached at tpippin@agnesscott.edu.

Abraham Smith is an Associate Professor of New Testament at Perkins School of Theology in Dallas, Texas. He is a literary critic and is the author of "'It Seems to Me We Do Agree' Said Booker T. and W. E. B.: Structures of Oppression in the Hermeneutics of Up from Slavery and The Souls of Black Folk" in *Reading Communities Reading Scripture: Essays in Honor of Daniel Patte* (ed. by Gary A. Phillips and Nicole Wilkinson Duran; Trinity, 2002); "Commentaries and Reflections on First and Second Thessalonians" in the *New Interpreter's Bible* (Abingdon, 2000); and *"Comfort One Another": Reconstructing the Audience of 1 Thessalonians* (Westminster/John Knox,1995). He may be reached at smith.abraham@att.net.

Demetrius Williams is Assistant Professor in the Department of Classical Studies at Tulane University in New Orleans, Louisiana. He is a historical critic and is the author of *Enemies of the Cross of Christ: Terminology of the Cross and Conflict in Philippians* (Sheffield, 2002). He may be reached at dwillia6@tulane.edu.